the *Genius*
Panasonic
microwave oven
cookbook

Microwave cooking is convenient, and time saving and versatile. Not only can it be used to warm leftovers, or prepare last-minute dinners, but also for leisurely breakfasts to elegant party menus.

This cookbook contains directions for cooking foods from appetizers to desserts to warming your bedtime milk. To be successful with microwave cooking, read the operating manual and instruction to the cookbook. Each chapter gives tips and techniques to help good results.

We have included some of our favorite recipes in this cookbook. After trying these recipes, we encourage you to experiment and adapt your favorites to microwave cooking. Use our recipes as a guide for cooking times and power levels, dish size and cooking technique. Relax and enjoy your new Panasonic microwave oven.

Yours truly,
MATSUSHITA APPLIANCE COMPANY

Please direct all inquiries to:

MATSUSHITA APPLIANCE COMPANY
Division of Matsushita Electric Corporation
of America
One Panasonic Way
Secaucus, New Jersey 07094
201-348-7841

In Canada:

PANASONIC HOME ECONOMIST
PANASONIC CANADA
Division of Matsushita Electric
of Canada Limited
5770 Ambler Drive
Mississauga, Ontario L4W2T3
(416) 624-5010

With special Thanks to Home Economists: Janet Briggs, Joy Williams, Lisa Camelotto, Marianne Marcketta.

Contents

INTRODUCTION

Cooking With Microwave Energy

Microwaves are a form of high frequency radio waves similar to those used by a radio including AM, FM, and CB. They are, however, much shorter than radio waves; approximately four to six inches long with a diameter of about one-fourth inch. Electricity is converted into microwave energy by the magnetron tube. From the magnetron tube, microwave energy is transmitted to the oven cavity where it is: reflected, transmitted and absorbed.

Reflection

Microwaves are reflected by metal just as a ball is bounced off a wall. A combination of stationary (interior walls) and rotating metal (turntable or stirrer fan) helps assure that the microwaves are well distributed within the oven cavity to produce even cooking.

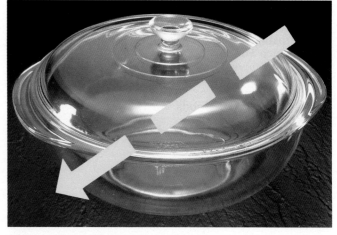

Transmission

Microwaves pass through some materials such as paper, glass and plastic much like sunlight shining through a window. Because these substances do not absorb or reflect the microwave energy, they are ideal materials for microwave oven cooking containers.

Absorption

During heating, microwaves will be absorbed by food. They penetrate to a depth of about ¾ to 1½ inches. Microwave energy excites the molecules in the food (especially water, fat and sugar molecules), and causes them to vibrate at a rate of 2,450,000,000 times per second. This vibration causes friction, and heat is produced. If you vigorously rub your hands together, you will feel heat produced by friction. The internal cooking of larger foods is done by conduction. The heat which is produced by friction is conducted to the center of the food. Foods also continue to cook by conduction during standing time (see page 15.)
Because microwaves dissipate, much like sunlight as it reaches the Earth's surface, they cannot be stored in food.

MICROWAVE COOKING UTENSILS

Microwave cooking opens new possibilities in convenience and flexibility for cooking containers. Although new microwave accessories are constantly being introduced, many utensils readily available in most kitchens may also be used for microwave cooking and heating.

Glass, Ceramic and China

Heat-Resistant glass cookware is invaluable in microwave cooking. Many of these items are readily available in most homes: glass measures, custard cups, mixing bowls, loaf dishes, covered casseroles, oblong baking dishes, pie plates and round or square cake dishes. Examples of this type of cookware are Pyrex® and Corning ware® by Corning, Fire-King® by Anchor Hocking, Heller Ovenware® by Heller Design and Glassbake® by Jeanette Glass.

Dinnerware can be used for microwave cooking. Many brands of dinnerware are microwave safe. Check the care information for reference to microwave use for dinnerware and serving pieces. If dinnerware is marked ovenproof, it frequently is safe to use in the microwave oven. However, to be sure, check by conducting microwave dish test. Examples of this type of dinnerware are: Corelle® by Corning, Temperware® by Lenox and Denby® dinnerware.

Several types of glassware and dinnerware are not recommended for use in the microwave oven. Remember these basic rules when using dinnerware and glassware. Do not use dishes with metallic trim or containers with metal parts. Arcing may occur and/or the dish may break.
Do not use ceramic mugs or cups with glued-on handles. The handles may fall off with continued heating.
Do not use delicate glassware. Although the glassware may be transparent to microwave energy, the heat from the food may cause the glassware to crack.

4

Jars and Bottles can be used to warm food to serving temperature, if the lid is removed first. Cooking should not be done in these containers since most are not heat resistant and during extended heating times, heat from food would cause cracking or breaking.

Browning Dishes are used to sear chops, meat patties, steaks etc. A special coating on the bottom of the dish absorbs the microwave energy and becomes very hot. When foods are added to the dish, the result is a seared effect. Preheat dish according to manufacturer's directions. Add food to be seared and cooked according to recipe or personal preference.
Use pot holders to remove dish from microwave oven.
Do not use browning dish with temperature probe.
Check information included with browning dish for detailed instructions and heating chart.

How to Test a Container for Safe Microwave Oven Use:

Fill a 1-cup glass measure with water and place it in the microwave oven along with the container to be tested; heat one minute at HIGH. If the container is microwave oven safe, it should remain comfortably cool and the water should be hot. If the container is hot, it has absorbed some microwave energy and should not be used. This test cannot be used for plastic containers.

Plastics

Plastic Dishes that are safe for microwave cooking are readily available in the marketplace. Look for statements such as, "For microwave cooking only." or "Suitable for conventional or microwave cooking." in manufacturers' brochures. Most microwave safe plastic dishes are suitable for cooking vegetables, meat, poultry, fish and baked goods. Some plastic dishes should not be used for cooking foods with a high fat or sugar content. Check manufacturers' care instructions for recommended cooking uses. Plastic food storage containers can become soft, pitted or distorted from microwave cooking and should not be used. Melamine plastic dishes are not microwave safe.

Cooking Bags designed to withstand boiling, freezing, or conventional heating are microwave safe. Prepare bags according to manufacturer's directions. Close cooking bag with nylon tie provided, otherwise, use a piece of cotton string, or a strip cut from the open end of the bag. Make six ½-inch slits in the top of bag to allow steam to escape. DO NOT use wire twist-tie to close bag. They can act as an antenna and cause arcing (blue sparks). Wire twist-ties could ingite and damage the oven.
DO NOT COOK IN PLASTIC FOOD STORAGE BAGS. They are not heat resistant and may melt.

Plastic Wrap such as SARAN WRAP™ (by Dow Chemical Co.) can be used to cover dishes in most recipes. Over an extended cooking time, some disfiguration of the wrap may occur. When using plastic wrap as a casserole dish cover, fold back a small section of plastic wrap from the edge of the dish to allow some steam to escape. When removing plastic wrap "covers", as well as any glass lid, be careful to remove it away from you to avoid steam burns. After cooking, loosen plastic but let dish stand covered.

Paper, Napkins, Wax Paper, Paper Towels, Plates, Cups, and Freezer Wrap

All are handy utensils for microwave cooking. Use them for foods with short cooking times and low fat content. Avoid wax coated paper goods, since the wax may melt onto the food when the food reaches high temperatures. Wax paper is suitable to use to prevent spatter. Disposable polyester coated paperboard pans are sturdy, come in a variety of sizes, and are ideal for microwaving.

CAUTION: DO NOT use recycled paper products, such as brown paper bags, since they contain impurities which may cause arcing (blue sparks) and damage the oven.

Straw, Wicker and Wood

Straw and wicker baskets may be used in the microwave oven for short periods of time to warm rolls or bread. Large wooden utensils, such as bowls or cutting boards should NOT be used for prolonged heating as the microwave energy may cause the wood to become dry and brittle.

Metal

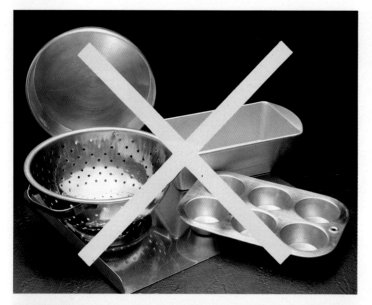

Metal containers or utensils, and those with metallic trim, should NOT be used in the microwave oven. Since microwave energy is reflected by metal, foods in metal containers will not cook evenly.
There is also the possibility of "arcing". This is a static discharge or blue spark between gaps in the metal or between the metal and the interior of the oven. Arcing may cause damage to the oven walls. If arcing occurs, turn the unit off and transfer food to a non-metallic container.

Although metal utensils must be avoided in microwave cooking, some metal can be helpful when used correctly.

Aluminum Foil can be used safely if certain guidelines are followed. Because it reflects microwave energy, foil can be used to an advantage in some recipes. It can be used to prevent overcooking. Small pieces of foil are used to cover areas such as chicken wings, tips of roasts, or other thin parts that cook before the rest of the recipe is finished. Foil is used in these cases to slow or stop the cooking process and prevent overcooking.

Foil Lined Containers, either cardboard or plastic, should NOT be used in the microwave oven. Foil lined milk cartons, frozen orange juice concentrate containers, or baking containers included in some cake mixes are examples of things to be avoided.

Frozen Dinner Trays can be used in the microwave oven, but results are only satisfactory if the container is no higher than ¾-inch. In metal containers, all the heating takes place from the top; the metal container reflects the energy directed to the sides and bottom. See Heating Convenience Foods, page 35.

Metal Skewers can be used if there is a large amount of food in proportion to the amount of metal. Take care in the placement of the skewers to avoid arcing between the skewers or between the skewers and the sides of the oven. Wooden skewers are the best and can be easily purchased at your local market, grocery store, or in the housewares section of many department stores.

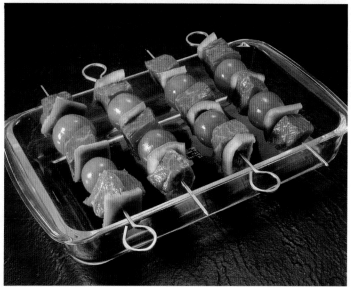

Thermometers are available for use in microwave ovens. DO NOT USE CONVENTIONAL MERCURY TYPE CANDY OR MEAT THERMOMETERS in food while heating in the microwave oven.

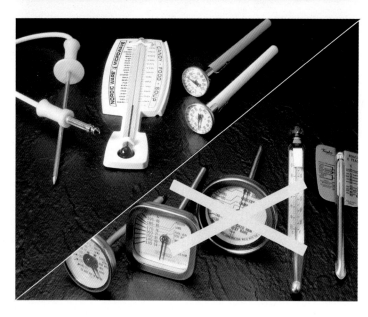

Metal Twist-Ties either paper or plastic coated, should NOT be used in the microwave oven. See pictures and information under COOKING BAGS page 6.

RECIPE PREPARATION and TECHNIQUES

There are few basic rules to be remembered when preparing recipes from this cookbook: All ingredients are taken from their common storage place. Milk, meat, eggs and butter are refrigerator temperature. Canned goods are room temperature. Recipes using canned ingredients include the liquid unless specified DRAINED. Other facts to remember:

- **Flour** is all-purpose unless another type such as whole wheat is specified.
- **Milk** is homogenized whole milk.
- **Sugar** is granulated white sugar.

- **Brown Sugar** may be light or dark, but should be measured packed.
- **Eggs** are Grade A large.
- **Amounts** given are in level measures.

Food Characteristics

Food characteristics which affect conventional cooking are more pronounced with microwave heating.

Size and Quantity—
Small portions cook faster than large ones.

Shape—Uniform sizes heat more evenly. To compensate for irregular shapes, place thin pieces toward the center of the dish and thicker pieces toward the edge of dish.

Bone and Fat—Both affect heating. Bones may cause irregular cooking. Large amounts of fat absorb microwave energy and meat next to these areas may overcook.

Starting Temperatures—Room temperature foods take less time to cook than refrigerator or frozen foods.

Density—Porous, airy foods take less time to cook than heavy, compact foods.

11

Browning

Meats and poultry, cooked 10 to 15 minutes, brown from their own fat. Foods cooked for shorter periods of time can be aided with the help of a browning sauce, Worcestershire sauce, or soy sauce. Simply brush one of these sauces over meat or poultry before cooking. Baked goods do not need long cooking time and, therefore, do not brown. When cakes or cupcakes will be frosted, no one will notice this visual difference. For quick breads or muffins, brown sugar can be used in the recipe in place of granulated sugar or the surface can be sprinkled with dark spices before baking.

Covering

As with conventional cooking moisture evaporates during microwave cooking. Because microwave cooking is done by time and not direct heat, the rate of evaporation cannot be easily controlled. This, however, can be easily corrected by using different materials to cover dishes. Casserole lids or plastic wrap are used for a tighter seal. Various degrees of moisture retention are also obtained by using wax paper or paper towels. However, unless specified, a recipe is cooked uncovered.

When using plastic wrap for a cover for cooking, it is best to leave an area around the edge of the dish opened to allow steam to escape.

Spacing

Individual foods, such as baked potatoes, cupcakes and hors d'oeuvres, will cook more evenly if placed in the oven equal distance apart. When possible, arrange foods in a circular pattern.

Similarly, when placing foods in a baking dish, arrange around the outside of dish, not lined up next to each other. Food should NOT be stacked on top of each other.

Piercing

The skin or membranes on some foods will cause steam to build up during microwave cooking and the food may burst. Foods must be pierced, scored or have a strip of skin peeled off before cooking to allow steam to escape.

Eggs—Pierce egg yolk twice and egg white several times with a toothpick.

Whole clams and Oysters—Pierce several times with a toothpick.

Whole Potatoes and Vegetables—Pierce with a fork.

Whole Apples and New Potatoes—Peel off 1-inch strip of skin before cooking.

Frankfurters and Sausages—Score smoked polish sausage and frankfurters. Pierce fresh sausage or brown and serve sausage with a fork.

Timing

A range in heating time is given in each recipe. The time range compensates for the uncontrollable differences in food shapes, starting temperature and regional preferences. Always cook food for the minimum cooking time given in the recipe and check for doneness. If the food is undercooked, continue cooking. It is easier to add time to an undercooked product. Once the food is overcooked, nothing can be done!

Stirring

Stirring is usually necessary during microwave cooking. We have noted when stirring is helpful, using the words once, twice, frequently or occasionally to describe the amount of stirring necessary. Always bring the cooked outside edges toward the center and the less cooked center portions toward the outside.

Turning and Rearranging

It is not possible to stir some foods to redistribute the heat. At times, microwave energy will concentrate in one area of a food. To help insure even cooking, some foods need to be turned or rearranged. Turn over large foods such as roasts or turkeys.
Generally, they are turned over once halfway through cooking.

Rearrange small items such as chicken pieces, shrimp, hamburger patties or pork chops. Rearrange pieces from the edge to the center and pieces from the center to the edge of the dish.

Standing Time

Most foods will continue to cook by conduction after the microwave oven is turned off. In meat cookery, the internal temperature will rise 5°F to 15°F if allowed to stand, covered, for 10 to 15 minutes. Casseroles and vegetables need a shorter amount of standing time, but this standing time is necessary to allow foods to complete cooking in the center without overcooking on the edges.

Testing for Doneness

The same test for doneness used in conventional cooking may be used for microwave cooking.

Cakes are done when toothpick comes out clean and cake pulls away from side of the pan.

Chicken is done when juices are clear yellow and drumstick moves freely.

Meat is done when fork-tender or splits at fibers.

Fish is done when it flakes and is opaque.

Converting Favorite Recipes

Select recipes that convert easily to microwave cooking such as casseroles, stews, baked chicken, fish and vegetable dishes. The results from foods such as broiled meats, cooked souffles or two-crust pies would be less than satisfactory. Never attempt to deep fat fry in your microwave oven.

A basic rule, when converting conventional recipes to microwave recipes, is to cut the suggested cooking time to one-fourth. Also, find a similar microwave recipe and adapt that time and power setting. Season meats with herbs and spices before cooking; salt after cooking.

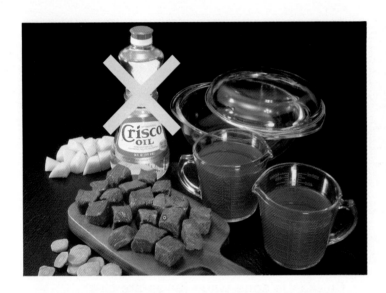

Stew meats are not browned before cooking. Omit any oil or fat that would be used for browning. Cut stew meat into 1½-inch pieces. Cut carrots, potatoes and other firm vegetables into small pieces. Carrots should be thinly sliced and potatoes cut into sixteenths. Reduce liquid by one-fourth. Cover with lid and cook at HIGH to bring liquid to a boil and cook at LOW until tender. Stir occasionally.

Casseroles microwave cook well. Cut foods into uniform pieces. Condensed soup makes a good base for casseroles. Select a dish that is large enough to allow for stirring. Cooking covered with a lid or plastic wrap reduces cooking time. Stir occasionally during cooking. To keep crumb toppings crisp sprinkle on before stand time.

SPECIAL FEATURES

The information in this section describes the special cooking features available on Panasonic microwave ovens. For each feature there is an explanation how the feature works, how to use the feature and cooking charts for the feature. The microwave oven you own will not be equipped with every feature. Refer to the oven control panel or operating manual to identify the features on your microwave oven.

AUTO SENSOR COOKING

The Auto Sensor system works by detecting a build-up of steam on the humidity sensor. As foods cook in a microwave, steam is produced. When foods are covered, the steam will build up and escape from the dish in a burst. This burst of steam is detected by the humidity sensor and then the oven automatically calculates the remaining cooking time.

When an Auto Sensor Cycle is selected A1 through A8 will appear in the display window. The oven door should not be opened for longer than one minute when A1 through A8 appears in the display window. Opening the door may cause inaccurate cooking results. Once the steam is detected, the remaining cooking time immediately appears in the display window and begins to count-down. At this time, the oven door may be opened, to stir, turn or add foods.

Look for the symbol **A** to indicate recipes and charts with Auto Sensor directions. Use these recipes and charts as a basis for determining which of your own similar conventional recipes may be converted to Auto Sensor cooking.

Auto Sensor Cycle Programs

Cook Cycle
The eight Auto Sensor Cook Cycles are designed for use with foods from their normal storage place. For example, meats and poultry are refrigerator temperature and canned goods and cake mixes are room temperature.
The Cook A1 cycle is completed when the burst of steam is detected. A cook time will NOT appear in the display window.

Frozen-Cook Cycles*
The eight Auto Sensor Frozen-Cook Cycles are designed for use with frozen foods. Frozen-Cook complete cooking cycle which will heat foods from the frozen state to serving temperature. When the Frozen-Cook Cycle number A1 through A8 disappears from the display window and is replaced by cooking time, the food will NOT be completely defrosted.
Foods should not be removed until the end of the cycle. To defrost foods use the Defrost Pad or the Weight Defrost Pad. Foods that are going to be cooked on the Frozen-Cook Cycles should be prepared for freezing according to the instructions given on page 21 in the "Preparing Foods for Freezer to Table" section. Your own precooked casseroles and stews may also be heated from freezer to table on Frozen-Cook A5.

Cook Warm* and Frozen-Cook-Warm* Cycles
The eight Cook-Warm and Frozen-Cook-Warm Cycles operate exactly as their corresponding Cook and Frozen-Cook-Cycles. These cycles also keep the food warm for one hour after cooking is complete. The first twenty minutes of the "Warm" Cycle is standing time and the remaining forty minutes keep the food warm. If the Cook-Warm of Frozen-Cook-Warm Cycles are used, foods may be removed after the cooking cycle is completed, but should be allowed to stand according to recipe directions. The Cook-Warm Cycles can be used instead of any Cook Cycle and the Frozen-Cook-Warm Cycles can be used instead of any Frozen-Cook Cycle.

*Not all models are equipped with this feature.

CYCLE	COOK (Warm)	FROZEN-COOK (Warm)
A1	Canned Foods, Leftovers, Noodles	Frozen Convenience Foods (1 to 11 oz.)
A2	Beef, Lamb (Well) Pork Whole Poultry	Frozen Convenience Foods (12 to 22 oz.)
A3	Beef, Lamb (medium) Rice	Frozen Pot Roasts
A4	Beef (rare) Cut-up Chicken	Frozen Cut-up Chicken
A5	Stews	Frozen Precooked Casseroles, Stews, Pork Chops
A6	Potatoes, Carrots	Frozen Hamburgers, Lamb Chops
A7	Beans, Cauliflower, Peas	Frozen Vegetables
A8	Fish, Chops, Broccoli	Frozen Fish Fillets, Scallops

Consult recipes or charts for procedures.

18

Auto Sensor Cooking Hints

For proper cooking results on the Auto Sensor Cycles, the directions given in the recipes and charts for container size and coverings must be followed. Lids should fit properly and be the one designed for the container.

Cover dishes without matching lids COMPLETELY with plastic wrap. Large dishes need two overlapping pieces of plastic wrap. Securely mold wrap around sides of dish. Foods with bones should not pierce through wrap. Steams build up under plastic wrap and lids, remove them away from you to avoid steam burns.

Do not open oven door longer than one minute when Auto Sensor Cycle number is in display window. Cooking results may be unsuccessful. Open the door during the second stage of cooking (i.e. when cooking time appears and counts down) to turn over pot roasts, or stir, glaze or shield foods.

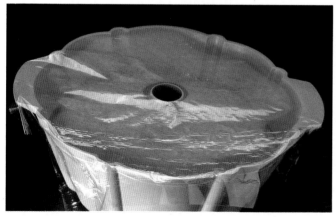

Do not use nonglossy plastic microwave safe cookware. Plastic wrap does not adhere tightly to nonglossy plastic dishes. Plastic wrap also may not adhere to some glass cookware with large decorative coatings on the outside of the dish.

Loosen or remove plastic wrap as recipe directs for stand time.

Reheating Food
(Refrigerated or Room Temperature)

Below are guidelines to follow when reheating various types of foods. Foods are heated covered on Auto Cook Cycle A1.

Plates of food—Arrange food on plate; top with butter, gravy, etc. Loosely, but completely cover plate with plastic wrap. Heat on Cook (Warm) A1. After Auto Sensor heating, release plastic wrap. Let stand, covered, 2 minutes before serving.

Canned foods—Empty contents into casserole dish or serving bowl; cover dish with casserole lid or plastic wrap. Heat on Cook (Warm) A1. After Auto Sensor heating, release plastic wrap. Let stand, covered, 2 minutes before serving.

Casseroles—Make sure container is dry on the outside and free from all moisture. Add 2 to 4 tablespoons liquid; cover with lid or plastic wrap. Let stand 2 to 3 minutes before serving. Heat on Cook (Warm) A1.

Note: *Only the foods listed above are suitable for reheating with the Auto Sensor Cycle. To reheat other foods refer to pages 33 to 39.*

Preparing Food for Auto Sensor Frozen-Cook (Warm)

Preparing Food for Freezer to Table Cooking

Both the Frozen-Cook and Frozen-Cook-Warm Auto Sensors Cycles can minimize kitchen preparation time for meals by following some easy planning tips before freezing the food. As a rule, most foods that can be stored frozen can be prepared for freezer to table cooking.

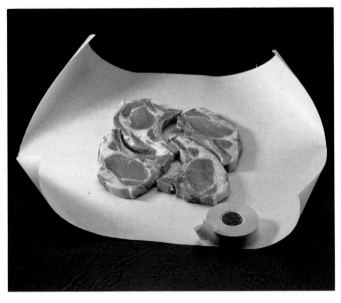

CHOPS, HAMBURGERS, CUT-UP POULTRY should be seasoned as desired, excluding salt.

Freeze in a single layer. Appropriately WRAP foods for freezing. Label and date package.

COOKED HOMEMADE STEWS and CASSEROLES should be frozen in an appropriate size dish which has been lined with plastic wrap. Once food is thoroughly frozen, remove from dish. Secure wrap to food. Label and date. To heat, use Frozen-Cook (Warm) A5.

To heat and serve your frozen foods, simply unwrap and place in an appropriate container. Cover and heat on the recommended Frozen-Cook (Warm) Cycle.

Note: *Containers should be at room temperature and completely dry in order to cook properly on the Auto Sensor Cycles.*

21

DEFROSTING

Defrosting frozen foods is one of the benefits of having a microwave oven. To receive the best results, follow our recommended techniques for freezing and defrosting.

Preparing Meat for Freezing

The finished quality of the prepared food will depend on the original quality before freezing, the care the food receives during freezing, and the techniques and times used for defrosting. Select good quality and fresh meat, poultry, or fish for freezing. Foods should be frozen as soon as possible after purchasing to preserve their quality. How foods are wrapped for freezing and the temperature at which they are frozen affect defrosting results. Proper wrapping materials should be used, and packaging techniques should be following for best results.

WRAPPING MATERIALS best suited for use in the freezer are odorless, and moisture and vapor proof. Meats need to be removed from their wrappings before defrosting. Therefore, containers such as glass freezer jars and plastic freezer containers are unsuitable. Heavy-duty plastic wraps and bags, and freezer wrap are suitable. If aluminum foil is used for Wrapping, all pieces of foil should be removed before defrosting in your microwave oven. Otherwise, arcing may occur. Meats may also be frozen in their store packaging for short periods of time.

When WRAPPING FOR FREEZING, arrange meat in thin uniform layers. Package ground meat in 1 to 2 inch thick rectangular, square or round shapes. Chicken pieces, chops and stew meat will defrost more easily if frozen in 1 or 2 piece layers rather than in bulky, thick packages. To aid in separating chops and hamburger patties during defrosting, place two pieces of wax paper between the layers.

REMOVE GIBLETS from fresh whole poultry.
(The giblets may be frozen separately, if desired.) Clean and dry poultry. Tie legs and wings with string; this helps poultry keep its shape during freezing. If poultry is packaged frozen, it may be defrosted even though the giblets are inside the cavity However, the cavity will be very icy after the defrosting cycle. It will be necessary to run cold water over the poultry.

23

FISH AND SEAFOODS are best frozen in single layers. Fillets may be frozen 2 or 3 deep, but place two pieces of wax paper or plastic wrap between each layer. Shrimp or scallops may be quick frozen on a cookie sheet. Once they are frozen, simply remove from the cookie sheet and place in a freezer bag or container. If they are thoroughly frozen before placing in the bag, they will not stick to each other.

REMOVE ALL AIR before sealing plastic bags. The drug store wrap is a good wrapping procedure to follow when using sheets of wrap such as freezer or plastic wrap. Center food to be wrapped on material. Bring two edges, up over the center and start folding down in 1 inch tucks until wrap is close to meat. Remove excess air from package. Shape ends into triangles and fold up over center. Tape securely.

LABEL package with type and cut of meat, date and weight.

FREEZE FOODS in a freezer which is maintained at 0°F or lower. Defrosting times given in the charts are for thoroughly frozen foods. (i.e. foods should be frozen at least 24 hours before defrosting.)

DEFROSTING CONTROLS
AUTO WEIGHT DEFROST

Auto Weight Defrost can be used to defrost many cuts of meat, poultry and fish by weight. To use, simply program the Auto Weight Defrost Category and the weight of the food in pounds (1.0) and tenths of a pound (0.1). The oven will determine the defrosting time and power levels. Once the oven is programmed the defrosting time will appear in the display window.

There are three categories for Auto Weight Defrost. Listed below are the recommended foods and the maximum weight that can be defrosted on each category.

Category	Food	Maximum Weight
1	Ground meats, roasts, ribs stew meat, chops, steaks, frankfurters	8 lb.
2	Whole or split cornish hens, Whole or cut-up chicken, Whole Turkey, Turkey breast	16 lb.
3	Shrimp (medium), Sea Scallops, Whole Fish	3 lb.

Before using Auto Weight Defrost make sure the meat, poultry, or fish has been properly frozen. See, "Preparing Meats for Freezing". For best results follow Defrosting Directions. After defrosting by Auto Weight Defrost always cook by Power and Time.

Foods that are not recommended for Auto Weight Defrost can be defrosted using Cyclic Defrost. Follow the times and information given in the Cyclic Defrosting section.

DEFROSTING DIRECTIONS FOR AUTO WEIGHT DEFROST

BEFORE STARTING

CONVERT ounces to tenths of a pound. Meats packaged in most grocery stores are labeled with the weight in pound and hundredths of a pound. See conversion chart below.

Conversion Chart
Follow this chart to convert ounces or hundredths of a pound into tenths of a pound.

Ounces	Hundredths of a Pound	Tenths of a Pound
0	.96–.05	0.0
1–2	.06–.15	0.1
3–4	.16–.25	0.2
5	.26–.35	0.3
6–7	.36–.45	0.4
8	.46–.55	0.5
9–10	.56–.65	0.6
11–12	.66–.75	0.7
13	.76–.85	0.8
14–15	.86–.95	0.9

Examples: *If a roast weighs 5.95 pounds or 5 pounds 14 ounces, program 5.9 pounds. If a roasts weighs 5.99 pounds or 6 pounds 0 ounces, program 6.0 pounds.*

REMOVE WRAPPER. Otherwise, the wrap will hold steam and juice close to the food which can cause the outer surface of the food to cook.

25

REMOVE ground meat from its TRAY. Place meat in an appropriate size dish.

PLACE ROAST FAT-SIDE DOWN and WHOLE POULTRY BREAST-SIDE DOWN on a microwave roasting rack in an oblong dish. The rack helps prevent the food from sitting in its own juice. The juice will get hot during defrosting and if the food is sitting in the juice, the bottom will begin to cook.

PLACE SMALL ITEMS, such as chops, chicken pieces, shrimp, scallops, fish on a microwave roasting rack in an oblong dish.

AT THE FIRST BEEP

TURN OVER ground meat or stew meat.
BREAK APART poultry pieces, shrimp or scallops.
REMOVE defrosted portion from ground meat, stew meat, shrimp or scallops.

AT THE SECOND BEEP

TURN OVER ground beef, stew meat, turkey, or whole fish.
BREAK APART stew meat, ground meat, poultry pieces, shrimp or scallops.
SEPARATE chops and hamburger patties.
REMOVE defrosted ground meat, stew meat, poultry pieces, shrimp or scallops.
SHIELD ends of roasts, fat or bones with foil.

AFTER DEFROSTING

LARGE ROASTS may still be icy in center. Allow to stand in the refrigerator to finish defrosting.

WHOLE POULTRY may still be icy in center. Run cold water in cavity. If poultry was frozen with giblets in cavity, after defrosting run cold water in the cavity until giblets can be removed.
SMALL ITEMS such as chops, steaks, cornish hens, or shrimp can stand 10 to 15 minutes. Use this time to prepare the remaining ingredients for cooking.

MEAT DEFROSTED on AUTO WEIGHT DEFROST should be cooked by Power and Time.

CYCLIC DEFROST

All Touch Control ovens have Cyclic Defrost. To use, touch the DEFROST pad and program the defrosting time. The oven will divide the defrost time into eight stages: 4 defrost and 4 stand periods.

During the programmed time, the oven will alternate between defrost power and stand times (no power). Follow Defrosting times and directions given in this section.

DEFROSTING MEATS

Meat should be frozen in moisture and vapor proof wrapping materials. Small items such as chops, hamburger patties, etc. should be frozen in 1 or 2 piece layers.

Remove meat from original wrapper and set on a microwave roasting rack placed in oblong dish. Set DEFROST and heat for the time recommended in the chart.

Turn meat over two or three times during defrost. Shield edges and unevenly shaped ends of roasts halfway through the defrost cycle.

Halfway through the defrost cycle break apart ground beef, separate chops and remove meat that is defrosted.

Large roasts may still be icy in center. Allow to stand.

	MEAT	DEFROST TIME (minutes per pound)
Beef	Roasts	
	Beef Tenderloin	10 to 12
	Chuck or rump	10 to 12
	Sirloin, rolled	10 to 12
	Steak	
	Boneless sirloin	12 to 14
	Flank	8 to 10
	Miscellaneous	
	Frankfurters	10 to 12
	Ground beef	10 to 12
	Liver	10 to 12
Pork	Chops	12 to 14
	Ribs	12 to 14
	Roasts	12 to 14
Estimated times for meats not listed above.		10 to 12

DEFROSTING POULTRY AND GAME

Poultry and game should be frozen in moisture and vapor proof wrapping materials. For best results cut-up chicken should be frozen in a single layer. Remove poultry or game from original wrapper and set on a microwave rack placed in an oblong dish.

Set Defrost and the time recommended in the chart. Turn poultry or game over two to four times during defrosting. Halfway through the defrost cycle shield end of drumsticks, wings and breast bones. Also, break apart cut-up chickens and remove small pieces such as wings, that may defrost before larger pieces.

Rinse poultry or game under cold water to remove ice crystals.

POULTRY	DEFROST TIME (minutes per pound)
Chicken	
Whole	12 to 14
Cut-up	8 to 10
Boneless breasts	12 to 14
Cornish hens, Whole	12 to 16
Duck, Whole	16 to 18
Goose, Whole	10 to 12
Pheasant, Whole,	16 to 18
Turkey	
Whole	12 to 14
Half	16 to 18
Estimated times for poultry not listed above.	10 to 12

DEFROSTING FISH AND SEAFOOD

Fish and seafood should be frozen in moisture and vapor proof wrapping materials. Small items such as scallops or shrimp should be frozen in a single layer. Remove fish from original wrapper and set on microwave roasting rack placed in an oblong dish.

Set Defrost and time recommended in chart. Halfway through the defrost cycle, turn whole fish or blocks of fillets over. Also, break apart shrimp or scallops. Remove any pieces that are defrosted.

FISH	DEFROST TIME (minutes per pound)
Crabmeat	30 to 32
Fish Fillets	8 to 12
Fish Steaks	10 to 12
Lobster Tails	12 to 14
Sea Scallops	16 to 20
Shrimp, medium	12 to 14
Whole Fish	10 to 12
Estimated times for fish and seafood not listed above.	12 to 14

DEFROSTING FROZEN CONVENIENCE FOODS

Food that normally takes several hours at room temperature to defrost, can be defrosted in the microwave oven. Cakes, rolls, and frozen fruits and vegetables are defrosted in a matter of minutes. Consult Chart for recommended defrosting times and techniques.

Remove layer cake from original container. Place on a microwave safe dish. Defrost according to time given in chart. Center will be slightly icy after defrost time. Allow to stand at room temperature.

Wrap roll or danish in paper towel. Defrost according to time given in chart.

Defrost frozen whipped topping in original plastic tub for time given in chart.

DEFROSTING FROZEN CONVENIENCE FOODS

ITEM	POWER	DEFROST TIME (in minutes)	SPECIAL HINTS
BAKED GOODS	DEFROST		Remove from original container; arrange on serving plate.
Brownies (13 oz.)		4 to 6	
Cupcakes (6) (10 to 11 oz.)		3 to 5	Add an additional 1 to 1½ minutes to serve warm.
Cheese Cake (17 oz.)		7 to 9	
Layer Cakes (17 to 18 oz.)		3 to 5	
Pound Cake (10¾ oz.)		2 to 4	
Coffee Cake (11 to 12 oz.)		6 to 8	
BAGELS	DEFROST		
2		4 to 6	
4		6 to 8	
DANISH	DEFROST		Each individually wrapped in a paper towel (for 1 or 2).
1		1 to 2	
2		3 to 4	Arrange on paper plate; cover with paper towel (for 4 to 6).
4 (9 oz. package)		5 to 7½	
6 (13 oz. package)		7 to 9½	
Dinner Rolls (6)	DEFROST	3 to 5	
Donuts	DEFROST		
Plain or Sugar coated			
1		1½ to 2	
2		2 to 3	
4		5 to 6	
6		8 to 9	
Hard Rolls (1 to 1¼ oz. ea.)	DEFROST		
1		1 to 1½	
2		2 to 3	
4		4 to 5	
MISCELLANEOUS (TO THAW)			
Frozen Juice Concentrates (6 oz.)	MEDIUM	1½ to 2½	Remove lid. If container is foil lined, remove to pitcher.
(12 oz.)		3 to 5	
Non-Dairy Creamer (16 oz.)	DEFROST	18 to 20 ⌉	Open carton. Shake vigorously 2 times during defrosting. Defrost original plastic tub.
Pancake/Muffin Batter (10 oz.)	DEFROST	8 to 10 ⌋	
Whipped Topping (9 oz.)	DEFROST	4 to 6	
Frozen Mixed Fruit (10 oz.)	DEFROST	9 to 11	Pierce pouch or remove metal lid; set on saucer.
Frozen Vegetables (6 oz.)	DEFROST	6 to 8	Remove from box. Break apart after 3 minutes. If vegetables are in a pouch, pierce pouch.
(10 oz.)		10 to 12	

CONVENIENCE FOODS

Quick and easy reheating of frozen foods, is one of the many benefits of microwave oven. Many frozen convenience foods are heated in less time than it would take in a conventional oven. The Frozen Convenience Food chart gives suggested power levels, cooking times and techniques for successful reheating results. In addition, check manufacturer's heating directions. Many convenience foods now include microwave directions.

FROZEN CONVENIENCE FOODS

Place bite-size appetizers on a paper towel lined paper plate. Arrange 12 appetizers in a circular pattern.

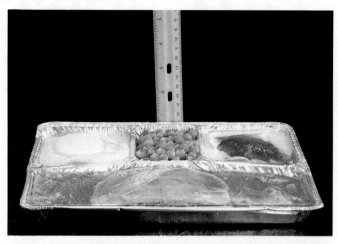

Frozen dinners may be heated in the foil tray, if the tray is less than ¾-inch high.

Frozen dinners and breakfasts are available in paperboard and microwave safe plastic tray. These dinners may be heated directly in the tray.

If there is a foil cover, remove it from the tray. Some foods such as breads, french fries or cake like desserts such as brownies do not microwave well. These can be removed from the tray.

Cover the tray with plastic wrap, or use plastic lid or film which accompanies some dinners. Vent lids according to manufacturers directions.

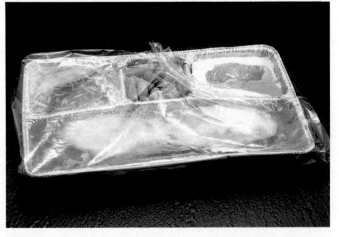

When using plastic do not cover desserts. Desserts cook better uncovered. Cake like desserts can be heated in a custard cup at HIGH 1½ to 2½ minutes.

34

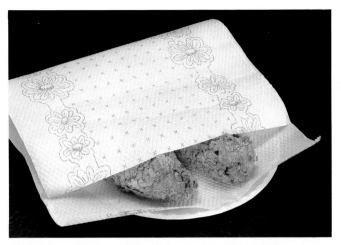

Remove foods from foil containers deeper than ¾-inch; place in appropriately sized dish. Heat, covered with lid or plastic wrap.

Place 2 pieces frozen fried chicken between paper toweling on a paper plate. Coating will not be crisp after heating.

HEATING FROZEN CONVENIENCE FOODS

ITEM	POWER	APPROX. COOKING TIME (in minutes)	SPECIAL HINTS
APPETIZERS Bite Size	M. HIGH	2½ to 4½	Heat 12 at a time on paper towel lined paper plate or microwave roasting rack. Brush pastry items with Worcestershire sauce.
MAIN DISH Frozen Dinners (17 oz.) (11 oz.) Entree (8 to 9 oz.) (21 oz.) (32 oz.) Macaroni and Cheese (8 oz.) Breakfast Entree (4 to 8 oz.)	M. HIGH M. LOW MEDIUM MEDIUM	 8 to 10 5 to 7 13 to 14 25 to 32 32 to 35 8 to 10 2 to 4	If container is ¾-inch deep, remove foil cover and cover with plastic wrap. For containers more than ¾-inch deep, remove food to similar size glass container; heat covered if no top crust. Stir occasionally, if possible.
French Toast 2 pieces 4 pieces Waffles 2 pieces 4 pieces Fried Chicken 2 pieces 4 pieces 6 pieces Fried Fish Fillets 2 fillets 4 fillets	MEDIUM M. LOW M. HIGH M. HIGH	 1 to 2 2 to 3 1½ to 2 3 to 3½ 4 to 5 5 to 6 7 to 8 2 to 3 3½ to 4½	Arrange on paper towel lined paper plate, cover with paper towel.
Fish Cakes 4 cakes	M. HIGH	3½ to 4½	Arrange on microwave roasting rack.
Pouch Dinners (5 to 6 oz.) (10 to 11 oz.)	M. HIGH	 4 to 5 7 to 8	Pierce pouch, set on saucer.
SIDE DISHES Baked Stuffed Potatoes 2 4	M. HIGH	 10 to 12 15 to 17	Heat in original paper board containers. If it has foil container, remove and place on dish. Let stand 5 times after heating.
Vegetables in Pouches Frozen Potato Puffs (10 oz.)	HIGH M. HIGH	7 to 9 2 to 3	Pierce pouch, set on saucer. Heat on paper plate, covered, with paper towel, stirring once.

HEATING FROZEN CONVENIENCE FOODS ON AUTO SENSOR

Froz-Cook A1 is an ideal cycle for heating TV dinners and frozen entrees.

Note: Not all models are equipped with special Froz-Cook feature.

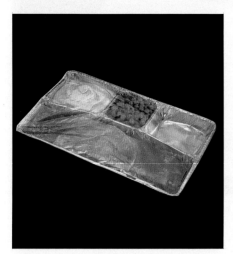

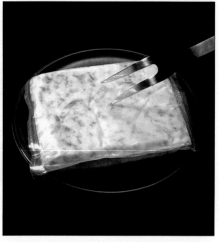

TV dinners may be heated in their foil tray, if the container is less than ¾-inch high. Follow recommendations for heating TV dinners on page 34. Remove cake-like desserts such as brownies before heating. Remove foil from tray and cover with plastic wrap.

Place entrees in an appropriately sized container. Cover with lid or plastic wrap.

Pouch dinners should be heated in their pouch. Place pouch on plate and pierce one hole in pouch.

HEATING FROZEN CONVENIENCE FOODS ON AUTO SENSOR A

ITEM	APPROXIMATE WEIGHT	FROZ-COOK CYCLE	APPROX. HEATING TIME (in minutes)	SPECIAL INSTRUCTIONS
FROZEN DINNER Small Large	6 to 11 oz. 12 to 22 oz.	FROZ-COOK A1 FROZ-COOK A2	6 to 10 12 to 25	Remove tray from box. Remove foil or plastic cover. Remove any cake-like desserts such as brownies; they may burn. Cover completely with plastic wrap.
FROZEN BREAKFAST	4 to 8 oz.	FROZ-COOK A1	4½ to 6½	Remove tray from box. Leave plastic film on breakfast. For breakfasts without film, cover completely with plastic wrap.
ENTREES Small Large	6 to 11 oz. 12 to 22 oz.	FROZ-COOK A1 FROZ-COOK A2	7 to 9 9 to 20	Remove from foil container and place in appropriately sized glass container. Cover with lid or cover completely with plastic wrap.
POUCH ENTREES Single Pouch Double Pouch	4 to 11 oz. 8 to 11 oz.	FROZ-COOK A1 FROZ-COOK A1	3 to 9 8 to 10	Pierce 1 hole in each pouch. Place on paper plate or glass dish. Double pouch entrees should be placed side by side.
VEGETABLE IN A POUCH	10 oz.	FROZ-COOK A1	7½ to 10	Pierce hole in pouch. Place on paper plate or pie plate.

Note: *Frozen convenience foods with pastry such as pot pies, pizzas, or hors d'oeuvres are not recommended for Auto Sensor heating.*
Frozen convenience potato products requiring crispness such as potato puffs, etc., are also not recommended.

HEATING CANNED GOODS

Empty contents of can into serving dish or casserole.

Choose a casserole large enough to allow for stirring.

Food spread out in a shallow dish will heat more quickly than the same food heated in a narrow deep dish.

Cover with a lid or plastic wrap. Stir occasionally during heating.

Let stand, uncovered, 3 minutes before serving.

Food	Approx. Cooking Time (in minutes) at MEDIUM-HIGH
Chili (15 oz.)	3½ to 4½
Corned Beef Hash (15½ oz.)	3 to 4
Gravy (10½ oz.)	2 to 3½
Pork and Beans 16 oz. 20¾ oz.	 3½ to 4½ 5 to 6
Soup 10¾ oz. plus 1 can liquid 20 oz.	 4 to 5 4 to 5
Spaghetti 7¾ oz. 14 to 19 oz.	 3 to 4 5 to 6
Spaghetti Sauce 15½ oz. 32 oz.	 3½ to 5 8 to 10
Vegetables 8 oz. 16 to 17 oz.	 2 to 3 3 to 4

Reheating Leftovers

The microwave oven is ideal for reheating leftovers. Most leftovers will reach serving temperature in a matter of minutes and will taste freshly cooked. Follow our guidelines listed below to prepare foods for reheating. Always use microwave safe plates and dishes. If there is any doubt if a dish is microwave safe, perform the dish test given on page 5.

The times given in the reheating chart are for foods that are refrigerator temperature.

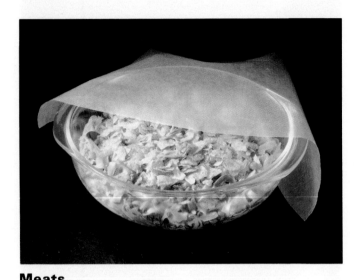

Meats

Sliced meat will heat more evenly and quickly than a roast, and thin slices more quickly than thick slices. Arrange slices flat on a plate. Cover with wax paper. Sauce or gravy may be poured over meat before reheating to help keep meat moist.

To reheat chops, arrange on a dish with the thicker portion toward the edge of the dish. Cover with wax paper.

Casseroles

For quick heating, spread out individual servings in a single serving casserole. Cover with lid or plastic wrap. For serveral servings, heat in a 1½-quart casserole. If necessary, stir in a small amount of liquid (water, milk, gravy or broth). Cover with a lid or plastic wrap. Casseroles with crumb toppings should be covered with wax paper. This will help prevent the crumb topping from becoming soggy. Stir casseroles several times during heating.

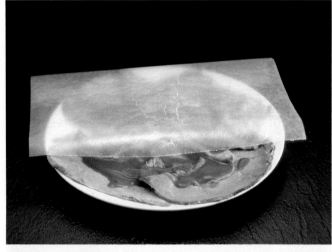

Plates of food

Arrange food on the plate with the thicker, denser food along the edge of the plate. Food that reheats quickly such as vegetables should be placed in the middle of the plate. However, mashed potatoes which are dense, should be spread out along the edge for quicker heating. Cover with wax paper or plastic wrap.

Pastries
Place pastry on a paper plate. Heat 10 to 40 seconds. The filling and glazes will be hotter than the pastry. Be careful when eating.

Slice of Pie
Place slice of pie on plate. Heat 1 to 1½ minutes.

Rolls
Wrap individual roll in paper towel. Heat 5 to 10 seconds. Arrange 4 to 6 rolls in a serving container. Cover with a paper towel or napkin. Heat 30 seconds. Test baked goods before adding more time; when overheated they become tough and hard.

Vegetables
Reheat covered just until very warm. If possible, stir or rearrange during heating.

Sandwiches
Wrap closed sandwiches in a paper towel and place on glass tray. Place open-faced sandwiches on plate and cover with wax paper. Heat until sandwiches are just warm.

REHEATING LEFTOVERS CHART

ITEM	APPROX. COOKING TIME (in minutes) at MEDIUM-HIGH	STAND TIME
Casseroles		
Individual serving (about 1 cup)	1½ to 2	1
Small casserole (about 3 cups)	6 to 10	2
Meats		
1 chop (about 5 oz.)	1¼ to 1½	1
2 chops (about 5 oz. ea.)	1¾ to 2	1
½ pound meat, sliced thin	2 to 2½	1
1 pound meat, sliced thin	2¾ to 3	1
½ pound meat, sliced thick	2½ to 3	1
1 pound meat, sliced thick	3 to 3½	1
Pastries		
1 doughnut	¼	1
2 doughnuts	½	1
4 doughnuts	¾ to 1	1
Pie		
1 slice	1 to 1½	1
2 slices	2 to 2½	1
Plate of Food (1)	2¼ to 3	2
Rolls		
2	¼	½
4	½	1
Sandwiches		
Open-faced		
1	1½ to 1¾	1
2	2 to 2¼	1
Closed		
1	1¼ to 1½	1
2	1¾ to 2¼	1
Vegetables		
1 cup	1 to 1½	1
3 cups	4 to 5	2

39

CANNING
DO NOT USE YOUR MICROWAVE OVEN FOR CANNING

Canning and sterilizing of canning jars should NOT be done in a microwave oven. Home canning destroys mold, yeast, bacteria and enzymes in foods to prevent spoilage.

Low acid and nonacid foods require a temperature of 240°F which is above the boiling point of water. In canning 240°F is obtained by using a pressure canner set at 10 pounds pressure (at sea level). Your microwave oven can only bring plain water to the boiling points. (212°F). High acid foods are processed in a hot water bath canner. The canning jars are covered with water which is kept at a rolling boil. Your microwave oven cannot duplicate this procedure. Since canning jars also need to be submerged in water for sterilization, it would be impossible to do this procedure in a microwave oven. Improperly canned food may spoil and be dangerous to consume. We recommend that canning be done only on a conventional range top following standard canning procedures.

In addition, certain canning lids and rings may cause arcing in the microwave oven.

PANASONIC RECOMMENDS THE FOLLOWING REGARDING COOKING IN YOUR MICROWAVE OVEN:

1. Small quantities of food or foods with low moisture content can burn, dry out or catch on fire. If a fire occurs, turn oven off and leave the oven door closed. Disconnect the power cord, or shut off power at the fuse or circuit breaker panel.

2. Popcorn must be popped in a microwave corn popper. Microwave corn poppers are available through many retail stores. In addition, special microwave popcorn is available in some areas of the country. This popcorn pops in its own package and does not require a microwave corn popper. It may be used in this oven.

3. Do not attempt to deep fat fry in your oven.

4. Dry only herbs in your microwave oven. Follow directions given in this cookbook and do not leave oven unattended. Drying meats, fruits, and vegetables are not recommended.

5. Do not use paper towels which contain a synthetic fiber woven into them, such as nylon. Synthetic fibers may cause the towel to ignite.

6. Do not use the oven for any reason other than the preparation of food. Exceptions would be specific uses indicated in this cookbook.

PRECAUTIONS TO AVOID POSSIBLE EXPOSURE TO EXCESSIVE MICROWAVE ENERGY

(a) **Do not attempt to operate this oven with the door open** since open-door operation can result in harmful exposure to microwave energy. It is important not to defeat or tamper with the safety interlocks.

(b) **Do not place any object** between the oven front face and the door or allow soil or cleaner residue to accumulate on sealing surfaces.

(c) **Do not operate the oven** if it is damaged. It is particularly important that the oven door close properly and that there is no damage to the :
   (1) door (bent)
   (2) hinges and latches (broken or loosened)
   (3) door seals and sealing surfaces

(d) **The oven should not be adjusted or repaired** by anyone except properly qualified service personnel.

OVEN MEALS

Total oven meals can be prepared in your microwave oven. Plan the order of the meal so that the foods that have the longest cooking and stand time are prepared first. The foods that need to be served immediately should be prepared last. Desserts can be prepared first and allowed to chill or stand, covered, or they can be prepared during the meal and served warm. At times it may be necessary to reheat a food for 1 or 2 minutes just before serving. To get you started, we have included Step-by-Step instructions for an easily prepared breakfast, lunch and dinner.

BREAKFAST

MENU:
Orange Juice
Baked Eggs in Bologna Cups
Raisin Bran Muffins

Prepare Raisin Bran Muffins, page 195.

Keep muffins covered until ready to use.
Prepare recipe for Baked Eggs in Bologna Cups on page 147.

Pour juice while eggs are cooking. Approximate cooking time is 15 minutes.

LUNCH

MENU:
Meat Loaf
Baked Potatoes
Fresh Broccoli
Raisin Bread Pudding
Iced Tea

Prepare Raisin Bread Pudding according to recipe on page 213.

Prepare Midget Meat Loaf according to recipe on page 90.

While meat loaf stands, bake potatoes according to chart on page 163.

After cooking wrap potatoes in foil. Prepare broccoli according to chart on page 162. Pour iced tea. Approximate cooking time is 45 minutes.

43

DINNER

MENU:
Apricot Glazed Chicken
Chicken Flavored Rice
(from mix)
Green Beans Amandine
Chilled Chocolate Almond
Souffle

Prepare Chocolate Souffle according to recipe on page 212. Souffle needs to be chilled for at least 3 hours so prepare early in the day.

Prepare rice according to chart on page 184.

Let rice stand, covered, until ready to serve. Meanwhile, prepare Apricot Glazed Chicken recipe on page 112. After cooking let stand, covered until ready to serve.

Assemble Green Bean Amandine, while chicken is cooking. Cook while chicken is standing.
If necessary, reheat rice or chicken 2 to 3 minutes while beans are standing.
Approximate cooking time is 1 hour.

APPETIZERS and BEVERAGES

Hot appetizers and beverages take minutes to heat in a microwave. Assembled and refrigerate appetizers before company arrives. When needed, place appetizers on microwave safe serving dish and heat. Hot appetizers can be easily prepared throughout a party.

CHILI DIP OLÉ

½ pound ground beef
1 large onion, finely chopped
1 envelope (1¼ oz.) chili seasoning mix
1 can (6 oz.) tomato paste
1 tablespoon sugar, optional
Corn chips

Yield: 2 Cups

Crumble ground beef in medium glass bowl. Stir in onions. Cook at **HIGH** 3 to 4 minutes, or until beef is browned; stir once. Drain. Stir in chili seasoning, tomato paste and sugar. Cook at **HIGH** 3 to 4 minutes. Serve warm with corn chips.

Crumble ground beef in medium bowl. Stir in onions.

Cook at HIGH 3 to 4 minutes, or until beef is browned. Stir once.

Remove grease from ground beef mixture. Stir chili seasoning, tomato paste and sugar. Cook at HIGH 3 to 4 minutes.

APPETIZER PÂTÉ A

1 pound chicken livers, halved
½ cup chicken broth
1 small onion, chopped
¼ teaspoon thyme
4 slices bacon, cooked (see page 83)
¼ cup butter or margarine, softened
  (see page 230)
1 tablespoon sherry, optional
½ teaspoon garlic salt
Dash pepper
Parsley flakes

Yield: 1⅓ Cups

In medium glass bowl, combine livers, broth, onion and thyme.

TO COOK BY AUTO SENSOR: Cover completely with plastic wrap. Cook on **COOK A3**. After time appears in display window, stir once.

TO COOK BY TIME: Cover with plastic wrap. Cook at **HIGH** 2 to 3 minutes and at **MEDIUM** 3 to 4 minutes; stir once.

TO COMPLETE: Drain and reserve ¼ cup liquid. With electric mixer, blender or food processor, puree liver and onion mixture, reserved broth, bacon, butter, sherry, garlic and pepper until smooth. Spoon into crock or small bowl. Sprinkle with parsley and chill. Serve as spread with crackers.

BACON BITES

4 slices bacon, halved
8 frozen potato puffs, defrosted (see page 32), canned pineapple chunks or water chestnuts

Yield: 8 Hors d'oeuvres

Place bacon between layers of paper towel on paper plate. Cook at **HIGH** 1½ to 2 minutes, or until partially cooked. Wrap bacon around potato and secure with wooden toothpick. Arrange on paper towel lined paper plate. Cook at **HIGH** 1½ to 2 minutes. Serve immediately.

COCKTAIL MEATBALLS A

½ pound ground beef
1 egg, beaten
¼ cup Italian flavored dry bread crumbs
1 clove garlic, finely chopped
2 tablespoons finely chopped green onion
½ teaspoon salt
¼ teaspoon basil leaves, crushed
Dash pepper
½ cup grape jelly
½ cup chili sauce
1 tablespoon prepared mustard

Yield: 24 Meatballs

In medium bowl, combine meat, egg, bread crumbs, garlic, onion and seasonings. Mix lightly. Shape in 24 bite-size meatballs. In 2-quart casserole, combine jelly, chili sauce and mustard. Mix until well blended. Add meatballs. Cover with lid.

TO COOK BY AUTO SENSOR: Cook on **COOK A3**. After time appears in display window, stir twice.

TO COOK BY TIME: Cook at **HIGH** 6 minutes and **MEDIUM-LOW** 9 minutes. Stir twice.

TO COMPLETE: Stir. Let stand, uncovered, 3 minutes before serving.

NEPTUNE'S CHEESE CANAPES

1 package (10 oz.) sharp Cheddar cold pack cheese food
⅓ cup butter or margarine
1 can (6 oz.) crabmeat, drained and flaked*
1 tablespoon flour
Dash hot pepper sauce
6 English muffins, split and toasted

Yield: 48 Canapes

Combine cheese and butter in medium glass bowl. Cook at **LOW** 1½ to 2 minutes, or until softened. Stir in crab, flour and pepper sauce; spread on muffins. Cut each muffin into quarters and garnish, if desired, with pimento or paprika. Arrange 12 canapes on a paper plate or microwave-safe serving plate. Cook at **MEDIUM** ½ to 1 minute, or until crab mixture begins to melt. Repeat procedure with remaining ingredients.

***Substitution:** Use 1 can (7 oz.) tuna, drained and flaked.*

HOLIDAY CHEESE BALL

1 package (3 oz.) cream cheese, softened
   (see page 230)
3 cups (12 oz.) shredded Cheddar cheese
¼ cup flour
¼ cup white wine
¼ teaspoon onion powder
⅛ teaspoon garlic powder
⅛ teaspoon Worcestershire sauce
⅓ cup finely chopped nuts or parsley
   flakes

Yield: 1 (6 inch) Ball

In medium glass bowl, combine cream
cheese, Cheddar cheese, flour, wine, onion,
garlic and Worcestershire. Cook at **WARM** 5
minutes. With electric mixer, beat until
smooth. Shape into ball and roll in nuts;
chill. Cook at **WARM** 3 minutes, or until
spreadable; serve.

CHEESE AND SPINACH ▣ CRUSTLESS QUICHE

4 eggs
⅓ cup half'n half
1½ cups (6 oz.) shredded Swiss cheese
1 package (10 oz.) frozen spinach, cooked
   and drained (see pages 163 and 165)
4 slices bacon, crisp-cooked and crumbled
   (see page 83)
1 teaspoon lemon juice
½ teaspoon salt

Yield: 10 Servings

Beat eggs with half'n half until light and
fluffy. Blend in cheese, spinach, bacon,
lemon juice and salt. Pour into lightly
greased 9-inch quiche dish.

TO COOK BY AUTO SENSOR: Cover
completely with plastic wrap. Cook on
COOK A7.

TO COOK BY TIME: Cook at **MEDIUM** 10 to
12 minutes.

TO COMPLETE: Quiche is done when knife
inserted near center comes out clean. Let
stand, uncovered, 5 minutes. Cut into 10
wedges to serve.

48

PARTY BLUE CHEESE SPREAD

1 envelope unflavored gelatin
¾ cup water
1 tablespoon lemon juice
1 package (3 oz.) cream cheese, softened
   (see page 230)
⅓ cup milk
¼ pound blue cheese, crumbled
½ cup sour cream
¼ cup diced green pepper or finely
   chopped walnuts
2 teaspoons Worcestershire sauce

Yield: 3 Cups

In small glass bowl, sprinkle unflavored gelatin over water. Heat at **HIGH** 2½ to 3 minutes, or until gelatin is dissolved; stir twice. Add lemon juice; cool slightly. Blend cream cheese and milk until smooth; stir in blue cheese, sour cream, green pepper, Worcestershire and gelatin mixture. Turn into 3-cup mold or bowl and chill until firm. Unmold and serve with crackers as a spread.

SURPRISE VEGETABLE DIP A

1 package (8 oz.) cream cheese (cut into 1-
   inch cubes)
1 jar (5 oz.) pasteurized process cheese
   spread with bacon
¼ cup beer
2 tablespoons chopped green onion
1 tablespoon chopped green pepper
1 tablespoon chopped pimento
1 teaspoon prepared horseradish
½ teaspoon prepared mustard

Yield: 2 Cups

Combine all ingredients in 1½-quart serving dish.

TO COOK BY AUTO SENSOR: Cover completely with plastic wrap. Cook on **COOK A1**.

TO COOK BY TIME: Cook at **HIGH** 3 to 4 minutes; stir once.

TO COMPLETE: Cheeses should be softened. Stir until well blended. Serve warm with assorted vegetable dippers.

MEXICALE FIESTA DIP A

1 pound pasteurized process cheese
   spread, cubed
1 can (16 oz.) whole tomatoes, drained
   and chopped
1 can (4 oz.) green chilies, drained and
   chopped
¼ teaspoon cumin seed
Dash hot pepper sauce
Taco Chips

Yield: 3 Cups

In large glass bowl, combine cheese, tomatoes, chilies, cumin seed and hot pepper sauce.

TO COOK BY AUTO SENSOR: Cover completely with plastic wrap. Cook on **COOK A4**. After time appears in display window, stir once. After cooking, release plastic wrap.

TO COOK BY TIME: Cook at **MEDIUM-LOW** 9 to 10 minutes. Stir occasionally.

TO COMPLETE: Stir; let stand, covered, 3 minutes. Stir before serving. Serve warm with taco chips.

SWISS FRUIT DIP A

1 package (8 oz.) cold pack cheese food,
   Swiss cheese flavor
¼ cup half'n half
1 tablespoon sherry
¼ teaspoon nutmeg

Yield: 1½ Cups

Combine all ingredients in 1-quart microwave-safe serving dish.

TO COOK BY AUTO SENSOR: Cover completely with plastic wrap. Cook on **COOK A1**.

TO COOK BY TIME: Cook at **HIGH** 3 to 4 minutes; stir once.

TO COMPLETE: Cheese should be softened. Stir until well blended. Serve warm with sliced apples, pears and grapes.

STUFFED MUSHROOMS

**1 pound medium fresh mushrooms
  (about 24), cleaned
4 slices bacon, chopped
¼ cup finely chopped onion
1 cup soft bread crumbs
¼ cup grated Parmesan cheese
¼ teaspoon pepper**

Yield: 24 Mushrooms

Remove mushroom stems and finely chop
1 cup; reserve. Combine bacon and onion
in medium glass bowl. Cook at **HIGH** 3 to
3½ minutes, or until bacon is crisp; stir
once. Drain. Stir in reserved mushroom
stems, bread crumbs, cheese and pepper.
Stuff mushroom caps with bread crumb
mixture and on glass platter, arrange 12 in
circular pattern. Cook, covered, at **HIGH** 6
to 7 minutes. Let stand, uncovered, 2 minutes
before serving; repeat procedure with
remaining ingredients.

Variation:
For SPINACH stuffed mushrooms, *partially
defrost 1 package (12 oz.) frozen spinach
souffle. Cut into squares and place in
mushroom caps; sprinkle, if desired, with
onion salt. Cook as directed above.*

SPICED NUTS

**2 tablespoons butter or margarine
1 to 2 tablespoons curry powder
1 tablespoon Worcestershire sauce
2 cups blanched almonds**

Yield: 2 Cups

Heat butter in 12×8-inch dish at **HIGH** 1
minute, or until melted. Stir in curry and
Worcestershire. Add almonds and coat
thoroughly. Cook at **HIGH** 4 to 5 minutes;
stir twice.

Variations:
For CHILI CASHEWS, *stir 1 to 2
tablespoons chili powder and 2 cups salted
cashews into melted butter.*
For GINGER WALNUTS, *stir 1 to 2
tablespoons ginger, 1 tablespoon soy sauce
and 2 cups walnuts into melted butter.*

NUTS AND BOLTS PARTY MIX

**½ cup butter or margarine
2 tablespoons Worcestershire sauce
½ teaspoon garlic salt
½ teaspoon salt
2 cups bite-size crispy corn squares
2 cups bite-size crispy rice squares
2 cups bite-size crispy wheat squares
1 cup salted peanuts
1 cup thin pretzel sticks**

Yield: 2 Quarts

Heat butter in 12×8-inch dish at **MEDIUM-
HIGH** 1 to 1½ minutes, or until melted. Stir
in Worcestershire, garlic and salt. Add
remaining ingredients, stir well.
Cook at **HIGH** 6 to 7 minutes, or until
butter is absorbed and mixture is crispy;
stir occasionally. Let cool before serving or
storing.

LAREDO STYLE NACHOS

Corn, taco or tortilla chips
Canned bean dip
Guacamole dip, optional
Jalapeno peppers, sliced, optional
Shredded Monterey jack cheese

Yield: 20 Hors d'oeuvres

Spread 20 chips with bean dip and guacamole dip; top with peppers and cheese. Arrange on wax paper lined glass oven tray or serving plate. Cook at **HIGH** 1 to 2 minutes, or until cheese is melted. Serve immediately. Repeat procedure as desired.

EASY OYSTER ROCKEFELLER A

2 cans (8 oz. ea.) oysters, drained
1 package (10 oz.) frozen creamed spinach, defrosted (see page 32)
2 tablespoons dry sherry
1 tablespoon finely chopped onion
½ teaspoon Worcestershire sauce
¼ teaspoon nutmeg
¼ teaspoon Tabasco sauce
½ cup fresh bread crumbs
¼ cup butter or margarine, melted
½ cup (2 oz.) natural shredded Swiss cheese
8 shell-shaped dishes or individual ramekin

Yield: 8 Servings

Place 5 oysters in each dish. With toothpick, pierce each oyster several times. Combine creamed spinach, sherry, onion, Worcestershire sauce, nutmeg and Tabasco sauce. Spoon over oysters. Toss bread crumbs with melted butter; sprinkle over spinach mixture. Top with 1 tablespoon cheese.

TO COOK BY AUTO SENSOR: Cover completely with plastic wrap. Cook on **COOK A1**.

TO COOK BY TIME: Cover with plastic wrap. Arrange 4 shells in a circle. Cook at **HIGH** 3 to 4 minutes.

TO COMPLETE: Let stand, uncovered, 3 minutes before serving. Repeat procedure with remaining shells.

IRISH COFFEE

2 to 3 cups strong coffee
4 teaspoons sugar
6 ounces Irish whiskey
Sweetened whipped cream

Yield: 4 Servings (about 6 oz. ea.)

Pour ½ to ¾ cup coffee into each of 4 cups. Heat at **HIGH** 3 to 3½ minutes. For each drink, stir in 1 teaspoon sugar and 1½ ounces Irish whiskey; top with whipped cream.

Note: *For **TWO Servings,** follow above procedure. Halve all ingredients; heat coffee 1½ to 2 minutes. For **ONE Serving,** heat coffee 1 to 1½ minutes.*

HEATING LIQUIDS CHART

For tea, instant coffee, hot chocolate mix, instant soups, hot cereal, recipes, etc.

DESIRED TEMPERATURE	LIQUID	AMOUNT	POWER	APPROX. COOKING TIME (in minutes)
Boiling (212°F)	Water	1 cup (8 oz.) 2 cups (16 oz.) 4 cups (32 oz.)	HIGH HIGH HIGH	2 to 3 4 to 5 8 to 9
Scalding (about 180°F)	Milk	1 cup (8 oz.) 2 cups (16 oz.)	MEDIUM MEDIUM	2½ to 3½ 4 to 5
Steaming (for beverages) (about 170°F)	Water	1 mug (8 oz.) 2 mugs (8 oz. ea.) 4 mugs (8 oz. ea.) 1 coffee cup (5 oz.) 2 coffee cups (5 oz. ea.) 4 coffee cups (5 oz. ea.)	HIGH HIGH HIGH HIGH HIGH HIGH	1 to 1½ 2 to 2½ 3½ to 4 ¾ to 1¼ 1½ to 2 3 to 3½
Steaming (about 160°F)	Milk	1 mug (8 oz.) 2 mugs (8 oz. ea.) 4 mugs (8 oz. ea.) 1 coffee cup (5 oz.) 2 coffee cups (5 oz. ea.) 4 coffee cups (5 oz. ea.)	MEDIUM MEDIUM MEDIUM MEDIUM MEDIUM MEDIUM	2 to 3 3½ to 6 6 to 7½ 1½ to 2 2 to 3 4 to 5

WARNING: *Heated liquids can erupt if not mixed with air. Do not heat liquids in your microwave oven without stirring first.*

CAFÉ BRÛLOT

⅓ to ½ cup brandy
1 tablespoon sugar
3 whole cloves
1 cinnamon stick, broken
Peel of 1 lemon or orange
2 cups hot strong coffee

Yield: 6 Demitasse Servings

In 1-cup glass measure, combine brandy, sugar, cloves, cinnamon and lemon peel. Heat at **HIGH** ¾ to 1 minute; stir. Carefully flame and strain brandy into coffee. Serve in demitasse cups.

Variation: If desired, pour coffee into cups. Top with heated brandy; flame.

MULLED WINE

3 cups dry red wine
8 teaspoons packed brown sugar, or to taste
2 cinnamon sticks, broken
Dash nutmeg

Yield: 4 Servings (6 oz. ea.)

Into each of 4 mugs, combine ¾ cup wine, 2 teaspoons brown sugar, ½ cinnamon stick and dash nutmeg. Heat at **MEDIUM** 4½ to 6 minutes.

Note: For TWO Servings, follow above procedure. Halve all ingredients; heat wine 3½ to 4½ minutes. For ONE Serving, heat wine 1½ to 2½ minutes.

HOT BUTTERED RUM

2⅔ cups apple cider or water
4 cinnamon sticks
4 tablespoons packed brown sugar
6 ounces rum
4 teaspoons butter or margarine
Dash nutmeg

Yield: 4 Servings (about 6 oz. ea.)

Into each of 4 mugs, combine ⅔ cup cider, 1 cinnamon stick and 1 tablespoon sugar. Heat at **HIGH** 3½ to 4 minutes. For each drink, stir in 1½ ounces rum; top with 1 teaspoon butter and dash nutmeg.

Note: For TWO Servings, follow above procedure. Halve all ingredients; heat cider 1½ to 2 minutes. For ONE Serving, heat cider 1 to 1½ minutes.

TEA JAMMER

3 cups water
4 tea bags
4 tablespoons apricot preserves*
4 tablespoons apricot brandy, optional*
Sugar to taste
Sweetened whipped cream or whipped topping
Dash nutmeg or cinnamon

Yield: 4 Servings (8 oz. ea.)

Pour ¾ cup water into each of 4 mugs. Heat at **HIGH** 3 to 3½ minutes. For each drink, add one tea bag; brew 3 to 5 minutes. Stir in 1 tablespoon preserves, 1 tablespoon brandy and sugar. Top with whipped cream and dash nutmeg.

* Variation: Try a variety of jelly, jam or preserves and fruit-flavored brandies.

Note: For TWO Servings, follow above procedure. Halve all ingredients; heat water 2 to 2½ minutes. For ONE Serving, heat water 1 to 1½ minutes.

CAPE COD WARMER A

3 cups cranapple or cranberry juice
8 whole allspice
8 whole cloves
4 cinnamon sticks, broken

Yield: 4 Servings (6 oz. ea.)

Combine all ingredients in 4-cup glass measure.

TO COOK BY AUTO SENSOR: Cover completely with plastic wrap. Cook on **COOK A1.** After cooking, release plastic wrap.

TO COOK BY TIME: Cook at **HIGH** 5 to 6 minutes and at **MEDIUM-LOW** 9 to 10 minutes.

TO COMPLETE: Cool slightly; strain into mugs.

Note: For TWO Servings, follow above procedure. Halve all ingredients and heat juice at HIGH 3 to 3½ minutes and at MEDIUM-LOW 5 minutes. For ONE Serving, heat juice at HIGH 1½ to 2½ minutes and at MEDIUM-LOW 3 minutes.

APRICOT BRANDY

8 ounces dried apricots, chopped
1 cup sugar
2 cups vodka

Yield: 2 Cups

Thoroughly combine all ingredients in medium glass bowl. Heat at **MEDIUM** 10 minutes, or until sugar is dissolved; stir twice. Heat at **WARM** 30 minutes; stir twice. Cover and let stand 3 to 4 days. Strain before serving.

PLUM BRANDY

1½ pounds fresh plums, halved
**   (pits remove)**
2 cups sugar
2 cups gin

Yield: 2 Cups

Thoroughly combine all ingredients in medium glass bowl. Heat at **MEDIUM** 10 minutes, or until sugar is dissolved, stir once. Heat at **WARM** 30 minutes; stir twice. Cover and let stand 3 to 4 days. Strain before serving.

COFFEE LIQUEUR

1½ cups hot water
2 cups sugar
⅓ cup freeze-dried coffee
2 cups vodka
1 vanilla bean

Yield: 2 Cups

Heat water in large glass bowl at **HIGH** 3 to 4 minutes, or until boiling. Stir in sugar and coffee until dissolved; add remaining ingredients. Heat at **MEDIUM** 5 minutes, and at **WARM** 30 minutes; stir twice. Cover and let stand 3 to 4 days. Strain before serving.

PEACH LIQUEUR

1½ pounds fresh peaches, peeled and
**   sliced**
1½ cups sugar
4 strips lemon peel
3 whole cloves
2 cinnamon sticks
2 cups bourbon

Yield: 2 Cups

Thoroughly combine all ingredients in medium glass bowl. Heat at **MEDIUM** 10 minutes, or until sugar is dissolved; stir once. Heat at **WARM** 30 minutes; stir twice. Cover and let stand 3 to 4 days. Strain before serving.

SAUCES and TOPPINGS

To add a special flair to your meals, try the recipes in this chapter. With the speedy assistance of your microwave oven, savory sauces and delicious dessert toppings are a snap to cook. Make a Creole Sauce to spice up leftovers, Strawberry Jam to make a special brunch or Hot Fudge Sauce for a latenight snack.

BASIC WHITE SAUCE **A**

2 tablespoons butter or margarine, melted
2 tablespoons flour
¼ teaspoon salt, optional
1 cup milk

Yield: 1 Cup

In 1½-quart bowl, combine melted butter, flour and salt. Gradually add milk; stir until smooth.

TO COOK BY AUTO SENSOR: Cover completely with plastic wrap. Cook on **COOK A4**. After time appears in display window, remove plastic wrap. Stir twice.

TO COOK BY TIME: Cook at **MEDIUM** 5 to 6 minutes, or until sauce is thickened. Stir occasionally with wire whisk.

Variations:
For CHEESE Sauce, stir in ½ to ¾ cup shredded cheese. Cook at MEDIUM 1 minute, if necessary, to completely melt cheese.
For CURRY Sauce, stir in 1 to 2 teaspoons curry powder.
For HORSERADISH Sauce, add 1 tablespoon prepared horseradish.
For MUSTARD Sauce, add 2 tablespoons prepared mustard and dash Worcestershire sauce.

Melt butter at MEDIUM-LOW 30 seconds in 1½ quart bowl. Stir in flour and salt. Gradually add milk; stir until smooth.

To Cook by Time: Cook at MEDIUM 5 to 6 minutes, or until sauce is thickened.

To Cook by Auto Sensor: Cover completely with plastic wrap. Cook on COOK A4.

Stir occasionally with wire wisk. For Auto Sensor cooking, stir after time appears in display window.

HOMEMADE SPECIAL SPAGHETTI SAUCE

2 tablespoons oil
¾ cup chopped onion
2 cloves garlic, finely chopped
1 can (28 oz.) whole tomatoes, chopped
1 can (6 oz.) tomato paste
½ cup water
1 bay leaf, crushed
½ teaspoon salt
¼ teaspoon basil
¼ teaspoon oregano

Yield: 1½ Quarts

In 3-quart glass bowl, combine oil, onion and garlic. Cook at **HIGH** 1½ to 2 minutes. Add remaining ingredients. Cook, covered with wax paper, at **HIGH** 6 to 7 minutes and at **LOW** 1 hour; stir occasionally.

Variation: Add ½ pound browned ground beef or sausage, drained with tomatoes.

BARBECUE SAUCE A

1 cup chili sauce
¾ cup water
¼ cup lemon juice
1 envelope (1⅜ oz.) onion soup mix
½ cup packed brown sugar
1 teaspoon dry mustard
⅛ teaspoon garlic powder

Yield: 2 Cups

Combine all ingredients in medium glass bowl.

TO COOK BY AUTO SENSOR: Cover completely with plastic wrap. Cook on **COOK A3.** After time appears in display window, stir occasionally. After cooking, release plastic wrap.

TO COOK BY TIME: Cook at **HIGH** 5 minutes and at **MEDIUM-LOW** 8 to 10 minutes; stir occasionally.

TO COMPLETE: Sauce should be slightly thickened. Use as basting sauce on chicken, ribs, hamburgers, etc.

CRANBERRY SAUCE

2 cups sugar
¼ cup water
1 pound fresh cranberries
1 medium orange

Yield: 3½ Cups

Combine sugar and water in large glass bowl. Cook at **HIGH** 3 to 4 minutes, or until sugar is dissolved; stir once. Add cranberries and cook, covered, at **HIGH** 5 to 6 minutes, or until berries are soft. Grate peel from orange and squeeze juice. Add peel and juice to cranberries. Mash berries with masher or stir well to crush; cool slightly. If desired, add additional sugar to taste; chill before serving.

HOMEMADE GRAVY

1 to 2 tablespoons butter or margarine
2 tablespoons flour
Salt and pepper to taste
Few drops browning sauce, optional
1 cup roast drippings*

Yield: 1 Cup

Heat butter in small glass bowl at **HIGH** ½ to ¾ minute, or until melted. Stir in flour, salt, pepper and browning sauce. Gradually add drippings; stir until smooth. Cook at **HIGH** 2½ to 3½ minutes, or until gravy is thickened; stir twice.

If necessary, add broth, milk or water to roast drippings to equal 1 cup. If using milk, cook at **MEDIUM 3 to 4 minutes.*

NEWBURG SAUCE

1 cup half'n half
1 cup milk
3 to 4 tablespoons sherry
3 tablespoons flour
3 egg yolks
Salt and pepper to taste

Yield: 2½ Cups

In medium glass bowl, combine half'n half, milk, sherry and flour. Cook at **MEDIUM** 5 to 6 minutes, or until sauce is slightly thickened; stir twice. With wire whisk, quickly stir in egg yolks; season with salt and pepper. Cook at **MEDIUM-LOW** 1½ to 2 minutes, or until sauce is thickened; stir twice.

SWEET AND SOUR SAUCE

Water
1 can (8¼ oz.) crushed pineapple in heavy
  syrup drained; reserve syrup
¼ cup packed brown sugar
1 tablespoon soy sauce, optional
1 tablespoon cornstarch
⅓ to ½ cup cider vinegar

Yield: 1½ Cups

In 2-cup glass measure, add enough water
to reserved syrup to equal ¾ cup; stir in
pineapple, brown sugar and soy sauce.
Cook at **HIGH** 2 to 2½ minutes; stir once.
Blend cornstarch with vinegar until smooth
stir into pineapple mixture. Cook at **HIGH** 2
to 2½ minutes, or until sauce is slightly
thickened; stir once.

*Variation: Add ½ cup finely chopped green
pepper with pineapple.*

PREPARING CONVENIENCE SAUCES

- Use a glass container twice the volume of the sauce.
- Prepare sauce ingredients according to package directions.
- A wire whisk is helpful in eliminating lumps, when stirring dry ingredients into liquids.
- If needed, melt butter at **MEDIUM-LOW**.
- Cook sauces according to directions in chart.
- To blend flavors, when necessary, cook at **MEDIUM-LOW**.
- Stir occasionally during cooking.

ITEM	POWER	APPROX. COOKING TIME (in minutes)
Packaged Sauce and Gravy Mixes (¾ to 1½ oz.) prepared with water prepared with milk	HIGH MEDIUM	2½ to 3½ 3½ to 5
Sauces from condensed cream-style soups	MEDIUM	5 to 6
Spaghetti Sauce Mix (2 cup yield) prepared with tomato sauce prepared with tomato paste	HIGH→ M. LOW HIGH→ M.LOW	2½ to 3 8 to 10 2½ to 3 10 to 12

RAISIN SAUCE FOR HAM Ⓐ

½ cup orange juice
½ cup water
1 tablespoon cornstarch
1 tablespoon rum, optional
½ cup raisins
⅓ cup currant jelly*
Dash allspice

Yield: 1½ Cups

In 1½-quart glass bowl, stir together
orange juice, water and cornstarch until
blended. Stir in rum, raisins, currant jelly
and allspice.

TO COOK BY AUTO SENSOR: Cover
completely with plastic wrap. Cook on
COOK A4. After time appears in display
window, remove plastic wrap. Stir twice.

TO COOK BY TIME: Cook at **HIGH** 6 to 7
minutes, or until sauce is thickened. Stir
occasionally.

Substitution: *Use pineapple or apricot
preserves for currant jelly.*

BANANA SPLIT TOPPING

1 can (8¼ oz.) chunk pineapple, drained;
  reserve syrup
1 can (17 oz.) dark sweet pitted cherries in
  heavy syrup, drained; reserve syrup
1½ tablespoons cornstarch
2 bananas, cut into 1-inch pieces
Favorite flavors ice cream

Yield: 3 Cups

Reserve ¼ cup syrup. In medium glass
bowl, combine remaining syrups, pineapple
and cherries. Cook at **HIGH** 3 to 4 minutes;
stir once. Blend cornstarch with reserved
syrup until smooth. Stir into hot mixture.
Cook at **HIGH** 2 to 2½ minutes, or until
sauce is thickened; stir once. Cool slightly;
slice bananas over ice cream and add
topping.

ORANGE LIQUEUR SAUCE

½ cup water
¼ cup orange juice
3 to 4 tablespoons sugar
1 tablespoon cornstarch
1 to 2 tablespoons orange flavored liqueur

Yield: 1 Cup

In small glass bowl, combine water, orange
juice, sugar and cornstarch. Cook at **HIGH**
1½ to 2 minutes, or until sauce is
thickened; stir once. Stir in liqueur; cool.
Serve, as desired, over rice pudding,
chocolate mousse or plain cake.

BRANDIED CHERRY SAUCE

1 can (17 oz.) dark sweet pitted cherries in
  heavy syrup, drained; reserve syrup
Water
½ cup sugar
1½ tablespoons cornstarch
¼ cup brandy

Yield: 6 Servings

Reserve ¼ cup syrup. To remaining syrup,
add enough water to equal 1¼ cups. In
medium glass bowl, combine syrup-water
mixture, cherries and sugar. Cook at **HIGH**
3 to 4 minutes; stir once. Blend cornstarch
with reserved syrup until smooth. Stir into
hot mixture. Cook at **HIGH** 2 to 2½
minutes, or until sauce is thickened; stir
once. Transfer to serving dish.
Heat brandy in 1-cup glass measure at
HIGH ½ to ¾ minute. Pour over cherries
and carefully flame. Serve, as desired, over
vanilla ice cream, angel food cake or
chocolate souffle.

CARAMEL SAUCE

1 package (14 oz.) caramels
2 tablespoons rum, optional
1 tablespoon water
¼ teaspoon cinnamon

Yield: 1¼ Cups

Combine all ingredients in small glass
bowl. Cook at **HIGH** 3 to 4 minutes; stir
until smooth.

LEMON SAUCE

1 cup water, divided
⅓ cup sugar
1 tablespoon cornstarch
1 tablespoon lemon juice
1 tablespoon butter or margarine

Yield: 1 Cup

Combine ¾ cup water and sugar in medium glass bowl. Cook at **HIGH** 2 to 2½ minutes, or until sugar is dissolved; stir once. Blend cornstarch with remaining ¼ cup water and lemon juice until smooth. Stir into hot mixture. Cook at **HIGH** 2 to 2½ minutes, or until sauce is thickened; stir once. Stir in butter; cool slightly before serving.

VANILLA SAUCE

1 cup milk, divided
⅓ cup sugar
1½ tablespoons cornstarch
1 tablespoon butter or margarine
1 teaspoon vanilla

Yield: 1½ Cups

Combine ¾ cup milk and sugar in medium glass bowl. Cook at **MEDIUM** 3½ to 4 minutes, or until sugar is dissolved; stir once. Blend cornstarch with remaining milk until smooth. Stir into hot mixture. Cook at **MEDIUM** 2 to 2½ minutes, or until sauce is thickened; stir once. Stir in butter and vanilla; chill. Serve, as desired, in place of whipped cream. Delicious on fresh berries.

CUSTARD SAUCE

1½ cups milk
3 tablespoons sugar
2 tablespoons flour
2 egg yolks
1 teaspoon vanilla

Yield: 2 Cups

In medium glass bowl, combine milk, sugar and flour. Cook at **MEDIUM** 4 to 4½ minutes, or until sauce is slightly thickened; stir twice. With wire whisk, quickly stir in egg yolks. Cook at **MEDIUM-LOW** 1 to 1½ minutes, or until sauce is thickened; stir twice. Stir in vanilla. Chill slightly before serving.

HOT FUDGE SAUCE

1 cup (6 oz.) semi-sweet chocolate pieces
½ cup light corn syrup
¼ cup half'n half or milk
1 tablespoon butter or margarine
1 teaspoon vanilla

Yield: 1½ Cups

Combine chocolate and syrup in small glass bowl. Cook at **MEDIUM-LOW** 4 to 4½ minutes; stir once. Gradually add half'n half, stir until smooth. Stir in butter and vanilla.

Variation:
For CHOCOLATE MINT SAUCE, use ½ to ¾ teaspoon mint extract for vanilla.

RUM SAUCE A

½ cup sugar
¼ cup butter or margarine
¼ cup evaporated milk
1 tablespoon rum extract
½ teaspoon vanilla

Yield: ½ Cup

Combine all ingredients in a 2-cup glass measure.

TO COOK BY AUTO SENSOR: Cover completely with plastic wrap. Cook on **COOK A1.**

TO COOK BY TIME: Cook at **HIGH** 4 to 5 minutes.
TO COMPLETE: Stir. Let stand, covered, 5 minutes.

MELBA SAUCE

1 package (10 oz.) frozen raspberries in heavy syrup, defrosted (see page 32)
1 can (8¼ oz.) sliced peaches, drained; reserve syrup
¼ cup water
1½ tablespoons cornstarch

Yield: 2 Cups

In small glass bowl, combine raspberries, reserved syrup, water and cornstarch. Cook at **HIGH** 4 to 4½ minutes, or until sauce is thickened; stir once. Chill; just before serving, add peaches. Serve, as desired, over pound cake, ice cream or shortcake.

STRAWBERRY JAM

**4 packages (10 oz. ea.) frozen strawberries
in heavy syrup, defrosted (see page 32)
5 cups sugar
2 tablespoons lemon juice
½–6 ounce bottle liquid pectin**

Yield: 6½ Cups

In 4-quart glass bowl, thoroughly combine
strawberries, sugar and lemon juice. Cook
at **HIGH** 20 to 22 minutes, or until mixture
comes to a full boil; stir occasionally
during first 7 minutes. Cook at **HIGH** an
additional 1 minute. Stir in pectin and skim
off any foam; stir and skim foam for about
7 minutes. Ladle into sterilized jars; seal
with paraffin.

Note: *Do not melt paraffin in your
microwave oven.*

Place defrosted strawberries
5 cups of sugar and lemon
juice in 4-quart glass bowl.

Cook mixture at HIGH for
7 minutes. Stir 3 times
during cooking.

Continue to cook at HIGH
until mixture comes to a full
boil about 13 to 15 minutes
and cook an additional
1 minute.

Stir in pectin and skim off
any foam. Continue to stir
and skim foam for about
7 minutes.

Sterilize glasses or jars.

Ladle strawberry jam into
hot sterilized jars. Seal with
⅛ to ¼-inch layer of
paraffin. Store jellies and
jams in a cool, dry place.

PEACH JAM

4 cups sliced, peeled fresh peaches (about 3 lb.)
7¼ cups sugar
¼ cup lemon juice
½–6 ounce bottle liquid pectin

Yield: 9 Cups

In 4-quart glass bowl, thoroughly combine peaches, sugar and lemon juice. Cook at **HIGH** 15 to 17 minutes, or until mixture comes to a full boil; stir occasionally during the first 5 minutes. Cook at **HIGH** an additional 1 minute. Stir in pectin and skim off any foam; stir and skim foam for about 7 minutes. Ladle into sterilized jars; seal with paraffin.

Note: Do not melt paraffin in your microwave oven.

GRAPE JELLY

2 cups grape juice
3½ cups sugar
½–6 ounce bottle liquid pectin

Yield: 3 Cups

Thoroughly combine juice and sugar in 4-quart glass bowl. Cook at **HIGH** 10 to 12 minutes, or until mixture is boiling; stir twice during first 4 minutes of cooking. Stir in pectin. Cook at **HIGH** 4 to 6 minutes, or until mixture comes to a full boil. Cook at **HIGH** an additional 1 minute; skim off any foam. Ladle into jars; seal with paraffin.

Note: Do not melt paraffin in your microwave oven.

APRICOT PINEAPPLE JAM

¼ pound dried apricots, finely chopped
1 can (20 oz.) crushed pineapple, drained; reserve syrup
Water
6½ cups sugar
½ cup lemon juice
½–6 ounce bottle liquid pectin

Yield: 6½ Cups

Combine apricots and reserved syrup in 4-cup glass measure. Cook at **HIGH** 1 to 2 minutes and at **MEDIUM** 3 to 4 minutes, or until apricots are soft. Add pineapple and enough water to equal 3½ cups. In large bowl, thoroughly combine fruit mixture, sugar and lemon juice. Cook at **HIGH** 19 to 21 minutes, or until mixture comes to a full boil; stir occasionally during first 7 minutes. Cook at **HIGH** an additional 1 minute. Stir in pectin and skim off any foam; stir and skim foam for about 7 minutes. Ladle into sterilized jars; seal with paraffin.

Note: Do not melt paraffin in your microwave oven.

SOUPS and STEWS

Satisfy hearty appetites with savory soups and stews prepared in your microwave oven. The lower power levels, MEDIUM-LOW and LOW allow flavors to blend and less tender cuts of meat to become tender. Follow our recipes for homemade soups and stew or adapt your favorites by using similar cooking power, times and techniques.

PREPARING CANNED SOUPS

Empty contents of can into casserole dish. Dilute according to label directions with milk or water.

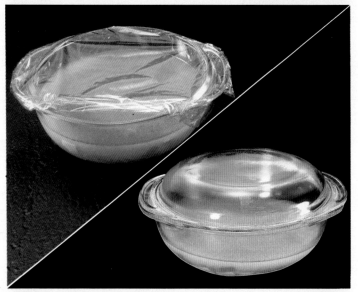

To Heat by Time:
Cover dish with lid or plastic wrap. Heat soup diluted with water at MEDIUM-HIGH. Heat soups diluted with milk at MEDIUM. Heat for times given in chart. Stir twice.

To Heat by Auto Sensor:
Cover dish with lid or completely with plastic wrap or casserole lid. Heat on COOK A1. Heating time should be 5 to 8 minutes.

After heating, stir. Let stand, covered, 3 minutes.

PREPARING CONVENIENCE SOUPS

SOUP	APPROX. COOKING TIME (in minutes) at MEDIUM-HIGH
Condensed (10½ to 11½ oz.)	4 to 6
Semi-condensed, single serving (7½ to 7¾ oz.)	2 to 4
Ready-to-heat (19 oz.)	6 to 8
(10¾ oz.)	3 to 5

PREPARING DRY SOUP MIXES

Select a casserole which is twice the volume of the water recommended on the soup mix package. Add water to the dish and stir. Bring to a boil. Stir in soup mix.

Cover with lid or plastic wrap or casserole lid. Heat at HIGH until water boils. Reduce power to MEDIUM-LOW. Heat 3 to 4 minutes for soups with narrow noodles, or 7 to 8 minutes for soups with broad noodles. Stir once during heating.

Stand, covered, 5 minutes, or until noodles and vegetables are tender.

MINESTRONE

2 tablespoons butter or margarine
2 medium carrots, thinly sliced
1 large onion, chopped
2 cups chicken broth
1 can (16 oz.) stewed tomatoes, chopped
1 cup shredded cabbage or zucchini
1 teaspoon basil
1 teaspoon parsley flakes
1 teaspoon salt
1 can (16 oz.) kidney beans, drained
¼ to ⅓ cup broken spaghetti (about 2-inch pieces)

Yield: 4 Servings

In 3-quart casserole, combine butter, carrots and onions. Cook, covered with lid, at **HIGH** 5 to 6 minutes. Add broth, tomatoes, cabbage, basil, parsley and salt. Cook, covered, at **HIGH** 7 to 8 minutes; stir once. Add kidney beans and spaghetti. Cook, covered, at **MEDIUM-LOW** 9 to 11 minutes, or until vegetables are tender; stir once. Let stand, covered, 10 minutes or until spaghetti is tender, before serving.

SUNDAY SUPPER SOUPS

Cheesy Tomato Soup

1 can (11 oz.) condensed Cheddar cheese soup
1 can (10¾ oz.) condensed tomato soup
1 can milk
1 can water
¼ teaspoon basil
Seasoned croutons or small pretzel rings, optional

Yield: 6 Servings

Stir both soups until smooth in a 3-quart casserole. Blend in remaining ingredients; mix well. Cover with lid. Cook at **MEDIUM-HIGH** 9 to 11 minutes. Stir occasionally.

Let stand, covered, 3 minutes before serving. Garnish, if desired, with seasoned croutons or small pretzel rings.

Garden Puree Soup

1 can (11¼ oz.) condensed split pea with ham soup
1 can (10¾ oz.) condensed tomato soup
1 can milk
1 can water
Seasoned croutons or small pretzel rings, optional

Yield: 6 Servings

Follow above procedure for Cheesy Tomato Soup.

SAVORY SPLIT PEA SOUP A

6 cups hot water
1 package (16 oz.) dried split peas
½ pound bacon, diced*
2 stalks celery, chopped
2 medium carrots, sliced
1 large onion, chopped
1 teaspoon salt
⅛ teaspoon thyme or basil

Yield: 6 Servings

Combine all ingredients in 4-quart casserole. Cover with lid.

TO COOK BY AUTO SENSOR: Cook on **COOK A5**. After time appears in display window, stir occasionally.

TO COOK BY TIME: Cook at **HIGH** 8 to 9 minutes and at **MEDIUM-LOW** 45 to 50 minutes. Stir occasionally.

TO COMPLETE: Peas should be tender. Put mixture through food mill or puree in food processor or blender. Reheat, adding additional water, if necessary.

***Substitution:** Use ham bone in place of bacon. Before putting soup through food mill, remove bone from soup and cut off any ham. Blend into soup before cooking.*

MANHATTAN CLAM A CHOWDER

1 can (10½ oz.) condensed vegetable soup
1½ cups tomato juice
1 can (7½ oz.) minced clams
Dash thyme

Yield: 4 Servings

Combine all ingredients in 1½-quart casserole; Cover with lid.

TO COOK BY AUTO SENSOR: Cook on **COOK A1**.

TO COOK BY TIME: Cook at **HIGH** 8 to 10 minutes; stir occasionally.

TO COMPLETE: Let stand, covered, 3 minutes; serve, if desired, with oysterette crackers.

MOM'S HOMEMADE CHICKEN A SOUP

2 to 2½ pounds chicken parts
3 stalks celery, cut up
2 bay leaves, crushed
1½ to 2 teaspoons peppercorns or pepper to taste
1 onion, sliced
8 cups hot water
2 carrots, shredded (about 1 cup)
1 to 1½ cups fine egg noodles
2 teaspoons salt

Yield: 8 Servings

In 5-quart casserole, combine chicken, celery, bay leaves, peppercorns, onion and water. Cover with lid.

TO COOK BY AUTO SENSOR: Cook on **COOK A4**.

TO COOK BY TIME: Cook at **HIGH** 10 minutes and at **MEDIUM-LOW** 35 to 37 minutes, or until chicken is tender.

TO COMPLETE: Strain broth into bowl and pour back into casserole. Add carrots, noodles and salt to broth. Cook, covered, at **MEDIUM-LOW** 7 to 8 minutes. Meanwhile, remove chicken from bone. Add chicken to soup and let stand, covered, 7 to 8 minutes or until noodles are tender.

67

FRENCH ONION SOUP ▗A▖

3 tablespoons butter or margarine
3 medium onions, sliced
3 cups beef broth
1 cup water*
1 teaspoon Worcestershire sauce
Salt and pepper to taste
Croutons
Grated Parmesan cheese

Yield: 4 Servings

TO COOK BY AUTO SENSOR: In 3-quart casserole, combine butter, onions, broth, water, Worcestershire, salt and pepper. Cover with lid. Cook on **COOK A3.**

TO COOK BY TIME: Combine butter and onions in 3-quart casserole; Cover with lid. Cook at **HIGH** 7 to 8 minutes. Stir in broth, water, Worcestershire, salt and pepper; cover. Cook at **HIGH** 9 to 10 minutes and at **MEDIUM** 10 minutes.

TO COMPLETE: Let stand, covered, 4 minutes before serving. Serve with croutons and cheese.

Variation: Use ½ cup water and ½ cup white wine.

CHICKEN GUMBO

1 pound chicken parts
¾ cup sliced onion
1 tablespoon flour
2 cups chicken broth
1 can (16 oz.) stewed tomatoes, chopped
1 package (10 oz.) frozen sliced okra, defrosted (see page 32)
1 can (8 oz.) whole kernel corn
1 teaspoon salt
2 dashes hot pepper sauce
⅛ teaspoon garlic powder
Pepper to taste

Yield: 6 Servings

Arrange chicken in 3-quart casserole. Cook, covered with lid, at **HIGH** 6 to 8 minutes, or until tender. Remove chicken and cool. Add onion to casserole. Cook at **HIGH** 3 minutes.
Blend flour with broth, until smooth. Stir into casserole. Stir in tomatoes, okra, corn, salt, hot pepper sauce, garlic and pepper. Cook, covered, at **HIGH** 5 to 7 minutes and at **MEDIUM** 8 to 10 minutes; stir occasionally. Meanwhile, remove chicken from bones. Add to soup and cook, covered, at **MEDIUM** 4 to 6 minutes. Let stand, covered, 5 minutes before serving.

NEW ENGLAND CHOWDER

4 slices bacon
1 small onion, finely chopped
2 tablespoons flour
Milk
1 can (7½ oz.) minced clams, drained; reserve liquid
2 small potatoes (about 4 oz. ea.) partially baked*, peeled and diced
1 teaspoon salt
⅛ teaspoon thyme
Dash pepper

Yield: 4 Servings

Arrange bacon in 3-quart casserole dish. Cook, covered with paper towel, at **HIGH** 3 to 4 minutes. Remove and crumble; set aside. Into bacon drippings, add onion. Cook at **HIGH** 2 minutes. Stir in flour. Add enough milk to reserved liquid to equal 2½ cups; gradually stir into dish. Add potatoes, salt, thyme and pepper. Cook, covered with lid, at **HIGH** 3 to 4 minutes and at **MEDIUM-LOW** 5 minutes; stir once. Stir in clams. Cook, covered, at **MEDIUM-LOW** 5 minutes. Let stand, covered, 3 minutes; top with bacon.

To partially bake potatoes, follow basic information for baking potatoes (page 163) except reduce cooking time to 3 to 4 minutes. Let stand, 5 minutes, before peeling.

CREAMY CORN CHOWDER

3 tablespoons butter or margarine
¼ cup finely chopped celery or green pepper
3 tablespoons flour
1 teaspoon dried chives or dried onion flakes
½ teaspoon salt
⅛ teaspoon pepper
2 cups milk
1 can (17 oz.) cream-style corn

Yield: 4 Servings

Combine butter and celery in 2-quart casserole. Cook at **MEDIUM** 2 to 3 minutes. Stir in flour, chives, salt and pepper. Gradually add milk, stir until smooth. Stir in corn. Cook at **MEDIUM** 7 to 9 minutes, or until soup is slightly thickened; stir twice. Let stand, covered, 3 minutes before serving.

VICHYSSOISE

3 tablespoons butter or margarine
3 medium leeks, white part sliced
1½ cups chicken broth
½ teaspoon salt
⅛ teaspoon pepper
2 medium potatoes, baked (see page 163)
1½ cups milk
1 cup heavy cream
1 tablespoon sherry, optional
Chopped chives, optional

Yield: 4 Servings

Combine butter and leeks in 2-quart casserole. Cook at **HIGH** 3 to 4 minutes; stir in broth, salt and pepper. Cook, covered, with lid, at **HIGH** 3 to 4 minutes and at **MEDIUM** 5 minutes.
Meanwhile, peel and dice potatoes. With electric mixer, blender or food processor, puree potatoes, broth mixture and milk. Return to dish. Cook, covered, at **MEDIUM** 3 to 4 minutes; stir in cream and sherry. Chill thoroughly and garnish, if desired, with chopped chives before serving.

Note: This soup is also delicious piping hot!

CREAM OF BROCCOLI SOUP

6 tablespoons butter or margarine
1 tablespoon finely chopped onion
5 tablespoons flour
1 cup chicken broth
2 cups milk
¾ teaspoon salt
Dash pepper
Dash nutmeg, optional
1 package (10 oz.) frozen chopped broccoli, defrosted (see page 32)

Yield: 4 Servings

Combine butter and onion in 2-quart casserole. Cook at **HIGH** 1½ to 2 minutes. Blend in flour. Gradually add broth, milk, salt, pepper and nutmeg; stir until smooth. Cook at **MEDIUM** 7 to 9 minutes, or until soup slightly thickened; stir occasionally. Add broccoli and puree in food processor or blender. Return to casserole. Cook at **MEDIUM** 3 to 4 minutes; stir once.

Variations:
For Cream of MUSHROOM Soup, follow above procedure. Substitute 2 cans (4 oz. ea.) sliced mushrooms, drained, for broccoli.
For Cream of SPINACH Soup, follow above procedure. Substitute 1 package (10 oz.) frozen spinach, defrosted, for broccoli.
For Cream of CHICKEN Soup, follow above procedure. With butter and onion, cook ¼ pound chicken meat, diced 2½ to 3 minutes, stir once. Use 2 cups chicken broth and 1 cup milk; omit broccoli.

BEEF STEW

2 pounds boneless beef, cut into 1-inch cubes
2 cups water, divided
1 envelope (1¾ oz.) onion soup mix
4 medium carrots, thinly sliced
2 potatoes (about 8 oz. ea.) peeled and cut into ½-inch cubes
1 bay leaf
1 can (8 oz.) green peas, drained
¼ cup flour

Yield: 8 Servings

In 4-quart casserole, combine beef, 1½ cups water, soup mix, carrots, potatoes and bay leaf. Cover with lid.

TO COOK BY AUTO SENSOR: Cook on **COOK A5**. After time appears in display window, stir occasionally.

TO COOK BY TIME: Cook at **HIGH** 7 to 8 minutes and at **MEDIUM-LOW** 55 to 60 minutes, or until tender. Stir occasionally

TO COMPLETE: Add peas and flour blended with remaining ½ cup water. Cook at **HIGH** 5 to 7 minutes, or until stew is thickened; stir occasionally.

In 4-quart casserole, combine beef, 1½ cups water, soup mix, carrots, potatoes and bay leaf.

Cover with lid.
To Cook by Time: Cook on HIGH for 8 minutes and MEDIUM-LOW 55 to 60 minutes, or until beef is tender. Stir occasionally.
To Cook by Auto Sensor: Cook on COOK A5. After time appears in the display window, stir occasionally.

Add peas. Blend flour with remaining ½ cup water. Stir into stew. Cook at HIGH 5 to 7 minutes, or until stew thickened; stir occasionally.

70

CHILI STEW

1 pound lean ground beef
2 medium onions, chopped
¼ teaspoon dried garlic pieces
1 can (16 oz.) pinto or red kidney beans
1 can (15 oz.) stewed tomatoes, chopped
1 can (15 oz.) tomato sauce
1 teaspoon salt
2 to 3 tablespoons chili powder

Yield: 4 Servings

TO COOK BY AUTO SENSOR: Crumble ground beef in 3-quart casserole dish. Stir in remaining ingredients. Cover with lid. Cook on **COOK A5**. After time appears in display window, stir occasionally.

TO COOK BY TIME: Crumble ground beef in 3-quart casserole. Stir in onion and garlic. Cook at **HIGH** 6 to 7 minutes. Stir once; drain. Stir in remaining ingredients. Cook, cover with lid, at **HIGH** 6 to 7 minutes and at **MEDIUM-LOW** 35 to 40 minutes; stir occasionally.

TO COMPLETE: Stir. Let stand, covered, 7 minutes before serving.

BAVARIAN STEW

1½ pounds boneless beef, cut into strips
2 cups water, divided
2 medium onions, sliced
¼ cup cider vinegar
1 tablespoon sugar
1 bay leaf
1 teaspoon salt
½ teaspoon caraway seeds
1 small head (about 1 lb.) red cabbage, shredded*
¼ cup flour

Yield: 6 Servings

In 4-quart casserole, combine beef, 1½ cups water, onions, vinegar, sugar, bay leaf, salt and caraway. Cook, covered with lid, at **HIGH** 6 to 7 minutes and at **LOW** 30 to 35 minutes; stir occasionally.
Add red cabbage. Cook, covered, at **LOW** 20 to 25 minutes, or until beef and cabbage are tender; stir occasionally.
Blend flour with remaining ½ cup water until smooth. Stir into hot liquid. Cook at **HIGH** 4 to 5 minutes, or until stew is thickened; stir once.

***Substitution:** Use 1 jar (16 oz.) red cabbage drained for fresh red cabbage.*

ZESTY BEEF STEW A

2 tablespoons flour
1 teaspoon salt
¼ teaspoon pepper
¼ teaspoon garlic powder
1½ pounds round steak, cut into 1-inch cubes
1 large onion, sliced
½ cup chopped green pepper
½ cup catsup
¼ cup packed brown sugar

Yield: 4–6 Servings

In small dish combine flour, salt, pepper and garlic powder. Coat meat with flour mixture. In 2-quart casserole, combine meat, onion, green pepper, catsup and sugar. Cover with lid.

TO COOK BY AUTO SENSOR: Cook on **COOK A5**. After time appears in display window, stir occasionally.

TO COOK BY TIME: Cook at **MEDIUM** 10 minutes and at **MEDIUM-LOW** 20 to 22 minutes, or until meat is tender. Stir occasionally.

TO COMPLETE: Stir, let stand, covered, 5 minutes. Serve, if desired, over noodles.

IRISH STEW A

2 pounds boneless lamb, cut into 1-inch cubes
2 medium carrots, sliced into ¼-inch pieces
2 potatoes (about 6 oz. ea.), peeled and cubed
2½ cups water, divided
1 envelope (1 oz.) onion-mushroom soup mix
1 bay leaf
¼ cup flour

Yield: 8 Servings

In 4-quart casserole, arrange lamb, carrots and potatoes forming three separate layers. In bowl, combine 2 cups hot water, onion-mushroom mix and bay leaf. Stir together until well blended. Pour mixture over potatoes. Cover with lid.

TO COOK BY AUTO SENSOR: Cook on **COOK A5**. After time appears in display window, stir twice.

TO COOK BY TIME: Cook at **HIGH** 7 to 8 minutes and at **LOW** 70 to 75 minutes. Stir twice.

TO COMPLETE: Blend flour with remaining ½ cup water until smooth. Stir into dish*. Cook at **HIGH** 4 to 5 minutes, or until stew is thickened.

*If desired, add ¼ teaspoon browning sauce.

APPLE CIDER STEW A

½ small turnip, diced (about 3 cups)
½ pound fresh green beans, cut into 1½-inch pieces*
½ cup water, divided
1 cup sliced onion
2 pounds boneless beef, cut into 1-inch cubes
2 cups apple cider
2 tablespoons catsup
2 teaspoons salt
1 bay leaf
¼ teaspoon pepper
⅛ teaspoon thyme
¼ cup flour

Yield: 8 Servings

TO COOK BY AUTO SENSOR: In 4-quart casserole, combine turnip, beans, ¼ cup water, onion, beef, cider, catsup, salt, bay leaf, pepper and thyme; mix well. Cover with lid. Cook on **COOK A5**. After time appears in display window, stir occasionally.

TO COOK BY TIME: In medium glass bowl, combine turnips, beans and ¼ cup water. Cook at **HIGH** 8 to 9 minutes; stir once. Drain; reserve vegetables. In 4-quart casserole, combine onion, beef, cider, catsup, salt, bay leaf, pepper and thyme. Cover with lid. Cook at **HIGH** 5 to 6 minutes and at **LOW** 60 minutes. Stir occasionally.
Add reserved vegetables and cook, covered, at **LOW** 15 minutes, or until tender.

TO COMPLETE: Blend flour with remaining ¼ cup of water until smooth. Stir into stew. Cook at **HIGH** 3 to 4 minutes, or until stew is slightly thickened. Stir once.

Substitution: Use 1 can (16 oz.) sliced potatoes, drained and 1 can (16 oz.) sliced green beans, drained. Do not precook, just add to stew.

TERRIFIC BEER STEW A

1½ pounds boneless beef, cut into 1-inch cubes
4 carrots, cut into ½-inch slices
1 can (10½ oz.) beef broth
1 cup beer
1 tablespoon packed brown sugar
1½ teaspoons salt
1 teaspoon thyme
½ teaspoon pepper
3 medium onions, cut in eighths
1 package (10 oz.) frozen green peas
¼ cup water
3 tablespoons flour
1 regular size (10×16-inch) oven cooking bag

Yield: 6 Servings

TO COOK BY AUTO SENSOR: In 4-quart casserole (do NOT use cooking bag), combine beef, carrots, beef broth, beer, sugar, salt, thyme, pepper and onions. Cover with lid. Cook on **COOK A5**. After time appears in the display window, add peas. Stir occasionally.

TO COOK BY TIME: Prepare cooking bag according to package directions. In cooking bag, combine beef, carrots, beef broth, beer, sugar, salt, thyme, pepper and onions. Turn bag several times to mix. Pull bag up around beef and close (3-inch from top) with nylon tie or cotton string. Make six half-inch slits in top of bag. Place in 2-quart casserole. Cook at **HIGH** 7 minutes and at **LOW** 30 minutes. Open bag, add peas, and reclose bag. Cook at **LOW** 20 to 30 minutes.

TO COMPLETE: Blend flour with water* until smooth. Stir into stew. Cook at **HIGH** 2 to 2½ minutes, or until slightly thickened.

If desired, add ½ teaspoon browning sauce.

FISHERMAN'S POT

1 can (28 oz.) whole tomatoes, chopped
1 cup chicken broth
1 stalk celery, thinly sliced
1 large onion, sliced
1 tablespoon sugar, optional
1 clove garlic, finely chopped
1 teaspoon parsley flakes
1 teaspoon salt
Dash thyme
1 pound fish fillets, cut into chunks*
¼ cup white wine, optional

Yield: 4 Servings

In 3-quart casserole, combine tomatoes, broth, celery, onion, sugar, garlic, parsley, salt and thyme. Cook, covered with lid, at **HIGH** 5 minutes and at **MEDIUM** 9 to 10 minutes; stir once. Add fish and wine. Cook, covered, at **MEDIUM** 10 minutes, or until fish is tender, stir once. Let stand, covered, 5 minutes before serving.

***Variation:** Use a combination of your favorite fish.*

BRUNSWICK STEW A

2½ to 3 pound chicken, cut into serving pieces
1 can (16 oz.) whole tomatoes, chopped
1¼ cups water, divided
1 medium onion, thinly sliced
2 teaspoons salt
2 bay leaves, crushed
¼ teaspoon pepper
1 package (10 oz.) frozen succotash, partially defrosted (see page 32)
1 package (10 oz.) frozen sliced okra, partially defrosted (see page 32)
¼ cup flour

Yield: 4 Servings

In 3-quart casserole, combine chicken, tomatoes, 1 cup water, onion, salt, bay leaves and pepper. Cover with lid.

TO COOK BY AUTO SENSOR: Cook on **COOK A4**. After time appears in display window, stir once.

TO COOK BY TIME: Cook at **HIGH** 6 to 7 minutes and at **MEDIUM** 14 to 16 minutes. Stir once.

TO COMPLETE: Stir in succotash and okra; cover. Cook at **HIGH** 10 to 12 minutes; stir once. Blend flour with remaining ¼ cup water until smooth. Stir into liquid. Cook at **HIGH** 5 to 6 minutes, or until thickened.

SPICY SAUSAGE STEW A

1 pound Italian sausage links, cut into 1½-inch pieces
1 pound boneless pork, cut into 1-inch cubes
1 can (28 oz.) whole tomatoes, chopped
1 can (8 oz.) tomato sauce
1 green pepper, cut into chunks
1 teaspoon basil
1 teaspoon oregano
½ teaspoon garlic powder

Yield: 6 Servings

Cook sausage in 3-quart casserole at **HIGH** 5 to 6 minutes; stir once. Drain. Stir in remaining ingredients. Cover with lid.

TO COOK BY AUTO SENSOR: Cook on **COOK A5**. After time appears in display window, stir occasionally.

TO COOK BY TIME: Cook at **HIGH** 5 to 6 minutes and at **LOW** 55 to 58 minutes, or until pork is tender. Stir occasionally.

TO COMPLETE: Skim off fat from liquid. Serve, if desired, with rice or pasta.

MEATS

Most roasts can be cooked rare, medium or even well-done in less than one hour. Less tender cuts of meat such as pot roast can be simmered fork-tender in a sauce or gravy by using LOW power. In this chapter, there are a variety of recipes to please everyone, everyday favorites, entertaining specials and calorie savers. Use these times and procedures as well as the information from the charts as a guideline when microwaving a favorite recipe for the first time.

GENERAL DIRECTIONS FOR ROASTING TENDER CUTS OF MEAT

For best results, select roasts that are uniform in shape.

Season as desired, but salt after cooking. Browning sauce mixed with equal parts of butter will enhance the color.

Meats can be shielded at the beginning of cooking or halfway through cooking. If you wish to shield at the beginning of cooking, remove foil halfway through the cooking time. Beef and pork rib roasts should be shielded by the bones. Foil should extend about 2-inches down from bones. The shank bone on a lamb roast should be cupped with foil. Thin ends of boneless roasts should also be shielded.

Half hams should be shielded by wrapping a 3-inch wide strip of foil around the large end of the ham. Secure to the body of the ham with wooden toothpicks. Fold 1½ inches over cut surface. For shank ham halves, shield shank bone by cupping it with foil.

One-third of the way through cooking, remove ham from oven and cut off skin. Turn fat-side up and reshield edges. If desired, glaze during last 10 to 20 minutes of cooking.

Canned hams should be shielded on the top cut-edge with a 1½-inch strip of foil. Wrap strip of foil around ham and secure to body of ham with wooden toothpicks. Fold 1-inch over cut surface. If desired, glaze last 10 to 20 minutes of cooking.

After cooking, check temperature using a meat thermometer. The thermometer should not touch bone or fat. If it does, the reading could be inaccurate. Lower temperatures are found in the center of the roast and in the muscle close to a large bone, such as a pork loin center rib roast. If the temperatures are low, return meat to the oven and cook a few more minutes at the recommended power level.
DO NOT USE A CONVENTIONAL MEAT THERMOMETER IN THE MICROWAVE OVEN. Let stand, tented with foil, 10 to 15 minutes. During stand time internal temperature rises 5°F to 15°F.

DIRECTIONS FOR COOKING TENDER CUTS OF MEAT BY TIME

Place meat on microwave roasting rack set in an oblong dish. Beef Rib Roast should be placed cut side down. Other bone-in roasts should be placed fat-side down. Boneless roast should be placed fat-side up. Halfway through cooking turn over bone-in roasts.

Loosely cover baking dish with wax paper to prevent spatter. If a large amount of juice accumulates in the bottom of the dish, drain occasionally. If desired, reserve for making gravy.
Multiply the weight of the roast by the minimum recommended minutes per pound. Program Power and Time.

DIRECTIONS FOR COOKING TENDER CUTS OF MEAT BY AUTO SENSOR

Place meat on microwave roasting rack set in an oblong dish. Cover completely with 2 overlapping pieces of plastic wrap.

Heat on Auto Sensor Cycle indicated in chart. When time appears in the display window, shield and/or turn meat or brush with glaze.

MEAT ROASTING CHART FOR TIME COOKING

MEAT	POWER	APPROX. COOKING TIME (Minutes per pound)	APPROXIMATE TEMPERATURE AFTER STANDING
Beef Roasts (up to 5 lb.)			
Rare	MEDIUM-LOW	8½ to 9½	125° to 135°F
Medium	MEDIUM-LOW	11 to 12½	135° to 145°F
Well	MEDIUM-LOW	13 to 14½	170° to 175°F
Beef Pot Roast (up to 4 lb.) *Chuck, Rump, Flank	LOW	20 to 25	———
Pork			
*Roast (up to 5 lb.)	MEDIUM-LOW	12 to 13½	170° to 175°F
Ham (fully cooked)			
Canned (3 to 5 lb.)	MEDIUM-LOW	9 to 10	120° to 130°F
Shank (8 lb.)	MEDIUM-LOW	9 to 10	120° to 130°F
Chops ½" thick	MEDIUM	8 to 11	———
Lamb Roast (up to 5 lb.)			
Medium	MEDIUM-LOW	11 to 12½	150° to 160°F
Well	MEDIUM-LOW	13 to 14½	170° to 175°F
Chops ½" thick	MEDIUM	7 to 10	———

*These meats should be cooked in a cooking bag or covered casserole surrounded with liquid.

MEAT ROASTING CHART FOR AUTO SENSOR COOKING [A]

MEAT	AUTO SENSOR CYCLE	APPROXIMATE COOKING TIME (Minutes per pound)	APPROXIMATE TEMPERATURE AFTER STANDING	SPECIAL INSTRUCTIONS
Beef Roasts (up to 5 lb.)				
Rare	COOK A4	4 to 6	125° to 135°F	
Medium	COOK A3	7 to 9	135° to 145°F	———
Well	COOK A2	10 to 13	170° to 175°F	
Beef Pot Roast (up to 4 lb.)				
Chuck, Rump, Flank	COOK A2	17 to 20	———	Use 1 cup liquid per pound beef. Cook in 4-quart casserole with lid. Turn roast over once after time appears in display window.
Pork				
Roast (up to 5 lb.)	COOK A2	11 to 13	170° to 175°F	To glaze hams, prepare as recipe directs, coat ham with ½ the glaze before cycle heating. Add remaining glaze with time appears in display window. Recover after glazing.
Ham (fully cooked)				
Canned (3 to 5 lb.)	COOK A3	4 to 5	120° to 130°F	
Slice	COOK A3	7 to 9	120° to 130°F	
Chops ½" thick	COOK A8	8 to 11	———	
Lamb Roast (up to 5 lb.)				
Medium	COOK A3	6 to 7	150° to 160°F	Use 8" square baking dish for 2 to 3 chops.
Well	COOK A2	10 to 11	170° to 175°F	
Chops ½" thick	COOK A8	7 to 10	———	

DIRECTIONS FOR COOKING LESS-TENDER CUTS BY TIME

Less tender cuts such as pot roasts should be cooked in liquid. Use ½ to 1 cup of soup, broth, etc. Use an oven cooking bag or covered casserole when cooking less tender cuts of meat. Select a covered casserole deep enough so that the meat does not touch the lid.

If an oven cooking bag is used, prepare the bag according to package directions. Do not use wire or metal twist-ties. Use the nylon tie provided, otherwise, use a piece of cotton string or a strip cut from the open end of the bag. Make six ½-inch slits in top of bag to allow steam to escape.

Multiply the weight of the roast by the minimum recommended minutes per pound. Program oven. Turn meat over halfway through cooking. Meat should be fork tender when done.

DIRECTIONS FOR COOKING LESS-TENDER CUTS BY AUTO SENSOR

Less tender cuts such as pot roasts should be cooked in liquid. Use 1 cup of liquid such as soup or broth per pound of meat. Cook in a 4-quart covered casserole. Do not use an oven cooking bag.

Cook on Cook A2. When time appears in display window turn meat over. Meat should be fork tender when done.

To Cook frozen pot roasts by Froz-Cook: season fresh meat and wrap for freezing. When ready to cook, add 8 to 9 ice cubes per pound of meat. Cover 4-quart casserole with lid.

Cook on FROZ-COOK A3. When time appears in the display window, turn roast over and add vegetables.

GENERAL DIRECTIONS FOR PREPARING CONVENIENCE MEATS

Brush hamburgers and fresh sausage links with browning sauce mixed with equal parts of melted butter to enhance appearance.

Pierce sausage links with fork and score frankfurters before cooking.

To Cook by Time

Arrange food in a single layer in baking dish. Loosely cover with wax paper to prevent spatter. Up to four slices of bacon may be placed between layers of paper towels on paper plate. Cook according to time given in chart.

Let stand according to recommended time in charts.

To Cook by Auto Sensor

Arrange food in a single layer in baking dish. Cover completely with plastic wrap. Cook on Auto Sensor Cycle as indicated in chart.

After cooking release plastic wrap and let stand 3 to 5 minutes before serving.

PREPARING CONVENIENCE MEATS A

ITEM	AMOUNT	TIME COOKING			AUTO SENSOR COOKING
		POWER	APPROX. COOKING TIME (in minutes)	STAND TIME (in minutes)	AUTO SENSOR CYCLE
Beef Patties, frozen (3½ oz. ea.)	1 2 4	M. HIGH	2½ to 3 3½ to 4½ 5½ to 6½	2 3 3	FROZ-COOK A6
Bacon, slices*	2 3 4 8	HIGH	1 to 1½ 1½ to 2 2 to 3 4½ to 5½	1 1 1 1	—————
Canadian bacon slices (2 oz.)	2 4 8	HIGH	1 to 1½ 2 to 3 3 to 4	3 3 3	—————
Frankfurters, scored	2 4	HIGH	1½ to 2 2½ to 3½	3 3	COOK A1 FROZ-COOK A1**
Ham, slices (about 2 oz. ea.)	2 4	HIGH	1½ to 2½ 2½ to 3½	3 3	—————
Hamburgers (4 oz. ea.)	1 2 4	M. HIGH	¾ to 1¼ 1½ to 2 3½ to 4	2 2 2	COOK A8
Frozen Lamb Chops (4 oz. ea)	1 2 4	—————	—————	3 3 3	FROZ-COOK A6
Frozen Pork Chops (4 oz. ea)	1 2 4	—————	—————	3 3 3	FROZ-COOK A5
Sausage Links, frozen, (precooked, brown and serve)	2 4 8	HIGH	1 to 1½ 1½ to 2 3 to 4	2 2 2	—————
Sausage Links, fresh (1 to 2 oz. ea.)	2 4 8	HIGH	2 to 3 4 to 5 6½ to 7½	3 3 3	—————
Sausage Links or Patties fresh (1 to 2 oz. ea.)	2 4	HIGH	1 to 2½ 2 to 4	2 2	—————

*Note: Cooking more than 4 pieces bacon on paper utensils at one time is not recommended.

**Note: Two to four frozen frankfurters can be heated on FROZ-COOK A1.

Special Hint: Pierce with fork and brush with browning sauce before cooking.

BEEF WITH BROCCOLI

1 tablespoon oil
1 pound boneless steak, cut into thin strips
1 clove garlic, finely chopped
⅛ teaspoon ginger
3 to 4 cups broccoli flowerets
1 tablespoon cornstarch
½ cup beef broth
1 tablespoon sherry
1 tablespoon soy sauce
Toasted sesame seeds (see page 231)

Yield: 4 Servings

Heat oil in 12×8-inch dish at **HIGH** 2 minutes. Stir in beef, garlic and ginger. Cook at **HIGH** 3½ to 4½ minutes; stir twice. Add broccoli. Cook, covered with plastic wrap, at **HIGH** 5 to 6 minutes, or until broccoli is tender crisp; stir once. Blend cornstarch with broth, sherry, and soy sauce until smooth. Stir into beef mixture. Cook at **HIGH** 3 to 4 minutes, or until sauce is thickened; stir once. Top with sesame seeds.

Hint: If desired, combine beef with garlic, ginger, broth, sherry and soy sauce; marinate 30 minutes. Drain and reserve marinade to thicken. Proceed as directed above.

BEEF STROGANOFF

3 tablespoons butter or margarine
1 large onion, thinly sliced
1 pound boneless steak, cut into thin strips
¼ pound fresh mushrooms, sliced
Beef broth
½ teaspoon salt
¼ teaspoon pepper
2 tablespoons flour
½ to 1 cup sour cream or plain yogurt
⅛ teaspoon browning sauce, optional

Yield: 4 Servings

Heat butter in 12×8-inch dish at **HIGH** 1½ to 2 minutes. Add onion. Cook at **HIGH** 2 to 2½ minutes; stir once. Add beef and mushrooms. Cook at **MEDIUM-HIGH** 6½ to 7 minutes; stir twice. Drain and reserve liquid; add enough broth to reserved liquid to equal ¾ cup. Sprinkle beef with salt and pepper. Into dish, blend in flour, then broth mixture. Cook at **MEDIUM** 2½ to 3 minutes, or until sauce is thickened. Blend in sour cream and browning sauce and cook, if necessary, at **MEDIUM** 2 to 3 minutes.

Note: For TWO Servings, following above procedure; halve all ingredients. Heat butter 1 minute, onion 1 to 1¼ minutes, beef 3 to 3½ minutes and sauce 1 to 1½ minutes.

84

TERIYAKI BEEF KABOBS

2 tablespoons packed brown sugar
2 tablespoons soy sauce
1 tablespoon lemon juice
1 tablespoon oil
1 pound boneless steak, cut into
    1½-inch cubes
½ pint cherry tomatoes
1 medium green pepper, cut into chunks

Yield: 4 Servings

In bowl, combine sugar, soy sauce, lemon juice and oil; add steak. If desired, cover and marinate in refrigerator at least 3 hours, stirring occasionally. On four 9 or 10-inch wooden skewers, alternately thread steak, tomatoes and green pepper. Arrange skewers on 8-inch square dish. Cook at **MEDIUM** 7 to 9* minutes.

Cooking time given is for beef Medium-Rare. Adjust time accordingly for desired doneness.
Note: *If wooden skewers are unavailable, metal skewers may be used. Refer to Introduction for special instructions.*

BEST BEEF GOULASH A

2 pounds boneless beef, cut into 1-inch
    cubes
2¼ cups water, divided
1 envelope (1⅜ oz.) onion soup mix
1 can (3 oz.) whole mushrooms, drained
2 tablespoons paprika
¼ teaspoon caraway seeds
3 tablespoons cornstarch

Yield: 6–8 Servings

In 4-quart casserole, combine beef, 2 cups water, onion soup mix, mushrooms, paprika and caraway seeds. Cover with lid.

TO COOK BY AUTO SENSOR: Cook on **COOK A5**. After time appears in display window, stir twice.

TO COOK BY TIME: Cook at **HIGH** 6 to 7 minutes and at **LOW** 55 to 60 minutes; stir twice.

TO COMPLETE: Blend cornstarch with remaining ¼ cup water until smooth. Stir into dish. Cook, uncovered, at **LOW** 3 minutes, or until thickened.

MUSHROOM STUFFED STEAK A ROLLS

¼ pound fresh mushrooms, finely chopped
1 small onion finely chopped
2 tablespoons butter or margarine
2 cups soft bread crumbs
1 tablespoon parsley flakes
1 to 1½ pounds top round steak, cut into 4
    pieces
Salt and pepper to taste
1 can (10¼ oz.) beef gravy

Yield: 4 Servings

In medium glass bowl, combine mushrooms, onion and butter. Cook at **HIGH** 2 to 3 minutes. Stir in bread crumbs and parsley flakes.
Butterfly steak and pound thin for rolling*. Season one side with salt and pepper. Place mushroom mixture on seasoned side of each steak and roll up jelly-roll style. Tie with cotton string or secure with wooden toothpicks. Arrange rolls around edge of 8-inch square dish; top with gravy.

TO COOK BY AUTO SENSOR: Cover dish completely with plastic wrap. Cook on **COOK A3**. After time appears in the display window turn rolls over. Recover. After cooking, release plastic wrap.

TO COOK BY TIME: Cover with plastic wrap. Cook at **HIGH** 5 minutes and at **MEDIUM** 10 to 12 minutes. Turn rolls over, halfway through cooking; recover.

TO COMPLETE: Let stand, covered, 5 minutes before serving.

***Hint**: In some markets steaks may be purchased ready for rolling.*

FLANK STEAK FLORENTINE A

¼ pound fresh mushrooms
1 large onion, finely chopped
1 clove garlic, finely chopped
3 tablespoons butter or margarine, softened
1 package (10 oz.) frozen chopped spinach, defrosted and well drained (see page 32)
1½ to 1¾ pound beef flank steak, pounded thin
2 beef bouillon cubes
1 cup hot water
1 can (10¾ oz.) condensed golden mushroom soup
2 tablespoons dry vermouth, optional

Yield: 4 Servings

Chop ½ cup of mushrooms. In medium glass bowl, combine chopped mushrooms, onions, garlic, butter and spinach. Cook at **HIGH** 2 to 3 minutes. Score flank steak; spread spinach mixture on steak in a lengthwise strip. Roll steak lengthwise around filling; tie with string or secure with wooden toothpick.
Place steak rolls in 12×8-inch dish seam-side down. Combine bouillon, water, soup and vermouth; add remaining mushrooms, sliced. Pour sauce over steak roll.

TO COOK BY AUTO SENSOR: Cover completely with 2 pieces of plastic wrap. Cook on **COOK A3.** After cooking, release plastic wrap.

TO COOK BY TIME: Cover with plastic wrap. Cook at **HIGH** 8 to 9 minutes and at **LOW** 20 to 25 minutes.

TO COMPLETE: Beef should be tender. Let stand, covered, 10 minutes before serving.

FILET AU JUS

4 beef tenderloin steaks, 1-inch thick (about ¼ lb. ea.)
½ teaspoon pepper
4 slices bacon
Browning sauce

Yield: 4 Servings

Rub steaks with pepper; wrap bacon around steaks and secure bacon with wooden toothpicks. Arrange steaks in 12×8-inch dish. Brush with browning sauce. Cook at **MEDIUM** 6 to 7 minutes*, turning steaks over halfway through cooking. Let stand, covered, 2 to 4 minutes before serving.

*Cooking time given is for beef-Rare. For Medium, cook 8 to 9 minutes and for Well, cook 10 to 11 minutes.

Note: For TWO Servings, follow above procedure; halve all ingredients. Cook 3½ to 4½ minutes (for Rare), 4½ to 5 ½ (for Medium) or 5½ to 6½ (for Well).

SWISS STEAK SPECIAL A

1½ pounds boneless round steak, cut into individual servings and pounded ¼-inch thin
1 can (16 oz.) whole tomatoes, chopped
1 can (8 oz.) tomato sauce
1 envelope (1⅜ oz.) onion or onion-mushroom soup mix
1 teaspoon basil
¼ teaspoon garlic powder
6 slices (6 oz.) mozzarella cheese

Yield: 6 Servings

In 12×8-inch dish, combine steak, tomatoes, sauce, soup mix, basil and garlic.

TO COOK BY AUTO SENSOR: Cover completely with plastic wrap. Cook on **COOK A5.**

TO COOK BY TIME: Cover with plastic wrap. Cook at **HIGH** 4 to 5 minutes and at **LOW** 40 to 45 minutes.

TO COMPLETE: Top with cheese. Let stand, covered, 10 minutes before serving.

SHORT RIBS WITH BARBECUE SAUCE

4 pounds beef short ribs
1 medium onion, sliced
2 stalks celery, sliced
1¼ cups catsup
¼ cup cider vinegar
¼ cup flour
1 tablespoon Worcestershire sauce
½ teaspoon salt
¼ teaspoon dry mustard

Yield: 4 Servings

In 12×8-inch dish, arrange ribs, meatiest portions toward edge of dish. Add onion and celery. Cook, covered with plastic wrap, at **MEDIUM** 10 minutes. Meanwhile, combine remaining ingredients; pour over ribs. Cook, covered, at **HIGH** 5 minutes and at **LOW** 60 minutes, or until ribs are tender. Rearrange ribs once and baste with sauce occasionally. Let stand, covered, 5 minutes, before serving.

CORNED BEEF DINNER

6 medium new potatoes (about 5 oz. ea.)
2½ to 3 pound corned beef brisket
2 onions, quartered
1½ cups water
1 small head cabbage (about 1½ lb.), cut into 6 wedges
1 regular size (10"×16") oven cooking bag

Yield: 6 Servings

Following the method for baking potatoes (page 163), cook potatoes 11 to 12 minutes. Cool, then peel.
Meanwhile, prepare cooking bag according to package directions; place corned beef, onion and water in bag. Set bag in 12×8-inch dish; pull bag up around beef. Close bag with nylon tie or cotton string; make 6 (½-in.) slits in top of bag. Cook at **HIGH** 6 to 7 minutes and at **LOW** 90 minutes, or until beef is tender. Remove to serving platter; let stand, covered, 15 minutes. Meanwhile, in 12×8-inch dish, arrange cabbage (thick sides toward edge of dish) and potatoes; add ½ cup cooking liquid. Cook, covered with plastic wrap, at **HIGH** 9 to 11 minutes, or until cabbage and potatoes are tender. Slice corned beef and serve with vegetables.

CHILI BEEF LIVER

6 slices bacon
1 pound beef liver, cut into strips
2 tablespoons flour
1 can (10½ oz.) condensed onion soup
1 can (4 oz.) sliced mushrooms, drained
¼ cup chili sauce or catsup

Yield: 4 Servings

Arrange bacon in 12×8-inch dish. Cook, covered with paper towel, at **HIGH** 4½ to 5½ minutes. Remove bacon; crumble and reserve. In dish, arrange liver lightly coated with flour; cook at **HIGH** 1 to 2 minutes. Turn liver over; add soup, mushrooms and chili sauce. Cook, covered, with plastic wrap, at **HIGH** 5 minutes and at **MEDIUM** 10 to 12 minutes, or until liver is tender. Top with reserved bacon. Serve, if desired, over rice.

87

RANCHERO POT ROAST

1 teaspoon garlic salt
½ to 1 teaspoon pepper
¼ teaspoon paprika
3 to 3¼ pound beef bottom round roast
1 cup beef broth, increase to 1½ cups for Auto Sensor
½ cup chili sauce
2 tablespoons dried onion flakes
1 regular size (10"×16") oven cooking bag*

Yield: 8 Servings

TO COOK BY AUTO SENSOR: In small bowl, combine garlic, pepper, and paprika; rub over roast. In 12×8-inch dish, arrange roast and add 1½ cups broth, chili sauce, onion and additional ½ cup water. Cover completely with 2 pieces of plastic wrap. Cook on **COOK A2.** When time appears in display window, turn roast over; recover. After cooking, release plastic wrap.

TO COOK BY TIME: Prepare cooking bag according to label directions. In small bowl, combine garlic, pepper and paprika; rub over roast. Place in cooking bag and add 1 cup broth, chili sauce and onion. Set bag in 3-quart casserole; pull bag up around roast. Close with nylon tie or cotton string; make 6 (½-inch) slits in top of bag. Cook at **HIGH** 5 minutes and at **LOW** 90 minutes.

TO COMPLETE: Beef should be tender. Let stand, covered, 10 minutes before serving.

*Hint: If thicker gravy is desired, remove roast to serving platter; let stand, covered. Pour gravy into glass bowl. Blend 3 to 4 tablespoons flour with ½ cup water until smooth. Stir into gravy. Cook at **HIGH** 3 to 4 minutes; stir once.*

***Note:** The cooking bag CANNOT be used on the Auto Sensor Cycle.*

PEPPER STEAK

2 tablespoons oil
1 pound boneless beef sirloin steak, cut into thin strips
2 tablespoons soy sauce
Dash ginger
Salt to taste
2 medium green peppers, cut into chunks
2 medium onions, sliced
1 tablespoon cornstarch
½ cup beef broth

Yield: 4 Servings

Heat oil in 12×8-inch dish at **MEDIUM-HIGH** 2 minutes. Add steak, soy sauce and ginger. Cook at **MEDIUM-HIGH** 5 to 6 minutes; stir once. Season with salt and stir in peppers and onions. Cook, covered with plastic wrap, at **MEDIUM-HIGH** 3 to 3½ minutes, or until vegetables are crisp-tender. Blend cornstarch with broth until smooth. Stir into dish. Cook at **MEDIUM-HIGH** 3 to 3½ minutes, or until sauce is thickened; stir once.

Note: For TWO Servings, follow above procedure; halve all ingredients. Cook oil 1 minute, steak 2 to 2½ minutes, vegetables 1½ to 2 minutes and broth 1½ to 2 minutes.

CITRUS SIMMERED STEAK A

2 to 2½ pounds boneless chuck steak
  (about 2-inch thick)
½ cup orange juice
2 tablespoons barbecue sauce or catsup
2 tablespoons dried onion flakes
1 teaspoon grated orange peel
2 tablespoons cornstarch
¼ cup water
1 can (4 oz.) sliced mushrooms, drained
1 orange, sliced and halved

Yield: 6–8 Servings

In 4-quart casserole, combine steak, juice, barbecue sauce, onion and orange peel. Cover with lid.

TO COOK BY AUTO SENSOR: Cook on **COOK A2**. After time appears in display window, turn steak over.

TO COOK BY TIME: Cook at **HIGH** 5 minutes and at **LOW** 60 minutes, or until steak is tender. Turn steak over, halfway through cooking time.

TO COMPLETE: Remove steak to serving platter. Let stand, covered, 10 minutes. Meanwhile, blend cornstarch with water until smooth. Stir into casserole. Add mushrooms and orange. Cook at **HIGH** 2 to 3 minutes, or until sauce is thickened. Serve over steak.

BRAISED BRISKET

3 to 3¼ pound beef brisket
1 cup water
1 envelope (1⅜ oz.) onion soup mix
1 regular size (10″×16″) oven cooking
  bag*

Yield: 8 Servings

Prepare cooking bag according to package directions. Place brisket, water and soup mix in bag. Set in 12×8-inch dish. Close bag with nylon tie or cotton string. Make 6 (½ in.) slits in top of bag. Cook at **HIGH** 5 minutes and at **LOW** 90 minutes, or until beef is tender. Let stand 10 minutes before serving.

***Note:** Brisket may also be cooked in covered casserole.*

BURGUNDY BEEF A

6 slices bacon, cut crosswise into sixths
2 medium onions, cut into chunks
½ pound fresh mushrooms, sliced
3 medium carrots, cut ¼-inch thick
1 clove garlic, finely chopped
2 pounds boneless beef, cut into 1-inch
  pieces
1 can (10½ oz.) condensed golden
  mushroom soup
1 cup Burgundy wine
1 tablespoon Worcestershire sauce
1 teaspoon browning sauce
1 bay leaf
½ teaspoon basil, crushed
½ teaspoon salt
¼ teaspoon pepper

Yield: 8 Servings

Cook bacon in 3-quart casserole, at **HIGH** 6 to 6½ minutes. Stir once. Remove bacon; reserve. Remove all but 2 tablespoons drippings. To dish, add onions, mushrooms, carrots and garlic. Stir to coat. Cook at **HIGH** 4 minutes. Add remaining ingredients; stir.

TO COOK BY AUTO SENSOR: Cover with lid. Cook on **COOK A5**. After time appears in display, stir occasionally. At end of cooking time, stir in bacon. Remove bay leaf before serving.

TO COOK BY TIME: Cover with lid. Cook at **MEDIUM-LOW** 30 minutes and at **LOW** 1 hour. Stir occasionally. At end of cooking time. Stir in bacon. Remove bay leaf before serving.

Hint: When stirring Burgundy Beef, push meat and vegetables beneath surface of liquid to prevent drying.

MARVELOUS MEAT LOAF [A]

1½ pounds ground beef
1 egg
½ cup dry bread crumbs
⅓ cup catsup
⅓ cup finely chopped onion
2 tablespoons milk or water
1 teaspoon Worcestershire sauce
½ teaspoon salt
¼ teaspoon pepper

Yield: 6 Servings

Combine all ingredients. In 12×8-inch dish, shape beef mixture into loaf (about 8″×4″).

TO COOK BY AUTO SENSOR: Cover completely with 2 pieces of plastic wrap. Cook on **COOK A2**. After cooking, release plastic wrap.

TO COOK BY TIME: Cover with wax paper. Cook at **MEDIUM** 20 to 24 minutes.

TO COMPLETE: Drain liquid occasionally. If necessary, shield ends of loaf with aluminum foil halfway through cooking. Let stand, covered, 5 minutes before serving.

Hint: While meat loaf is standing, cook 1 cup gravy or seasoned tomato sauce; pour over loaf.

MIDGET MEAT LOAF [A]

1 pound ground beef
1 egg
⅓ cup dry bread crumbs
⅓ cup catsup
2 tablespoons milk or water
1 envelope (¼ oz.) instant onion soup

Yield: 4 Servings

Combine all ingredients. In 8-inch square dish, shape beef mixture into loaf.

TO COOK BY AUTO SENSOR: Cover completely with plastic wrap. Cook on **COOK A2**. After cooking, release plastic wrap.

TO COOK BY TIME: Cover with wax paper. Cook at **MEDIUM** 14 to 16 minutes.

TO COMPLETE: Drain liquid occasionally. If necessary, shield ends of loaf with aluminum foil halfway through cooking. Let stand, covered, 5 minutes before serving.

Hint: For even quicker cooking, shape meat into ring shape in 9-inch pie plate. Cook 9 to 10 minutes.

Note: ***For TWO Servings,*** *follow above procedure using ½ pound ground beef, 1 egg, ¼ cup bread crumbs, 2 tablespoons catsup and 1 envelope instant onion soup. Shape into two loaves. Cook 7 to 8 minutes.*

STUFFED GREEN PEPPERS

1 pound ground beef
1 medium onion, finely chopped
2 cans (8 oz. ea.) tomato sauce, divided
¼ cup water
3 tablespoons Parmesan cheese, divided
1 teaspoon salt
⅛ teaspoon pepper
½ cup instant rice
4 medium green peppers (about 1 lb.)

Yield: 4 Servings

TO COOK BY AUTO SENSOR: In medium bowl, combine ground beef, onion, 1 can tomato sauce, water, 1 tablespoon cheese, salt, pepper and rice. Cut peppers in half lengthwise; remove seeds and rinse. Spoon beef-rice filling into each half. Place in 12×8-inch dish. Top with remaining sauce and cheese. Cover completely with plastic wrap. Cook on **COOK A4**. After cooking, release plastic wrap.

TO COOK BY TIME: Crumble ground beef in medium glass bowl. Stir in onion. Cook at **HIGH** 3½ to 4½ minutes, or until beef is brown.
Stir once; drain. Stir in 1 can tomato sauce, water, 1 tablespoon cheese, salt and pepper. Cook, covered with plastic wrap, at **HIGH** 2½ to 3½ minutes. Stir in rice; let stand, covered 5 minutes.
Cut peppers in half lengthwise; remove seeds and rinse. Spoon beef-rice filling into each half; place in 12×8-inch dish. Top with remaining sauce and cheese. Cover with plastic wrap. Cook at **HIGH** 10 to 12 minutes, or until peppers are tender.

TO COMPLETE: Let stand, covered, 5 minutes before serving.

CHEESEBURGER PIE

1 pound ground beef
1 package (5 oz.) instant mashed potato flakes (2¼ cups), divided
1¼ cups milk, divided
1 egg
¼ cup catsup
1 tablespoon dried onion flakes
1½ teaspoons salt, divided
¼ teaspoon pepper, divided
6 slices American cheese, divided
1 cup hot water
2 tablespoons butter or margarine

Yield: 4 Servings

Combine ground beef, 1⅓ cups instant mashed potato flakes, 1 cup milk, egg, catsup, onion, 1 teaspoon salt and ⅛ teaspoon pepper. Spread into 9-inch pie plate. Cook at **MEDIUM-HIGH** 6½ to 7½ minutes; drain. Arrange 2 slices cheese on top. Let stand, loosely covered, 7 minutes. Meanwhile, in medium glass bowl, combine water, butter, remaining milk, salt and pepper. Cook at **MEDIUM-HIGH** 5 to 6 minutes. Add remaining instant mashed potato flakes and cheese, diced and stir until potatoes are fluffy. Spread over "cheeseburger". Cook at **MEDIUM-HIGH** 2 to 3 minutes or until heated through.

PIZZA WHEELS

1 pound ground beef
2 tablespoons finely chopped onion
½ teaspoon salt
Oregano
¼ cup spaghetti sauce
4 slices mozzarella cheese, cut into strips

Yield: 4 Servings

Combine ground beef, onion, salt and ¼ teaspoon oregano. Shape into 4 patties raising the edge ¼ inch to form a center well. In 12×8-inch dish, arrange patties. Cook at **MEDIUM-HIGH** 3 to 4 minutes; drain. Fill center well with spaghetti sauce and sprinkle with oregano. Cook at **MEDIUM-HIGH** 1 to 1½ minutes. Top with cheese and let stand, covered, 3 minutes before serving.

Note: For TWO Servings, follow above procedure; halve all ingredients. Cook patties 1½ to 2 minutes and with sauce ½ to 1 minute.

SALISBURY STEAK Ⓐ

1 can (4 oz.) sliced mushrooms, drained, divided
1½ pounds ground beef
1 can (10¾ oz.) condensed cream of mushroom soup, divided
1 egg
¾ cup milk, divided
½ cup dry bread crumbs
1 small onion, finely chopped
⅛ teaspoon pepper
Parsley, optional

Yield: 6 Servings

Chop half of mushrooms. In large bowl, combine chopped mushrooms, ground beef, ¼ can of soup, egg, ¼ cup milk, bread crumbs, onion and pepper. Shape into 6 patties and arrange in 12×8-inch dish.

TO COOK BY AUTO SENSOR: Cover completely with plastic wrap. Cook on **COOK A4**.

TO COOK BY TIME: Cover with wax paper. Cook at **MEDIUM-HIGH** 13 to 14 minutes.

TO COMPLETE: Drain. Let stand, covered, 5 minutes. Meanwhile, in small glass bowl, combine remaining soup, mushrooms and milk. Cook at **MEDIUM** 3 to 4 minutes. Stir once. Pour sauce over patties* and garnish, if desired, with parsley.

If desired, brush top of patties with browning sauce blended with water.

ITALIAN MEATBALLS

1 pound ground beef
1 egg
1½ cups soft bread crumbs
¼ cup water or milk
2 to 3 tablespoons grated Parmesan cheese
¾ teaspoon oregano
1 teaspoon parsley
1 teaspoon onion salt

Yield: 4 Servings

Combine all ingredients and shape into 1½-inch meatballs (about 20). Arrange in 12×8-inch dish. Cook at **MEDIUM-HIGH** 7½ to 8½ minutes; drain. Let stand, 3 minutes before serving.

SAVORY CABBAGE ROLLS

1 small head cabbage
1 pound ground beef
2 medium onions, finely chopped
1 can (15 oz.) tomato sauce, divided
½ cup cooked rice (see chart, page 184)
1 teaspoon salt
⅛ teaspoon pepper
2 tablespoons packed brown sugar
2 tablespoons cider vinegar

Yield: 4 Servings

Cut core from cabbage; rinse. In medium glass bowl, cook covered with plastic wrap, at **HIGH** 4 to 5 minutes. Remove 10 leaves; cut out hard center rib from each leaf (make a V-shape cut). Use remaining cabbage in other recipes. Crumble ground beef into medium bowl. Add onions, ½ tomato sauce, rice, salt and pepper; mix. To stuff cabbage, place beef-rice filling in cabbage leaf; roll up, folding edges in. Arrange seam-side down in 12×8-inch dish. Blend remaining tomato sauce with brown sugar and vinegar. Pour over rolls.

TO COOK BY AUTO SENSOR: Cover completely with plastic wrap. Cook on **COOK A7**. After cooking, release plastic wrap.

TO COOK BY TIME: Cover with plastic wrap. Cook at **MEDIUM** 28 to 30 minutes.

TO COMPLETE: Let stand, covered 5 minutes before serving.

ORIENTAL PEPPER BURGERS

1 pound ground beef
¼ teaspoon salt
⅛ teaspoon pepper
1 large onion, sliced
1 medium green pepper, cut into chunks
1 can (8 oz.) tomato sauce
¼ teaspoon ginger
4 teaspoon soy sauce

Yield: 4 Servings

Combine beef, salt and pepper; shape into 4 patties and arrange in 12×8-inch dish. Cook at **MEDIUM-HIGH** 4½ to 5½ minutes; drain. Add onion, green pepper and tomato sauce blended with ginger and soy sauce. Cook, covered with plastic wrap, at **MEDIUM-HIGH** 5½ to 6½ minutes, or until vegetables are tender. Let stand, covered, 5 minutes before serving.

SWEDISH MEATBALLS

1 pound ground beef
1 egg
½ cup dry bread crumbs
½ cup milk, divided
1 small onion, finely chopped
2 teaspoons parsley flakes
½ teaspoon salt
⅛ teaspoon allspice
⅛ teaspoon pepper
1 can (10¾ oz.) condensed cream of
  mushroom soup

Yield: 4–6 Servings

Combine ground beef, egg, bread crumbs, ¼ cup milk, onion, parsley, salt, allspice and pepper. Shape into 1¼-inch meatballs (about 30) and arrange in 12×8-inch dish. Cook at **MEDIUM-HIGH** 5½ to 6½ minutes. Push meatballs to one side of dish. Blend in soup and remaining milk; combine with meatballs. Cook, covered, with plastic wrap, at **MEDIUM-HIGH** 3 to 4 minutes, or until heated through. Serve, if desired, over buttered noodles, sprinkled with additional parsley.

93

VEAL PAPRIKA A

1 pound boneless veal, cut into 1½-inch cubes
½ pound fresh mushrooms, sliced
1 cup chicken broth, divided
1 large onion, finely chopped
½ to 1 teaspoon paprika
½ teaspoon salt
⅛ to ¼ teaspoon pepper
Dash caraway seeds
2 to 3 tablespoons flour
½ cup sour cream

Yield: 4 Servings

In 2-quart casserole, combine veal, mushrooms, ½ cup broth, onion, paprika, salt, pepper and caraway. Cover with lid.

TO COOK BY AUTO SENSOR: Cook on **COOK A2.** After time appears in display window, stir occasionally.

TO COOK BY TIME: Cook at **HIGH** 7 minutes and at **MEDIUM-LOW** 21 minutes; stir occasionally.

TO COMPLETE: Blend flour with remaining ½ cup broth until smooth. Stir into dish. Cook at **HIGH** 2 to 3 minutes, or until sauce is thickened. Blend in sour cream.

VEAL CUTLETS CORDON BLEU

4 veal cutlets (about 1 lb.), pounded thin*
2 thin slices cooked ham, halved
2 slices (rectangular) Swiss cheese, halved
1 cup seasoned dry bread crumbs
½ teaspoon salt
⅛ teaspoon pepper
Dash allspice
1 egg, beaten with ¼ cup water
3 tablespoons oil

Yield: 4 Servings

On one side of each cutlet, place ham and cheese; fold cutlet in half. Pound edges together to seal or secure with wooden toothpicks. Dip cutlets in bread crumbs mixed with salt, pepper and allspice; dip in egg, then again in bread crumbs. Coat bottom of 12×8-inch dish with half of oil; place cutlets in dish. Sprinkle remaining oil on cutlets. Cook at **MEDIUM-HIGH** 7 to 8 minutes, turning cutlets over once. Let stand, covered with wax paper, 5 minutes before serving.

Variation: Use chicken cutlets for veal.

WURST MIT KRAUT

6 tablespoons butter or margarine
1½ cups chopped onion (about 2 medium)
2 cups sliced apples (about 2 medium)
2 cans (16 oz. ea.) sauerkraut, drained and rinsed
½ cup beef broth
¼ teaspoon caraway seeds
¼ teaspoon pepper
6 knockwurst sausages (about 3 oz. ea.)

Yield: 6 Servings

In 12×8-inch dish, combine butter and onion. Cook at **HIGH** 3 to 3½ minutes. Stir in apples. Cook at **HIGH** 3 to 4½ minutes. Stir in sauerkraut, broth, caraway and pepper.
Score knockwurst diagonally and arrange on sauerkraut mixture. Cook at **HIGH** 8 to 9 minutes. Rearrange knockwurst once. Let stand, covered, 5 minutes.

APPLE STUFFED PORK CHOPS ▉A▉

4 pork chops, 1-inch thick
¼ cup butter or margarine, melted
½ cup chopped apple
½ cup herb seasoned stuffing mix
¼ cup (1 oz.) shredded Cheddar cheese
2 tablespoons chopped celery
1 tablespoon chopped onion
1 teaspoon chopped raisins
2 tablespoons orange juice
¼ teaspoon salt

Yield: 4 Servings

Cut pocket in each chop. In bowl, combine butter, apples, stuffing mix, cheese, celery, onion, raisins, orange juice and salt; mix well. Fill each pocket with stuffing; secure opening with wooden toothpicks*.

TO COOK BY AUTO SENSOR: Arrange chops on microwave roasting rack set in 12×8-inch dish. Cover completely with 2 pieces of plastic wrap. Cook on **COOK A8**. After cooking, release plastic wrap.

TO COOK BY TIME: Arrange pork chops in 12×8-inch dish. Cover with wax paper. Cook at **MEDIUM** 17 minutes.

TO COMPLETE: Let stand, covered, 5 minutes. Place remainder or stuffing in bowl. Cover with plastic wrap. Cook at **MEDIUM** 2 to 3 minutes, or until hot.

*****Note:** Break toothpicks in half, otherwise they may poke through plastic.

OVEN-FRIED PORK CHOPS ▉A▉

6 rib pork chops, ½-inch thick
1 package (1⅜ oz.) seasoned coating mix for pork

Yield: 6 Servings

Coat chops as package directs.

TO COOK BY AUTO SENSOR: Arrange chops on microwave roasting rack 12×8-inch dish. Cover completely with plastic wrap. Cook on **COOK A8**.

TO COOK BY TIME: Line 12×8-inch dish with paper towel; arrange chops, ribs toward center. Cook at **MEDIUM** 15 to 17 minutes.

TO COMPLETE: Let stand, uncovered, 5 minutes before serving.

***NOTE:** *For FOUR pork chops,* follow above procedure. Cook 11½ to 13 minutes.
For TWO pork chops, cook 6½ to 8 minutes.
For ONE pork chop, cook 3 to 4½ minutes.*

95

PEACHY PORK ROAST

Water
1 can (8½ oz.) sliced peaches, drained and chopped; reserve syrup
1 package (6 oz.) stuffing mix for pork with seasoning packet
1 egg
⅓ cup chopped walnuts
¼ cup butter or margarine
3 to 3¼ pound pork rib roast (about 6 ribs)*
¼ cup peach preserves

Yield: 6 Servings

In 2-cup glass measure, add enough water to reserved syrup to equal 1½ to 1¾ cups. Cook at **HIGH** 2 to 3 minutes, or until hot. In medium glass bowl, combine liquid with peaches, stuffing mix (and included seasoning packet), egg, walnuts and butter; stir until liquid is absorbed and butter is melted.
Cut pockets in pork roast, one opposite each bone. Stuff each pocket with 2 tablespoons stuffing. Secure with cotton string or wooden toothpicks.
Place roast fat-side down on microwave roasting rack set in 12×8-inch dish. Cook at **MEDIUM-LOW** 12 to 13½ minutes per pound. Halfway through cooking, turn over; brush on peach preserves. Let stand, covered, 10 minutes before serving. Meanwhile, heat remaining stuffing at **MEDIUM-LOW** 6 to 7 minutes; stir twice. Serve with roast. To carve roast, remove string; cut in between each bone.

Hint: For easy carving, when buying roast, have the backbone (chine bone) cracked.

FRUITED GLAZED HAM

1 cup packed brown sugar
¾ cup light corn syrup
⅓ cup prepared mustard
10 pound cooked ham (bone-in)
1 can (20 oz.) sliced pineapple, drained
8 to 10 maraschino cherries

Yield: 12–14 Servings

In small glass bowl, combine sugar, syrup and mustard. Cook at **MEDIUM** 3 to 4 minutes, or until sugar is dissolved and mixture boils; stir once. Place ham fat-side up on microwave roasting rack set in 12×8-inch dish. Shield ham by wrapping 3-inch wide strip of foil around the large end of the ham. Secure to the body of ham with wooden toothpicks. Fold 1½ inches over cut surface. For shank ham halves, shield shank bone by cupping it with foil. Cook, covered with wax paper, at **MEDIUM-LOW** 30 minutes. Remove skin from ham and score fat. Place ham fat-side up. Reshield ham. Cook at **MEDIUM-LOW** 30 minutes. Brush with glaze; reshield. Cook at **MEDIUM-LOW** 20 minutes. Remove foil; drain liquid. Arrange pineapples and cherries on ham, securing pineapple with wooden toothpicks. Brush with glaze. Cook at **MEDIUM-LOW** 15 to 20 minutes or until ham registers 120°F when tested with a conventional meat thermometer. (Remove ham from oven before reading temperature.) Brush fruit with remaining glaze. Let stand, covered, 15 minutes before serving.

CHINESE PORK AND SNOW PEAS

2 tablespoons oil
1 pound boneless pork, cut into thin strips
2 tablespoons soy sauce
⅛ teaspoon garlic powder
1 package (6 oz.) frozen pea pods, defrosted (see page 32)
2 tablespoons cornstarch
1 cup beef broth

Yield: 4 Servings

Heat oil in 12×8-inch dish at **MEDIUM-HIGH** 2 minutes. Stir in pork, soy sauce and garlic. Cook at **MEDIUM-HIGH** 4 to 5 minutes; stir twice. Add pea pods. Cook, covered with plastic wrap, at **MEDIUM-HIGH** 3 minutes; stir once. Blend cornstarch with broth until smooth. Stir into pork. Cook at **MEDIUM-HIGH** 4 minutes; stir twice.

96

HAM STEAK WITH RAISIN SAUCE

½ cup water
⅓ cup raisins
⅓ cup currant jelly
½ teaspoon grated orange peel
Dash allspice
1 tablespoon cornstarch
⅓ cup orange juice
1 pound ham steak (1-inch thick)

Yield: 4 Servings

In glass bowl, combine water, raisins, jelly, orange peel and allspice. Cook at **HIGH** 3 to 4 minutes; stir once. Blend cornstarch with orange juice until smooth. Stir into sauce. Cook at **HIGH** 1 minute, or until sauce is thickened; stir once. Cook ham in 12×8-inch dish at **HIGH** 6 to 7 minutes; turn ham over. Pour raisin sauce over ham; cook at **MEDIUM-HIGH** 1 minute. Let stand, covered 5 minutes before serving.

POLISH SAUSAGE (KIELBASA) WITH RED CABBAGE

1 small head (about 2 lb.) red cabbage, shredded*
1 small apple, chopped
¼ cup sugar
¼ cup cider vinegar
1 tablespoon dried onion flakes
½ teaspoon caraway seeds
½ teaspoon salt
1 ring (1¾ to 2 lb.) Kielbasa sausage

Yield: 6 Servings

In 12×8-inch dish, combine cabbage, apple, sugar, vinegar, onion, caraway and salt. Cook, covered with plastic wrap, at **HIGH** 7 to 8 minutes; stir twice.
Meanwhile, make ¼-inch slits every few inches in Kielbasa; arrange on red cabbage. Cook, covered with plastic wrap, at **HIGH** 12 to 13 minutes, or until cooked through. Let stand, covered, 5 minutes before serving.

***Substitution:** Use 2 jars (16 oz ea.) red cabbage, drained for fresh cabbage. Do not cook cabbage separately. Arrange Kielbasa on red cabbage blended with remaining ingredients. Cook covered, 15 to 17 minutes or until cooked through.*

SWEET 'N SOUR PORK

1 can (8¼ oz.) chunk pineapple in heavy syrup, drained; reserve ⅓ cup syrup
¼ cup cider vinegar
1 tablespoon cornstarch
2 tablespoons oil
1 pound boneless pork, cut into ¾-inch cubes
¼ cup soy sauce
1 bunch green onions, thinly sliced (about 3 tbsp.)
1 green pepper, cut into small chunks

Yield: 4 Servings

In small glass bowl, combine reserved syrup, vinegar and cornstarch. Cook at **MEDIUM-HIGH** ¾ to 1 minute, or until thickened; stir once.
Heat oil in 8-inch square dish at **MEDIUM-HIGH** 2 minutes. Stir in pork, soy sauce and onion. Cook at **MEDIUM-HIGH** 7 to 8 minutes; stir twice. Add green pepper and pineapple. Cook, covered with plastic wrap, at **MEDIUM-HIGH** 2 to 3 minutes, or until pork is tender. Stir in sauce and let stand, covered, 5 minutes before serving.

CRANBERRY GLAZED HAM

¾ cup cranberry juice
¼ cup orange juice
¼ cup packed brown sugar
¼ cup raisins
1 tablespoon cornstarch
Dash cloves
3 to 5 pound canned ham
Whole cloves

Yield: 12–20 Servings

In small glass bowl, combine juices, sugar, raisins, cornstarch and cloves. Cook at **HIGH** at 2½ to 3¼ minutes, or until glaze is thickened; stir twice. Decorate ham with whole cloves. Place ham on microwave roasting rack set in 12×8-inch dish. Cook at **MEDIUM-LOW** 9 to 10 minutes per pound. Halfway through cooking, shield top cut-edge of ham with a 1½-inch strip of foil. Wrap strip of foil around ham and secure to body of ham with wooden toothpicks. Fold 1-inch over cut surface. When 10 minutes of cooking remain, remove foil and glaze ham. Let stand, covered, 10 minutes before serving.

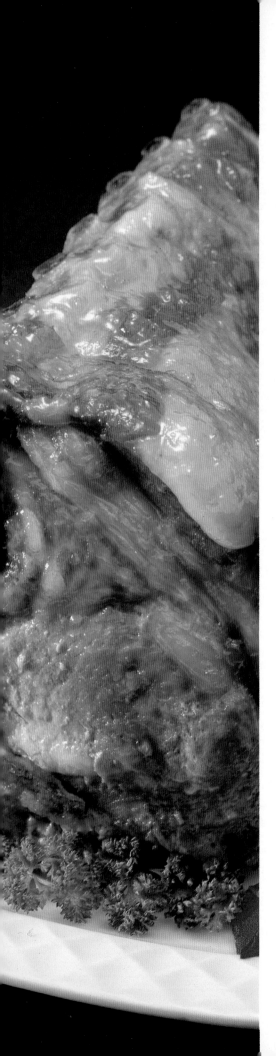

APRICOT GLAZED PORK ROAST

1 jar (12 oz.) apricot preserves
½ teaspoon ginger
1 tablespoon lemon juice
4 to 5 pound pork rib roast*
Pepper

Yield: 6–8 Servings

In small glass bowl, combine preserves, ginger and lemon juice. Cook at **HIGH** 1 to 2 minutes, or until hot. Season roast with pepper. Place roast fat-side down on microwave roasting rack set in 12×8-inch dish. Cook at **MEDIUM-LOW** 12 to 13½ minutes per pound, or until roast registers 170°F when tested with a conventional meat thermometer. (Remove roast from oven before reading the temperature.) Halfway through cooking, turn roast fat-side up. Baste roast with glaze 3 times. Occasionally drain liquid. Let stand, covered, 15 minutes before carving.

Hint: For easy carving, when buying a roast, have backbone (chine bone) cracked.

SOUTHERN BARBECUED RIBS

2 pounds pork backribs or spareribs, cut into individual ribs
1 cup barbecue sauce
2 tablespoons honey or dark corn syrup
2 tablespoons flour
1 tablespoon soy sauce

Yield: 4 Servings

Arrange ribs, meaty-side down in 12×8-inch dish. Combine remaining ingredients; pour over ribs. Cover with wax paper. Cook at **HIGH** 10 minutes and at **MEDIUM-LOW** 25 to 30 minutes, or until ribs are tender. Halfway through cooking, turn ribs over; rearrange. Spoon sauce over ribs.

MINT GLAZED LAMB

4 to 5 pound leg of lamb
3 cloves garlic
1 teaspoon crushed rosemary
¼ teaspoon pepper
½ cup mint jelly
1 can (8½ oz.) pear slices, drained and mashed; reserve 1 tablespoon syrup

Yield: 8 Servings

Make 6 slits in lamb, insert ⅓ clove garlic in each. Rub rosemary and pepper over lamb. Place lamb fat-side down on microwave roasting rack set in 12×8-inch dish. In small glass bowl, combine remaining garlic, finely chopped, jelly and reserved syrup. Cook at **MEDIUM** 2 to 3 minutes or until melted; stir in pears. Spoon ⅓ mint glaze over lamb.
Cook at **MEDIUM-LOW** 11 to 12½ minutes per pound for Medium, or 13 to 14½ minutes per pound for Well. Halfway through cooking, turn meat over. Drain liquid and brush with glaze. Continue cooking. Let stand, covered, 15 minutes before carving.

PERSIAN LAMB WITH PEACHES

Water
1 can (16 oz.) peach slices, drained; reserve syrup
1½ pounds boneless lamb, cut into 1½-inch cubes*
1 envelope (1 oz.) onion-mushroom soup mix
1 tablespoon lemon juice
¼ teaspoon cinnamon
⅛ teaspoon cloves
2 tablespoons cornstarch
¼ cup raisins

Yield: 6 Servings

Add enough water to reserved syrup to equal 1 cup. In 2-quart casserole dish, combine syrup, lamb, soup mix, lemon juice, cinnamon and cloves. Cover with lid.

TO COOK BY AUTO SENSOR: Cook on **COOK A5**. After time appears in display window, stir twice.

TO COOK BY TIME: Cook at **HIGH** 6 to 7 minutes and at **LOW** 30 minutes, or until lamb is tender. Stir twice.

TO COMPLETE: Blend cornstarch with ¼ cup water until smooth. Stir in cornstarch, peaches and raisins. Cook at **HIGH** 4 to 5 minutes, or until sauce is thickened. Stir once.

***Substitution:** Use beef cubes for lamb.*

CURRY LAMB

1 small onion, finely chopped
¼ cup butter or margarine
3 tablespoons flour
1 pound boneless lamb, cut into 1½-inch
cubes
1 can (10¾ oz.) chicken broth
⅓ cup raisins
⅓ cup peanuts
3 tablespoons lemon juice
1 tablespoon curry powder
½ teaspoon ginger
½ teaspoon salt
½ cup flaked coconut
2 cups cooked rice (see page 184)

Yield: 4 Servings

Cook onion and butter in 2-quart casserole
at **HIGH** 5 to 6 minutes; stir once. Stir
flour, then lamb, broth, raisins, peanuts,
lemon juice, curry powder, ginger and salt.
Cook, covered with lid, at **HIGH** 5 minutes
and at **LOW** 20 to 25 minutes, or until
lamb is tender; stir twice. Sprinkle with
coconut. Let stand, covered, 5 minutes
before serving over hot rice.

CROWN ROAST OF LAMB

¼ cup orange marmalade
2 racks of lamb (about 2¾ lb.), cut and
tied into crown roast
¼ cup thinly sliced celery
¼ cup finely chopped onion
2 tablespoons butter or margarine
2 to 3 cups cooked rice (see page 184)
1 small orange, peeled, sectioned and
chopped
1 small grapefruit, peeled, sectioned an
chopped
½ teaspoon salt
⅛ teaspoon sage
⅛ teaspoon pepper
Browning sauce

Yield: 6 Servings

Heat marmalade in small glass bowl at
MEDIUM 1 minute, or until marmalade is
melted; set aside.
Place roast on microwave roasting rack set
in 12×8-inch dish. Cook at **MEDIUM-LOW**
11 to 13 minutes. Let stand, covered, 5
minutes.
Meanwhile, in medium glass bowl,
combine celery, onion, and butter. Cook at
MEDIUM 2½ to 3 minutes, or until celery
is tender. Stir in rice, orange, grapefruit,
salt, sage and pepper. Cook at **MEDIUM** 2
to 3 minutes.
Transfer roast to microwave safe serving
platter; gently fill center with stuffing
mixture. Brush outside of roast with
browning sauce, then marmalade.
Cook at **MEDIUM-LOW** 10 to 12 minutess
for Medium, 18 to 20 minutes for Well or
until roast registers 150°F, or 170°F when
tested with conventional meat
thermometer. (Remove roast from oven
before reading temperature.) Let stand,
covered, 10 minutes before serving.

Note: *If desired, add ½ pound browned
ground lamb, drained, to stuffing mixture;
reduce rice to 1½ to 2 cups.*

POULTRY

Roast turkey is not only for special holidays! The long preparation once associated with cooking poultry vanishes when you microwave this family favorite. All types of poultry can be easily cooked in microwave minutes. You will please everyone with delicious moist meals while saving yourself time and effort.

GENERAL DIRECTIONS FOR ROASTING WHOLE POULTRY

Season as desired, but salt after cooking. Browning sauce mixed with equal parts of butter will enhance the appearance.

If a large amount of juice accumulates in the bottom of the baking dish, occasionally drain it. If desired, reserve for making gravy.

During cooking it may be necessary to shield legs, wings and the breast bone to prevent overcooking. Wooden toothpicks can be used to hold foil in place.

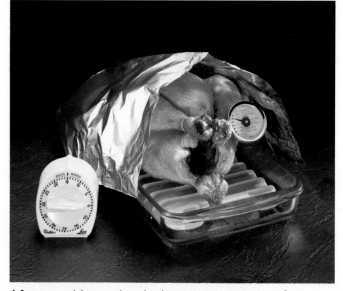

After cooking, check the temperature of large chickens and turkeys with a meat thermometer. Check the temperature in both thigh muscles. If thermometer touches bone, the reading may be inaccurate. Small chickens and game birds are cooked when juices run clear and drumstick readily moves up and down. If poultry is undercooked, cook a few more minutes at the recommended power level. Let stand, tented with foil, 10 to 15 minutes before carving.

DIRECTIONS FOR ROASTING WHOLE POULTRY BY TIME

Poultry may be stuffed or unstuffed. Tie legs together with cotton string. Place on microwave roasting rack set in 12×8-inch dish. Place over 4 pounds breast-side down; turn over halfway through cooking. Cover with wax paper to prevent spatter.

Less tender hens should be cooked in liquid such as soup or broth. Use ¼ cup per pound of poultry. Use an oven cooking bag or covered casserole. Select a covered casserole deep enough so that hen does not touch the lid.

If an oven cooking bag is used, prepare according to package directions. Do not use wire twist-ties to close bag. Do use nylon tie, a piece of cotton string, or a strip cut from the open end of the bag. Make six ½-inch slits in top of bag.

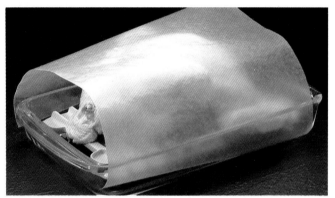

Multiply the weight of the poultry by the minimum recommended minutes per pound. Program Power and Time.

POULTRY ROASTING CHART FOR TIME COOKING

POULTRY	POWER	APPROX. COOKING TIME (minutes per pound)	APPROX. TEMPERATURE AFTER STANDING
Cornish Hens	HIGH	7½ to 8½	————
Chickens (up to 3 lb.)	HIGH	7½ to 8½	————
Chickens (3 to 7 lb.)	MEDIUM	10 to 11½	180° to 190°F
Turkey (See page 116)	MEDIUM MEDIUM-LOW	4 to 5 5 to 6	180° to 190°F
Turkey Parts	MEDIUM	9½ to 11½	180° to 190°F
Goose	MEDIUM	9½ to 10½	180° to 190°F
Duck	MEDIUM	9½ to 10½	180° to 190°F
Pheasant	MEDIUM	8 to 9½	————

DIRECTIONS FOR ROASTING WHOLE POULTRY BY AUTO SENSOR

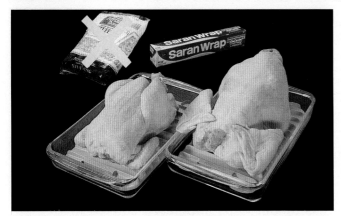

Tie legs together with cotton string. Place on microwave roasting rack set in an oblong dish. Place poultry over 4 pounds breast-side down. Cover completely with 2 overlapping pieces of plastic wrap. Do not stuff poultry cooked by Auto Sensor.

Cook according to Auto Sensor Cycle that is indicated in the chart. When time appears in the display window, turn poultry over 4 pounds breast-side up; shield and/or brush with glaze.

POULTRY ROASTING CHART FOR AUTO SENSOR COOKING A

POULTRY	AUTO SENSOR CYCLE	APPROX. COOKING TIME (minutes per pound)	APPROXIMATE TEMPERATURE AFTER COOKING
Cornish Hens (1 to 3)	A2	14 to 16	———
Chickens Whole (up to 7 lbs.)	A2	8 to 10	180 to 190°F
Chicken Parts (up to 3 lbs.)	A4	5 to 7	———

DIRECTIONS FOR COOKING POULTRY PIECES

Arrange pieces skin-side up, with meatier portions toward edge of the dish.

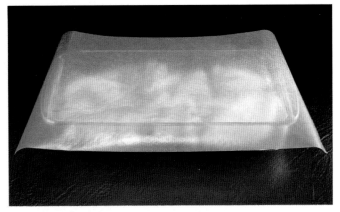

To Cook by Time: Cover with wax paper, Multiply the weight by 5 to 6 minutes per pound. Cook at HIGH.

To Cook by Auto Sensor: Cover completely with plastic wrap and cook on COOK A4.

Poultry is cooked when juices are clear (no pink color). If there is a slight pink color in the juice, return poultry parts to the oven and cook 1 or 2 minutes longer at the recommended power level.

To Cook frozen poultry **by Froz-Cook:** Season fresh poultry and wrap in a single layer for freezing. The poultry should be arranged so that it will fit into a baking dish. When ready to cook, follow directions for Auto Sensor cooking, and cook on FROZ-COOK A4 cycle.

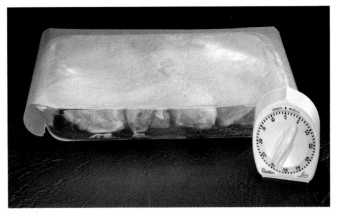

Let stand 5 minutes before serving or as recipe indicates.

BAKED CHICKEN WITH CORN BREAD STUFFING

1¼ to 1½ cups hot water
½ cup butter or margarine
1 package (6 oz.) corn bread stuffing mix
 with seasoning packet
3 chicken breasts, split (about 2½ lb.)
1 tablespoon butter or margarine, melted
¼ teaspoon browning sauce
1 can (10½ oz.) chicken gravy

Yield: 6 Servings

In 12×8-inch dish, combine water, ½ cup butter and seasoning packet. Cook at **HIGH** 3½ to 4 minutes; stir in stuffing crumbs. Arrange chicken on stuffing with meatier portion toward edge of dish. Brush with melted butter mixed with browning sauce. Cook, covered with wax paper, at **HIGH** 12 to 13 minutes, or until chicken is tender. Let stand, covered, 5 minutes.
Meanwhile, in small glass bowl, cook gravy at **HIGH** 3 to 3½ minutes stirring once; serve over chicken.

CHICKEN PARMESAN

2 boneless chicken breasts, skinned, split
 and pounded thin (about 1 to 1¼ lb.)
¾ cup seasoned dry bread crumbs
¼ cup grated Parmesan cheese
¼ teaspoon paprika
1 egg, beaten with ¼ cup water
2 tablespoons oil
1 can (8 oz.) tomato sauce or 1 cup
 spaghetti sauce
Oregano
1 cup (4 oz.) shredded mozzarella cheese

Yield: 4 Servings

Dip chicken in bread crumbs mixed with Parmesan cheese and paprika, then in egg and again in bread crumb mixture. Coat bottom of 12×8-inch dish with 1 tablespoon oil. Place chicken in dish; sprinkle with remaining oil. Cook at **HIGH** 2 to 2½ minutes; turn chicken over and cook an additional 2 to 2½ minutes. Top with tomato sauce and season with oregano. Cook at **HIGH** 3½ to 4½ minutes, or until sauce is hot. Sprinkle with mozzarella cheese and let stand, covered, 5 minutes or until cheese is melted.

Note: For TWO Servings, follow above procedure; halve all ingredients. Cook chicken 1 to 1½ minutes on each side and tomato sauce 2 to 2½ minutes.

CHICKEN CACCIATORE A

2½ to 3 pound chicken, cut into serving pieces
1 can (15 oz.) tomato sauce
1 jar (4½ oz.) sliced mushrooms, drained
½ cup chopped onion
1 tablespoon sugar, optional
1 teaspoon oregano
1 teaspoon salt
1 clove garlic, finely chopped
¼ teaspoon pepper

Yield: 4 Servings

Arrange chicken in 12×8-inch dish with meatier portions toward edge of dish. Combine remaining ingredients, pour over chicken.

TO COOK BY AUTO SENSOR: Cover completely with plastic wrap. Cook on **COOK A2**. After time appears in display window, rearrange chicken; recover. After cooking, release plastic wrap.

TO COOK BY TIME: Cover with wax paper. Cook at **HIGH** 18 to 20 minutes. Rearrange chicken pieces once.

TO COMPLETE: Chicken should be tender. Let stand, covered, 5 minutes. Serve, if desired, with spaghetti.

BARBECUED CHICKEN

2½ to 3 pound chicken, cut into serving pieces
1 cup barbecue sauce*

Yield: 4 Servings

Arrange chicken in 12×8-inch dish with meatier portions toward edge of dish. Spread sauce evenly over chicken.

Cover with wax paper. Cook at **HIGH** 10 to 13 minutes. Baste chicken with sauce. Cook, uncovered, at **HIGH** 3 to 5 minutes. Chicken should be tender. Let covered, 5 minutes before serving.

***Hint:** Use bottled barbecue sauce or see page 57 for tangy homemade sauce.*

CALIFORNIA CHICKEN A

2 chicken breasts, split (1¾ to 2 lb.)
2 teaspoons lemon juice
1 teaspoon dried onion flakes
Basil
Pepper
⅔ cup (2⅔ oz.) shredded Cheddar cheese
½ small avocado, thinly sliced
4 thin slices tomato

Yield: 4 Servings

Arrange chicken in 8-inch square dish with meatier portions toward edge of dish. Sprinkle with lemon juice, onion flakes, basil and pepper.

TO COOK BY AUTO SENSOR: Cover completely with plastic wrap. Cook on **COOK A4.**

TO COOK BY TIME: Cover with wax paper. Cook at **HIGH** 8½ to 9½ minutes, or until chicken is tender.

TO COMPLETE: Top chicken with ⅓ cup cheese, avocado, tomato and remaining cheese. Cook, covered with wax paper at **HIGH** 2½ to 3 minutes. Let covered, 5 minutes before serving.

*Note: **For TWO Servings,** follow above procedure; halve all ingredients. Cook chicken 6 to 6½ minutes and vegetables 1½ to 2 minutes. **For ONE Serving,** cook chicken 4 to 4½ minutes and vegetables ¾ to 1¼ minutes.*

IN-A-JAM KABOBS

⅓ cup orange marmalade
2 tablespoons orange juice
2 tablespoons soy sauce
½ teaspoon lemon juice
Dash ginger
2 boneless chicken breasts, skinned and cut into 1½-inch pieces (about 1 to 1¼ lb.)
1 package (10 oz.) frozen brussel sprouts, defrosted (see page 32)

Yield: 4 Servings

In medium glass bowl, combine marmalade, orange juice, soy sauce, lemon juice and ginger. Cook at **HIGH** 2½ to 3 minutes. Add chicken and marinate, if desired, 30 minutes.
On four 9 or 10-inch wooden skewers*, alternately thread chicken and brussel sprouts. Arrange skewers on 8-inch square dish. Cook at **HIGH** 5 to 6 minutes, or until chicken is tender. Rearrange skewers once and brush with marinade twice.

***Note:** If wooden skewers are unavailable, metal skewers may be used. Refer to page 9 for special instructions.*

CHICKEN LIVERS SUPREME

½ pound fresh mushrooms, sliced
1 medium onion, chopped
¼ cup butter or margarine
1 pound chicken livers, halved
2 to 3 tablespoons flour
1 teaspoon salt
½ teaspoon pepper
½ teaspoon thyme
Cooked rice, optional

Yield: 4 Servings

In 2½-quart casserole, combine mushrooms, onion and butter. Cook, covered with lid, at **HIGH** 3 to 4 minutes, or until onion and mushrooms are tender; stir once. Stir in livers tossed with flour, salt, pepper and thyme. Cook, covered, at **HIGH** 2 minutes and at **MEDIUM** 5 to 6 minutes, or until liver is tender, stir twice. Serve, if desired, with rice.

TANGY CHICKEN CUTLETS

1 large onion, chopped
1 clove garlic, finely chopped
1 tablespoon water
4 chicken cutlets (1 lb.)
½ pound mushrooms, sliced
1 tablespoon tarragon or white wine
    vinegar
2 tablespoons flour
¼ cup water
½ teaspoon salt
⅛ teaspoon pepper
1 cup plain yogurt

Yeld: 4 Servings

Combine onion, garlic and water in 12×8-inch dish. Cover with plastic wrap. Cook at **HIGH** 4 to 5 minutes; stir once. Place cutlets in dish. Top with mushrooms and sprinkle with vinegar. Cover. Cook at **HIGH** 5½ to 6 minutes, or until chicken is tender. Place chicken and vegetables on serving platter. Pour ¼ cup liquid into 1-quart glass bowl. Blend flour with ¼ cup water until smooth. Stir into liquid. Stir in salt, pepper and yogurt. Cook at **MEDIUM** 5 to 6 minutes, or until thickened. Stir frequently. Pour sauce over cutlets and serve immediately.

HURRY CURRY CHICKEN A

2½ to 3 pound chicken, cut into serving
    pieces
1 can (10¾ oz.) condensed cream of
    chicken soup
1 tomato, cut into wedges, optional
½ cup raisins or peanuts
1 tablespoon curry powder
1 tablespoon dried onion flakes
⅛ teaspoon garlic powder

Yield: 4 Servings

Arrange chicken in 12×8-inch dish with meatier portions toward edge of dish. Combine remaining ingredients; mix well. Spoon over chicken.

TO COOK BY AUTO SENSOR: Cover completely with plastic wrap. Cook on **COOK A4**. After cooking, release plastic wrap.

TO COOK BY TIME: Cover with wax paper. Cook at **HIGH** 13 to 15 minutes.

TO COMPLETE: Chicken should be tender. Let stand, covered, 5 minutes. Remove chicken to serving platter, stir sauce until smooth and serve over chicken.

TENDER CRISPY CHICKEN A

8 small chicken pieces (about 2 lb.)
1 package (2⅜ oz.) seasoned coating mix
    for chicken

Yield: 4 Servings

Coat chicken according to package directions. Arrange in 12×8-inch dish with meatier portions toward edge of dish.

TO COOK BY AUTO SENSOR: Cover completely with plastic wrap. Cook on **COOK A4**.

TO COOK BY TIME: Cover with wax paper. Cook at **HIGH** 9 to 10½ minutes, or until chicken is tender.

TO COMPLETE: Let stand, uncovered, 5 minutes before serving.

Note: For TWO Servings (4 pieces), follow above procedure. Halve all ingredients and cook chicken 5½ to 6 minutes.
For ONE Serving (2 pieces), cook chicken 3½ to 4 minutes.

MOROCCAN CHICKEN

2 cups hot water
1 cup rice
1 envelope (1 oz.) onion-mushroom soup
    mix, divided
½ cup raisins
½ teaspoon cinnamon, divided
2½ to 3 pound chicken, cut into serving
    pieces
1 cup plain yogurt
2 tablespoons flour
1 to 2 tablespoons milk

Yield: 4 Servings

In 12×8-inch dish, combine water, rice, ½ envelope soup mix, raisins and ¼ teaspoon cinnamon. Cook, covered with plastic wrap, at **HIGH** 4 to 5 minutes and at **MEDIUM-LOW** 13 to 15 minutes, or until rice is almost tender; stir once. Arrange chicken on rice with meatier portions toward edge of dish. Sprinkle with remaining cinnamon. Cook, covered with wax paper, at **HIGH** 12 to 14 minutes, or until chicken is tender. Rearrange chicken and stir rice once. Combine yogurt, flour, milk and remaining soup mix. Spoon over chicken. Let stand, covered, 5 minutes. If necessary, reheat at **MEDIUM-LOW** 1½ to 2 minutes before serving.

109

FIESTA CHICKEN ROLL-UPS A

2 boneless chicken breasts, skinned, split and pounded thin (about 1 to 1¼ lb.)
Chili powder
Pepper
2 ounces Cheddar cheese, cut into quarters
¼ cup sliced green olives
¼ cup butter or margarine, melted*
¾ cup crushed taco or corn chips
1 can (8 oz.) taco or seasoned tomato sauce

Yield: 4 Servings

Season one side of each chicken breast with chili powder and pepper. Place one stick of cheese on each breast. Sprinkle 1 tablespoon of olives down center. Fold edges over to enclose filling. Secure with wooden toothpicks. Carefully roll in melted butter, then crushed corn chips. Arrange seam-side down in 8-inch square dish.

TO COOK BY AUTO SENSOR: Cover completely with plastic wrap. Cook on **COOK A4.** After cooking, release plastic wrap.

TO COOK BY TIME: Cover with wax paper. Cook at **MEDIUM** 8 to 9 minutes, or until chicken is tender.

TO COMPLETE: Let stand, covered, 5 minutes. Meanwhile, in small glass bowl, heat taco sauce at **HIGH** 2 to 3 minutes, or until hot. Serve over chicken.

FRUITED GLAZED CHICKEN

¼ cup peach or apricot preserves
¼ teaspoon browning sauce
2½ to 3 pounds chicken, cut into serving pieces
1 package (10 oz.) frozen mixed fruit, defrosted (see page 32)
1 tablespoon cornstarch
½ teaspoon lemon juice, optional
Dash ginger or cinnamon

Yield: 4 Servings

Combine preserves and browning sauce in small glass bowl. Cook at **HIGH** ½ to 1 minute. Arrange chicken in 12×8-inch dish with meatier portions toward edge of dish. Brush with ½ preserves. Cook, covered with wax paper, at **HIGH** 12 to 13 minutes. Brush with remaining preserves halfway through cooking. Remove chicken to serving platter. Let stand, covered, 5 minutes. Drain liquid, reserving ½ cup. In baking dish, combine reserved liquid and remaining ingredients. Cook at **HIGH** 3 to 4 minutes, or until sauce is slightly thickened; stir twice. Serve over chicken.

CHICKEN VERONIQUE

2½ to 3 pound chicken, cut into serving pieces
3 tablespoons butter or margarine
1 teaspoon browning sauce
3 tablespoons flour
½ cup milk or half'n half
¼ cup white wine
1 cup halved green grapes
Toasted slivered almonds

Yield: 4 Servings

Prepare Butter Baked Chicken, page 111, using chicken, butter and browning sauce. Remove chicken to serving platter; drain liquid, reserving ¾ cup. Blend flour with milk until smooth. Into baking dish, stir milk, wine, reserved liquid and grapes. Cook at **MEDIUM** 3½ to 4½ minutes, or until sauce is thickened; stir twice. Pour sauce over chicken and garnish with almonds.

HONEY GLAZED CHICKEN A

2 chicken breasts, split
¼ cup honey
2 tablespoons orange juice
1 tablespoon chili sauce
1 teaspoon prepared mustard
1 teaspoon browning sauce, optional

Yield: 4 Servings

Arrange chicken breasts in 12×8-inch dish
with meatier portions toward edge of dish.
Combine honey, orange juice, chili sauce,
mustard and browning sauce; stir well.
Pour honey mixture over chicken.

TO COOK BY AUTO SENSOR: Cover
completely with plastic wrap. Cook on
COOK A4.

TO COOK BY TIME: Cover with wax paper.
Cook at **HIGH** 8 to 9 minutes and at
MEDIUM-LOW 8 to 9 minutes.

TO COMPLETE: Chicken should be tender.
Let stand, uncovered, 5 minutes before
serving.

HERB BAKED CHICKEN A

1 teaspoon garlic salt
1 teaspoon paprika
½ teaspoon oregano
¼ teaspoon pepper
Juice and grated peel of 1 lemon
2½ to 3 pound chicken, cut into serving
    pieces
1 jar (4½ oz.) sliced mushrooms, drained

Yield: 4 Servings

Combine garlic, paprika, oregano, pepper
and lemon peel. Rub over chicken. Arrange
chicken in 12×8-inch dish with meatier
portions toward edge of dish. Drizzle with
lemon and top with mushrooms.

TO COOK BY AUTO SENSOR: Cover
completely with plastic wrap. Cook on
COOK A4. After cooking, release plastic
wrap.

TO COOK BY TIME: Cover with wax paper.
Cook at **HIGH** 10½ to 12 minutes.

TO COMPLETE: Chicken should be tender.
Let stand, covered, 5 minutes before
serving.

BUTTERED BAKED CHICKEN A

2½ to 3 pound chicken, cut into serving
    pieces
3 tablespoons butter or margarine, melted
1 teaspoon browning sauce

Yield: 4 Servings

Arrange chicken in 12×8-inch dish with
meatier portions toward edge of dish.
Combine butter and browning sauce.

TO COOK BY AUTO SENSOR: Brush all of
the butter sauce over chicken. Cover
completely with plastic wrap. Cook on
COOK A4. After cooking, release plastic
wrap.

TO COOK BY TIME: Brush half of butter
mixture over chicken. Cover with wax
paper. Cook at **HIGH** 11 to 13 minutes.
Halfway through cooking, brush remaining
butter mixture on chicken.

TO COMPLETE: Chicken should be tender.
Let stand, covered, 5 minutes before
serving.

Note: For TWO Servings, *follow above
procedure. Halve all ingredients and
cook 5½ to 6½ minutes.*
For ONE Serving, *cook chicken 3½
to 4½ minutes.*

111

APRICOT GLAZED CHICKEN

2½ to 3 pound chicken, cut into serving
   pieces
¾ cup apricot preserves
½ cup bottled red Russian dressing
2 envelopes (¼ oz. ea.) instant onion soup

Yield: 4 Servings

Arrange chicken in 12×8-inch dish with
meatier portions toward edge of dish.
Cook, covered with wax paper, at **HIGH** 9
to 10 minutes, or until chicken is almost
tender; drain. Combine remaining
ingredients and spoon over chicken. Cook
chicken, uncovered, at **MEDIUM** 5 to 5½
minutes, or until chicken is tender. Let
stand, 5 minutes before serving.

CHICKEN IN WINE SAUCE

1 medium onion, sliced
¼ cup butter or margarine
2 boneless chicken breasts, skinned and
   thinly sliced (about 1 lb.)
Salt and pepper to taste
1 medium green pepper, cut into thin
   strips
⅓ cup white wine
1 jar (4½ oz.) sliced mushrooms, drained
2 tablespoons flour
⅔ cup chicken broth

Yield: 4 Servings

Combine onion and butter in 12×8-inch
dish. Cook at **HIGH** 3 to 3½ minutes, or
until onion is tender; add chicken. Cook at
HIGH 3 to 3½ minutes; stir once. Season
with salt and pepper; add green pepper
and wine. Cook, covered with plastic wrap,
at **HIGH** 2½ to 3 minutes; add mushrooms.
Blend flour with broth until smooth. Stir
into dish. Cook at **HIGH** 3 to 4 minutes, or
until sauce is thickened; stir twice.

CHICKEN WITH CREAMY ▣ MUSHROOM SAUCE

2½ to 3 pounds chicken, cut into serving
   pieces
1 medium onion, sliced
½ cup white wine
Salt, pepper and garlic to taste
½ pound fresh mushrooms, sliced*
1 can (10¾ oz.) condensed golden
   mushroom soup
1 cup sour cream

Yield: 4 Servings

TO COOK BY AUTO SENSOR: Arrange
chicken in 12×8-inch dish with meatier
portions toward edge of dish. Season with
salt, pepper and garlic salt. Top with
onions and mushrooms; pour wine over
chicken. Cover completely with plastic
wrap. Cook on **COOK A2**.

TO COOK BY TIME: Arrange chicken in
12×8-inch dish with meatier portions
toward edge of dish. Top with onion and
add wine. Cover with wax paper. Cook at
HIGH 10 to 20 minutes. Season with salt,
pepper and garlic salt. Add mushrooms
and cook, covered, at **HIGH** 3 to 3½
minutes.

TO COMPLETE: Chicken and mushrooms
should be tender. Drain liquid; reserve ⅓
cup. Blend reserved liquid, soup and sour
cream until smooth; spoon over chicken.
Cover with wax paper. Cook at **MEDIUM** 4
to 5 minutes or until heated through. Let
stand, covered, 5 minutes. Remove chicken
to serving platter; stir sauce until smooth
and serve over chicken.

***Substitution:** Use 1 jar (4½ oz.) sliced
mushrooms, drained, for fresh
mushrooms.*

112

ORIENTAL CHICKEN AND CASHEWS

3 tablespoons oil
2 boneless chicken breasts, skinned and thinly sliced (about 1 to 1¼ lb.)
2 cloves garlic, finely chopped
2 tablespoons soy sauce
1 tablespoon sherry
1 tablespoon cornstarch
¼ teaspoon ginger
1 medium green pepper, cut into small chunks
½ cup cashew halves or chopped walnuts

Yield: 4 Servings

Heat oil in 12×8-inch dish at **HIGH** 2½ to 3 minutes.
Meanwhile, combine chicken, garlic, soy sauce, sherry, cornstarch and ginger. Add to dish and cook at **HIGH** 3 to 4 minutes; stir twice. Add green pepper and cashews. Cook, covered with plastic wrap, at **HIGH** 2½ to 3½ minutes, or until chicken and green pepper are tender; stir once. Let stand 3 minutes before serving.

CHICKEN WITH SNOW PEAS

6 chicken legs, thighs detached (about 2¾ lb.)
1 tablespoon butter or margarine, melted
1 tablespoon soy sauce
1½ teaspoons paprika
½ teaspoon crushed rosemary
¼ teaspoon salt
1 package (6 oz.) frozen pea pods, defrosted (see page 32)
1 jar (2½ oz.) sliced mushrooms, drained

Yield: 6 Servings

Arrange chicken in 12×8-inch dish. Combine butter, soy sauce, paprika, rosemary and salt. Brush over chicken. Cook, covered with wax paper, at **HIGH** 8 to 9 minutes. Top with pea pods and mushrooms. Cook, covered, at **HIGH** 5 to 6 minutes, or until chicken and vegetables are tender. Let stand, covered, 5 minutes before serving.

CHICKEN TERIYAKI A

2½ to 3 pound chicken cut into servings pieces
1 can (8 oz.) chunk pineapple in pineapple juice
1 clove garlic, finely chopped
¼ cup soy sauce
2 tablespoons packed brown sugar
½ teaspoon salt
¼ teaspoon ginger

Yield: 4–6 Servings

Arrange chickens in 12×8-inch dish with meatier portions toward edge of dish. Combine remaining ingredients; stir well. Pour sauce over chicken.

TO COOK BY AUTO SENSOR: Cover completely with plastic wrap. Cook on **COOK A4**. After cooking, release plastic wrap.

TO COOK BY TIME: Cover with wax paper. Cook at **HIGH** 9 to 10 minutes and at **MEDIUM-LOW** 9 to 10 minutes.

TO COMPLETE: Chicken should be tender. Let stand, covered, 5 minutes. To serve, spoon pineapple sauce over chicken.

113

HAWAIIAN ISLAND CHICKEN

2½ to 3 pound chicken, cut into serving
    pieces
2 tablespoons soy sauce
¼ teaspoon ginger
1 green pepper, cut into chunks
1 can (11 oz.) mandarin oranges, drained;
    reserve syrup
1 can (8¼ oz.) pineapple slices, drained
    and halved; reserve syrup
1 tablespoon cornstarch

Yield: 4 Servings

Arrange chicken in 12×8-inch dish with
meatier portions toward edge of dish.
Brush with soy sauce blended with ginger.
Add green pepper. Cook, covered with wax
paper, at **HIGH** 13 to 15 minutes; drain. Let
stand, covered, 5 minutes. Blend
cornstarch with 1 cup reserved syrup until
smooth. Cook at **HIGH** 2 minutes; stir
once. Add fruit and pour over chicken; if
necessary, reheat at **HIGH** 3 to 4 minutes.

SPIRITED CHICKEN 🄰

2¾ pounds chicken legs, thighs detached
½ cup dry sherry
¼ cup soy sauce
1 tablespoon Worcestershire sauce
½ teaspoon garlic powder

Yield: 6 Servings

Combine all ingredients and marinate 30
minutes.

TO COOK BY AUTO SENSOR: Arrange
chicken in 12×8-inch dish with meatier
portions toward the edge of dish. Cover
completely with plastic wrap. Cook on
COOK A4. After cooking, release plastic wrap.

TO COOK BY TIME: Arrange chicken in
12×8-inch dish with meatier portions
toward the edge of dish. Cover with wax
paper. Cook at **HIGH** 14 to 16 minutes, or
until chicken is tender.

TO COMPLETE: Let stand, covered, 5
minutes before serving.

CITRUS CHICKEN

½ cup orange juice
¼ cup lime juice
½ teaspoon grated lime peel
½ teaspoon salt
¼ teaspoon thyme
⅛ teaspoon sage
⅛ teaspoon pepper
2½ pound chicken, cut into serving pieces
1 tablespoon cornstarch
1 tablespoon water

Yield: 4 Servings

Combine juices, peel, salt, thyme, sage and
pepper. Arrange chicken in 12×8-inch dish
skin-side down and meatier portions
toward edge of dish. Pour juice over
chicken. Cover with wax paper. Cook at
HIGH 17 to 20 minutes, or until chicken is
done. Turn chicken skin-side up halfway
through cooking.
Place chicken on platter. Skim fat from
liquid and pour liquid into 4-cup measure.
Blend cornstarch with water until smooth.
Stir into measure. Cook at **HIGH** 3 minutes,
or until thickened; stir twice. Pour sauce
over chicken and serve immediately.

STUFFED CORNISH HENS WITH ORANGE SAUCE

2½ cups hot water
1 can (6 oz.) frozen orange juice concentrate, defrosted and divided (see page 32)
1 package (6 oz.) long grain and wild rice mix
4 slices bacon, cooked and crumbled (see page 83)
4 cornish hens (1 lb. ea.)
⅓ cup honey
¼ to ½ teaspoon browning sauce

Yield: 4 Servings

In 2-quart casserole, combine water, ¼ cup orange juice concentrate and rice. Cook, covered with lid, at **HIGH** 5 to 6 minutes and at **MEDIUM-LOW** 20 minutes, or until rice is tender; stir in bacon. Stuff hens with rice mixture. With cotton string, tie legs together. Place hens in 12×8-inch dish. Cook, covered with wax paper, at **HIGH** 28 to 30 minutes, or until hens are tender.
Meanwhile, combine remaining orange juice concentrate, honey and browning sauce; brush hens every 10 minutes. Let stand, covered, 10 minutes before serving.

CORNISH HENS WITH PEACH A SAUCE

2 cornish hens (about 1 lb. ea.) split
Browning sauce
Paprika
Pepper
1 can (16 oz.) sliced peaches in heavy syrup, drained; reserve ⅓ cup syrup
⅔ cup orange juice
1 tablespoon cornstarch
⅛ teaspoon ginger
Slivered almonds, optional

Yield: 4 Servings

Arrange hens in 12×8-inch dish so that wings are in center of dish. Brush with browning sauce and season with paprika and pepper.

TO COOK BY AUTO SENSOR: Cover completely with 2 overlapping pieces of plastic wrap. Cook on **COOK A4**. After cooking, release plastic wrap.

TO COOK BY TIME: Cover with wax paper. Cook at **HIGH** 10 to 11 minutes.

TO COMPLETE: Hens should be tender. Let stand, covered, 5 minutes.
Meanwhile, in small glass bowl, combine reserved syrup, orange juice, cornstarch and ginger; blend until smooth. Cook at **HIGH** 1½ to 2½ minutes or until sauce is thickened; stir once. Add peaches and spoon over hens. If necessary, cook 1½ to 2 minutes before serving. Garnish, if desired, with slivered almond.

Note: *For TWO servings, follow above procedure. Halve all ingredients. Cook hens 7 to 8 minutes. Add enough reserved syrup to orange juice to equal ½ cup. Cook sauce 1 to 1½ minutes.*

115

ROAST DUCK WITH ORANGE

4 to 5 pound duck
¼ cup bottled fruit sauce (for poultry)
2 tablespoons orange liqueur or orange juice
¼ teaspoon browning sauce
1 can (11 oz.) mandarin oranges, drained, optional

Yield: 4-6 Servings

Pierce skin of duck several times. Place duck breast-side up on microwave roasting rack set in 12×8-inch dish. Combine fruit sauce, orange liqueur and browning sauce; set aside. Cook duck at **MEDIUM** 30 minutes; drain. Brush half of sauce on duck. Cook at **MEDIUM** 20 to 25 minutes, or until duck is tender. Brush with remaining sauce. Let stand, covered, 10 minutes before serving. Garnish with orange.

PECAN STUFFED PHEASANT

1 stalk celery, thinly sliced
2 tablespoons butter or margarine
⅔ cup dry bread crumbs
⅓ cup chopped pecans
1 teaspoon salt, divided
⅛ teaspoon pepper
2 pheasants (1 to 1½ lb. ea.)
1 cup water, divided
2 to 3 tablespoons sherry
1½ teaspoons browning sauce
2 tablespoons cornstarch

Yield: 4 Servings

Combine celery and butter in small glass bowl. Cook at **HIGH** 1 to 2 minutes. Stir in bread crumbs, pecans, ½ teaspoon salt and pepper. Stuff pheasant with pecan mixture. With string, tie wings and legs to body of pheasant. Arrange pheasant breast-side up, in 8-inch square dish. Add ¾ cup water, sherry and browning sauce. Cook, covered with plastic wrap, at **HIGH** 8 to 10 minutes and at **MEDIUM-LOW** 18 to 20 minutes, or until pheasant is tender. Remove pheasant to serving platter. Let stand, covered, 5 minutes. Blend cornstarch with remaining ¼ cup water until smooth. Stir cornstarch and salt into dish. Cook at **HIGH** 2 to 3 minutes, or until thickened, stir once. Serve with pheasant.

ROAST WHOLE TURKEY

12 pound turkey
Salt
Poultry seasoning
Browning sauce

Yield: 12 Servings

Season inside of turkey with salt and poultry seasoning. With cotton string, tie legs and wings securely to body of bird.

Place turkey, breast-side down on microwave roasting rack set in 12×8-inch dish. Brush with browning sauce. Cook, covered with wax paper, at **MEDIUM** 48 minutes; drain liquid once. Arrange turkey breast-side up; brush with browning sauce. Cook, covered with wax paper, at **MEDIUM-LOW** 1¼ hours, or until turkey registers 190°F when tested with conventional meat thermometer. Insert in both thigh joints.
(Remove turkey from oven before reading temperature.)
Drain liquid occasionally. Let stand, covered, 20 minutes before serving.

Hints: Turkey may be stuffed before heating by time. Close cavity with string or wooden toothpicks. Halfway through cooking at MEDIUM-LOW, shield legs and wings with aluminum foil to prevent overcooking.

116

TURKEY DIVAN

2 packages (10 oz. ea.) frozen broccoli spears, defrosted (see page 32)
2 to 3 cups cut-up cooked turkey or chicken*
Salt and pepper to taste
1 can (11 oz.) condensed Cheddar cheese soup
½ cup milk
¼ cup buttered bread crumbs
½ teaspoon paprika

Yield: 4 Servings

Arrange broccoli in 12×8-inch dish; top with turkey. Cook, covered with plastic wrap, at **MEDIUM-HIGH** 5 to 6 minutes; drain. Season with salt and pepper. In small glass bowl, combine soup and milk. Cook at **MEDIUM-HIGH** 2 to 3 minutes; stir until smooth. Pour sauce over turkey. Cook, covered, at **MEDIUM-HIGH** 5 to 6 minutes, or until heated through. Top with bread crumbs mixed with paprika; let stand, covered, 5 minutes before serving.

If desired, turkey may be thinly sliced.

ROAST GOOSE WITH APPLE STUFFING

¼ cup butter, margarine or goose fat
2 stalks celery, thinly sliced
2 medium onions, sliced finaly chopped
3 to 5 cups fresh bread cubes
2 medium apples chopped
1 egg, beaten
¼ cup brandy
1 tablespoon parsley flakes
1 teaspoon salt
¼ teaspoon pepper
9 to 10 pound goose
Browning sauce

Yield: 6–8 Servings

In large glass bowl, combine butter, celery and onion. Cook at **HIGH** 5 to 6 minutes, or until celery and onion are tender. Add bread, apples, egg, brandy, parsley, salt and pepper; combine thoroughly. Stuff goose with apple mixture; secure opening with wooden toothpicks or cotton string. Secure wings and legs to body of bird with cotton string. Pierce skin several times. Arrange bird, breast-side down, on microwave roasting rack set in 12×8-inch dish. Brush with browning sauce. Cook at **MEDIUM** 30 minutes; turn bird over and drain fat. Cook at **MEDIUM** 25 to 30 minutes, or until bird is tender.
Let stand, covered, 15 minutes before serving.

TURKEY ROAST

2 pound frozen turkey roast

Yield: 6 Servings

Place turkey roast in 9×5×3-inch loaf dish gravy-side up; cover with plastic wrap. Cook at **MEDIUM-LOW** 17 minutes. Turn roast over; recover. Cook at **MEDIUM-LOW** 17 to 20 minutes or until roast registers 160°F when tested with a conventional meat thermometer. (Remove roast from oven before reading temperature).
Let stand, covered, 7 minutes before serving.

APPLE SAUSAGE STUFFING

½ pound bulk pork sausage
2 stalks celery, thinly sliced
1 large onion, finely chopped
5 cups fresh bread cubes
3 cups chopped apple (3 medium)
2 eggs, beaten
1 to 1½ teaspoons salt
¼ to ½ teaspoon poultry seasoning

Yield: 8 Servings (about 6 cups)

Crumble sausage in 12×8-inch; stir in celery and onion. Cook at **HIGH** 4½ to 5½ minutes, or until sausage is browned, stir twice. Drain. Add remaining ingredients; combine thoroughly.* Cook, covered with plastic wrap, at **HIGH** 3 to 4 minutes and at **MEDIUM-LOW** 5 to 6 minutes, or until heated through.

This makes enough to stuff a 7 to 9 lb. bird.

CORN BREAD STUFFING

3 stalks celery, thinly sliced
1 large onion, chopped
½ cup butter or margarine
2 packages (12 oz. ea.) corn bread or corn muffin mix, baked and crumbled (see page 191)
2 eggs
1½ cups orange juice or chicken broth
1½ teaspoons salt
¾ teaspoon sage
¼ teaspoon pepper

Yield: 12 Servings (about 9 cups)

In 3-quart casserole, combine celery, onion and butter. Cook at **HIGH** 6 to 7 minutes, or until celery and onion are tender; stir twice. Add remaining ingredients; combine thoroughly.* Cook, covered with lid, at **MEDIUM-LOW** 10 to 11 minutes, or until heated through. Let stand, covered, 5 minutes before serving.

This makes enough to stuff a 9 to 12 pound bird.

CONVENIENCE STUFFING MIXES

1½ to 1¾ cups hot water
¼ cup butter
1 package (6 to 6½ oz.) stuffing mix (chicken, cornbread, pork or rice varieties) with seasoning packet

Yield: 6 Servings

In 2-quart casserole, combine water, butter and seasoning packet. Cook at **HIGH** 4½ to 5 minutes; stir in stuffing crumbs.* Let stand, covered, 5 minutes before serving.

This makes enough to stuff a 2½ to 3 pound bird.

Variations: Add one of the following with seasoning packet:
- 1 cup chopped fresh cranberries or apple
- ½ cup raisins, chopped nuts, or chopped apricots
- ½ pound browned ground sausage, drained
- 1 can (8 oz.) whole kernel corn, drained

FISH and SEAFOOD

Fish for dinner is always a delightful surprise to daily meal planning. And how lucky you seafood lovers are—fish prepared in the microwave oven is moist and delicious (not to mention quick).

Just follow the simple instructions in the charts or one of these tasty recipes and your efforts are sure to be applauded.

GENERAL DIRECTIONS FOR COOKING FISH AND SEAFOOD

Clean fish before starting the recipe. Arrange fish in a single layer; do not overlap edges. Place thicker pieces toward outside edge of dish. Shrimp and scallops should be placed in a single layer.

To Cook by Time: Cover dish with plastic wrap. Cook on the power level and for the minimum time recommended in the chart. Halfway through cooking rearrange or stir shrimp or scallops.

To Cook by Auto Sensor: Cover dish completely with plastic wrap. Cook on Auto Sensor Cycle COOK A8. When time appears in the display window, stir shrimp or scallops.

Let stand, covered, 5 minutes.

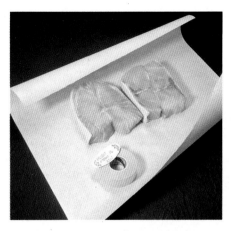

Test for doneness before adding extra heating time. Fish and seafood should be opaque in color and fish should flake when tested with a fork. If undercooked, return to oven and continue to cook for 30 to 60 seconds.

To Cook frozen fish and seafood **by Auto Sensor Froz-Cook:** Prepare fresh fish for freezer. Fish fillets and steaks, whole fish, should be frozen individually. Scallops and shrimp must be frozen in a single layer.

When ready to cook, follow directions for Auto Sensor cooking and special instructions given in the chart. Cook on the Froz-Cook Cycle indicated in the chart.

COOKING FISH AND SEAFOOD A

FISH OR SEAFOOD	AMOUNT	POWER	APPROX. COOKING TIME (in minutes)	APPROX. COOKING TIME (in minutes) on COOK A8
Fish Fillets	1 lb.	HIGH	4 to 6	————
Fish Steaks	4 (6 oz. ea.)	HIGH	6 to 8	————
Scallops (sea)	1 lb.	MEDIUM	6½ to 8½	8 to 9
Shrimp medium size (shelled and cleaned)	1 lb.	MEDIUM	4½ to 6½	10
Whole fish (stuffed or unstuffed)	1½ to 1¾ lb.	HIGH	9 to 11	5 to 6

Note: *Fish and seafood not listed above are not suitable for Auto Sensor.*

PREPARING AND COOKING FROZEN FISH AND SEAFOOD A

FISH OR SEAFOOD	AUTO SENSOR CYCLE	APPROX. COOKING TIME (min. per pound)	SPECIAL INSTRUCTIONS
Fish Steaks,* 1 lb.	FROZ-COOK A8	20 to 21	Individually frozen. Add ¼ cup water per pound.
Fish Fillets,* 1 lb.	FROZ-COOK A8	18 to 19	Individually frozen. Arrange in single layers.
Frozen Lobster Tails, (8 oz. ea.)	FROZ-COOK A8	15 to 19	————
Scallops, 1 lb.	FROZ-COOK A8	21 to 22	Arrange in single layer.
Shrimp, 1 lb. (peeled or in shell)	FROZ-COOK A6	22	Arrange in single layer.
Whole Fish, 1 lb.	FROZ-COOK A6	20 to 21	Arrange in single layer. Add ¼ cup water per pound.

Not suitable for cooking frozen blocks of fish.
Note: *Fish and seafood not listed above are not suitable for Auto Sensor Cooking.*

121

SCROD WITH GRAPE SAUCE

2 tablespoons butter or margarine
1 tablespoon dried onion flakes
¾ cup chicken broth
Pepper to taste
1½ pounds scrod or sole fillets
3 tablespoons flour
¾ cup milk or half'n half
1 cup halved green grapes
Parsley

Yield: 4–6 Servings

In 12×8-inch dish, combine butter, onion, broth and pepper. Cook at **HIGH** 2 to 3 minutes. Arrange fillets in single layer. Cook, covered with wax paper, at **HIGH** 7 to 8 minutes, or until fish is done. Arrange fillets on serving platter; cover. Strain broth into small glass bowl. Blend flour with milk until smooth. Stir milk and grapes into broth.
Cook at **MEDIUM** 3½ to 5 minutes, or until sauce is thickened; stir twice. Pour some sauce over fillets, sprinkle with parsley. Serve remaining sauce with fillets.

Variation: Add 2 tablespoons white wine when cooking fish.

TROUT AMANDINE A

⅓ cup butter or margarine
½ cup slivered almonds
2 whole trout (about 12 oz. ea.) cleaned
Salt and pepper to taste
Lemon juice

Yield: 2–4 Servings

Combine butter and almonds in 2-cup glass measure. Cook at **HIGH** 3 to 4 minutes, or until almonds are lightly browned; stir twice.
Arrange fish in 12×8-inch dish. Season inside of fish with salt, pepper and lemon juice. Pour butter and almonds inside and over fish.

TO COOK BY AUTO SENSOR: Cover completely with plastic wrap. Cook on **COOK A4**. After cooking, release plastic wrap.

TO COOK BY TIME: Cover with wax paper. Cook at **HIGH** 6 to 7 minutes.

TO COMPLETE: Fish should be tender. Let stand, covered, 5 minutes before serving.

FILLET PROVENCALE

2 small onions, sliced
2 tablespoons butter or margarine
1 clove garlic, finely chopped
1 can (16 oz.) stewed tomatoes, chopped
1 jar (4½ oz.) sliced mushrooms, drained
¼ cup white wine
⅛ teaspoon basil
6 flounder fillets (about ¼ lb. ea.)
Salt

Yield: 6 Servings

In 12×8-inch dish, combine onion, butter and garlic. Cook, covered with plastic wrap, at **HIGH** 3 to 3½ minutes. Stir in tomatoes, mushrooms, wine and basil. Cook, covered, at **HIGH** 3 minutes and at **MEDIUM** 3 to 4 minutes. Meanwhile, season fish with salt, skin side only. Roll up (skin-side in) and arrange seam-side down in sauce; spoon sauce over fish. Cook, covered, at **HIGH** 5 to 6 minutes, or until fish is done. Let stand, covered, 5 minutes before serving.

PARCHMENT SEAFOOD SPECTACULAR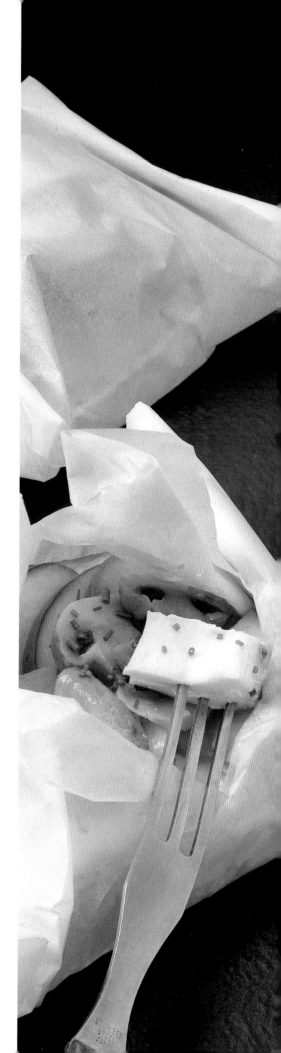

2 tablespoons brandy
1 tablespoon lemon juice
4 halibut or other seafood steaks (about 6 oz. ea.)
½ tablespoon butter or margarine, increased to 2
   tablespoons for Time cooking
1 teaspoon dried chives, increased to 2 tablespoons for
   Time heating
Salt and pepper to taste
1 cup slice fresh mushrooms (about ¼ lb.)
1 small apple, thinly sliced

Yield: 4 Servings

Combine brandy and lemon juice.

TO COOK BY AUTO SENSOR: Arrange fish in 12×8-inch
dish; do NOT use parchment paper. Brush brandy mixture
over fish; dot with ½ tablespoon butter, 1 teaspoon chives
and season with salt and pepper. Mound mushrooms and
apples on top. Cover completely with plastic wrap. Cook
on **COOK A8**. After cooking, release plastic wrap.

TO COOK BY TIME: Place each fish steak on a 10″×5″
piece of parchment paper. Brush fish with brandy mixture.
Dot with 2 tablespoons butter. Season with 2 tablespoons
chives, salt and pepper. Mound mushrooms and apples on
top; bring paper up around fish. Fold edges over twice to
seal top; fold side edges up. Places on glass oven tray.
Cook at **HIGH** 7½ to 9 minutes. Serve packet directly on
dinner plate.

TO COMPLETE: Let stand, covered, 5 minutes before
serving.

FLOUNDER WITH SHRIMP SAUCE A

4 flounder fillets (about ¼ lb. ea.)
1 can (10¾ oz.) condensed cream of shrimp soup
¼ cup white wine or milk
½ cup (2 oz.) shredded Swiss cheese
Parsley or slivered almonds

Yield: 4 Servings

Roll up fillets and arrange seam-side down in 8-inch square
dish. Combine soup, wine and cheese; spoon over fillets.

TO COOK BY AUTO SENSOR: Cover completely with
plastic wrap. Cook on **COOK A8**. After cooking, release
plastic wrap.

TO COOK BY TIME: Cover with plastic wrap. Cook at
MEDIUM 11 to 12 minutes, or until fish is done.

TO COMPLETE: Let stand, covered, 5 minutes. Sprinkle
with parsley or almonds before serving.

BAKED SNAPPER À LA ORANGE 🅰

1 medium orange
6 tablespoons butter or margarine
1 small onion, finely chopped
1 tablespoon parsley flakes
½ teaspoon basil
⅛ teaspoon pepper
2 cups soft bread crumbs (about 4 slices bread)
2 whole red snappers (1¼ to 1½ lb. ea.), dressed and heads removed
Salt
1 can (6 oz.) frozen orange juice concentrate, defrosted (see page 32)

Yield: 4 Servings

Slice half of orange; peel and chop remaining half. In small glass bowl, combine butter, onion, parsley, basil and pepper. Cook at **HIGH** 2½ to 3 minutes or until onion is tender. Stir in bread crumbs and chopped orange. Arrange fish in 12×8-inch dish, season inside with salt. Stuff cavity with bread crumb mixture.

TO COOK BY AUTO SENSOR: Top fish with orange slices; pour orange juice over fish. Cover completely with plastic wrap. Cook on **COOK A4**. After cooking, release plastic wrap.

TO COOK BY TIME: Cover with wax paper. Cook at **HIGH** 13 to 15 minutes. Pour orange juice over fish; add orange slice. Cook, covered with wax paper, at **HIGH** 2 minutes.

TO COMPLETE: Let covered, 3 minutes before serving.

SALMON STEAKS WITH DILL 🅰

1 stalk celery, very thinly sliced
¼ cup butter or margarine, melted
¼ cup white wine
½ teaspoon dill weed
¼ teaspoon salt
¼ teaspoon pepper
4 salmon steaks 1-inch thick (about 8 oz. ea.)

Yield: 4 Servings

In 12×8-inch dish, combine celery, butter, wine, dill weed, salt and pepper. Arrange salmon in dish; with thickest portion toward edge of dish. Spoon sauce over each steak.

TO COOK BY AUTO SENSOR: Cover completely with plastic wrap. Cook on **COOK A8**. After cooking, release plastic wrap.

TO COOK BY TIME: Cover with wax paper. Cook at **HIGH** 9 to 11 minutes.

TO COMPLETE: Let stand, covered, 3 minutes before serving.

SALMON ROMANOFF

1 package (8 oz.) medium egg noodles, cooked and drained (see page 180)
1½ cups cottage cheese
1½ cups sour cream
1 can (16 oz.) salmon, drained and flaked
1 can (4 oz.) sliced mushrooms, drained
½ cup (2 oz.) shredded Cheddar cheese
2 teaspoons dried onion flakes
2 teaspoons Worcestershire sauce
½ teaspoon salt
⅛ teaspoon dried garlic pieces
Shredded Cheddar cheese or buttered bread crumbs
Paprika

Yield: 4–6 Servings

In 3-quart casserole, thoroughly combine noodles, cottage cheese, sour cream, salmon, mushrooms, ½ cup cheese, onion, Worcestershire, salt and garlic. Cook, covered with lid, at **MEDIUM** 10 to 12 minutes, or until heated through; stir twice. Top with shredded cheese and sprinkle with paprika. Let stand, covered, 5 minutes before serving.

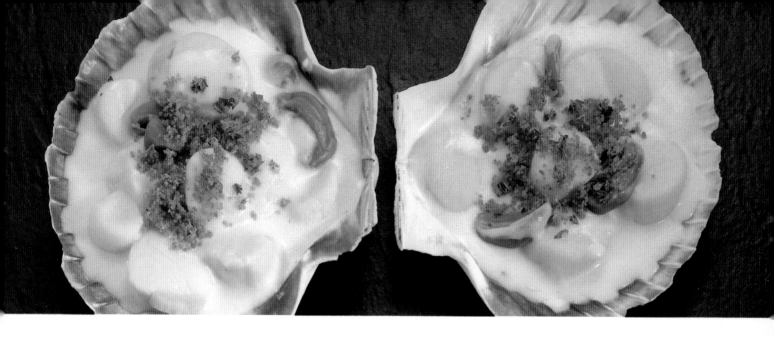

COQUILLE ST. JACQUES

¼ cup white wine
1 pound sea scallops
2 tablespoons butter or margarine
1 tablespoon dried onion flakes
2 tablespoons flour
Dash white pepper
¾ cup milk or half'n half
1 jar (2½ oz.) sliced mushrooms, drained
⅓ cup (1⅓ oz.) shredded Swiss cheese
¼ cup buttered bread crumbs
Parsley flakes

Yield: 4 Servings

Arrange scallops in 8-inch round dish. Pour wine over scallops. Cook, covered with plastic wrap, at **MEDIUM** 5 to 6 minutes, or until scallops are tender; stir once. Drain liquid and reserve ¼ cup; let scallops stand, covered.
Cook butter and onion in medium glass bowl, at **MEDIUM** ¾ to 1 minute. Stir in flour and pepper. Gradually add milk and reserved liquid, stirring until smooth. Cook at **MEDIUM** 3 to 3½ minutes, or until mixture is thickened; stir twice. Stir in mushrooms and cheese; add scallops. Spoon mixture into 4 individual glass ramekins or serving dishes, top with bread crumbs and parsley. Arrange ramekins on glass oven tray. Cook at **MEDIUM** 1 to 2 minutes, or until heated through.

*Note: **For TWO Servings,** follow above procedure; halve all ingredients. Cook scallops 2 to 3 minutes, butter ½ minute, cream mixture 1½ to 2 minutes and ramekin 1 minute.*

BOUILLABAISSE

1 medium onion, sliced
2 tablespoons oil
2 cloves garlic, finely chopped
6 small clams, scrubbed (littleneck)
1 can (28 oz.) whole tomatoes, chopped
2 bottles (8 oz. ea.) clam juice
2 bay leaves
½ teaspoon salt
⅛ teaspoon pepper
Dash thyme
Pinch saffron, optional
½ pound sea scallops
½ pound sole fillet, cut into 1½-inch
    pieces
2 lobster tails (8 oz. ea.) cut into 1½-inch
    pieces

Yield: 6 Servings

In 4-quart casserole, combine onion, oil and garlic. Cook, covered with lid, at **HIGH** 2 to 3 minutes. Add clams, tomatoes, clam juice, bay leaves, salt, pepper, thyme and saffron. Cook, covered, at **HIGH** 5 minutes and at **MEDIUM** 15 to 20 minutes, or until clams are open; stir once. Add scallops, fillet and lobster. Cook, covered, at **HIGH** 5 to 7 minutes, or until fish is done. Let stand, covered, 10 minutes. Remove bay leaves before serving.

BAKED STUFFED LOBSTER TAILS

4 lobster tails (about 8 oz. ea.)
3 tablespoons butter or margarine, melted
⅓ cup seasoned dry bread crumbs
⅛ teaspoon onion powder
⅛ teaspoon paprika
⅛ teaspoon salt

Yield: 4 Servings

With kitchen shears, cut lobster through center of soft shell (underneath) to the tail. Lift lobster out of shell by loosening with fingers, leaving meat attached to tail section. (Lobster meat will rest on shell). Arrange on 12-inch glass plate, tails toward center.
Combine remaining ingredients; sprinkle over lobster. Cook, covered with wax paper, at **MEDIUM** 8½ to 9½ minutes, or until lobster is done. Let stand 5 minutes. Serve, if desired, with Lemon Butter*.

***Lemon Butter:** In small bowl, heat ½ cup butter and 1 to 2 tablespoons lemon juice at **MEDIUM-LOW** 1 to 1½ minutes, or until butter is melted.*

***Note:** For TWO Servings, follow above procedure. Halve all ingredients; cook lobster 5½ to 6½ minutes.*

STEAMED WHOLE LOBSTER

1 quart hot water
½ teaspoon salt
1 fresh lobster (about 1½ to 2 lb.), pegged

Yield: 2 Servings

Combine water and salt in 5-quart casserole. Heat, covered with lid, at **HIGH** 5 to 6 minutes, or until boiling. Tilt dish; place lobster in dish, head first. Cook, covered, at **MEDIUM** 14 to 16 minutes, or until shell turns red. Let stand, covered, 2 minutes. To test for doneness, slit tail section; lobster meat should be opaque. If necessary, cook, covered, at **MEDIUM**, an additional 1 to 2 minutes.

SHRIMP AND VEGETABLES MANDARIN

Water
1 can (11 oz.) mandarin oranges; drained reserve liquid
2 envelopes (¼ oz. ea.) instant chicken broth
1½ tablespoons cornstarch
⅛ teaspoon garlic powder
1 pound medium shrimp, shelled and cleaned
1 bunch green onions, thinly sliced (about ½ cup)
1 package (6 oz.) frozen pea pods, defrosted (see page 32)
1 jar (4½ oz.) sliced mushrooms, drained
Slivered almonds

Yield: 4 Servings

Add enough water to reserved syrup to equal 1½ cups. In 2-quart casserole, combine syrup mixture, broth, cornstarch and garlic. Cook at **HIGH** 3½ to 4½ minutes, or until mixture is thickened; stir twice. Stir in shrimp, onions, pea pods and mushrooms. Cook, covered with lid, at **HIGH** 2 minutes and at **MEDIUM** 5 to 6 minutes, or until shrimp is tender; stir once. Stir in oranges and almonds and let stand, covered, 5 minutes before serving.

SHRIMP CREOLE A

½ cup <u>each</u> finely chopped celery, green pepper and onion
2 tablespoons oil
2 cloves garlic, finely chopped
1 can (15 oz.) tomato sauce
1 pound medium shrimp, shelled and cleaned
1 teaspoon salt
¼ teaspoon pepper
¼ to ½ teaspoon hot pepper sauce

Yield: 4 Servings

TO COOK BY AUTO SENSOR: In 2-quart casserole, combine all ingredients, omitting oil. Cover with lid. Cook on **COOK A7**. After time appears in display window, stir once.

TO COOK BY TIME: In 2-quart casserole, combine celery, green pepper, onion, oil and garlic. Cook at **HIGH** 4 to 5 minutes, or until vegetables are tender. Stir in remaining ingredients; cover with lid. Cook at **HIGH** 3 minutes and at **MEDIUM** 5 to 6 minutes; stir once.

TO COMPLETE: Stir; let stand, covered, 5 minutes before serving.

SHRIMP SCAMPI A

1 clove garlic, finely chopped
⅓ cup butter or margarine
¼ cup chopped parsley
½ teaspoon salt
¾ pound medium frozen shrimp, cleaned
1 tablespoon lemon juice

Yield: 4 Servings

Combine garlic and butter in 1-quart casserole. Cook at **HIGH** 1½ to 2 minutes. Add parsley and salt. Stir in shrimp, coating each with butter sauce.

TO COOK BY AUTO SENSOR: Cover completely with plastic wrap. Cook on **COOK A8**. After time appears in display window, stir once. After cooking, release plastic wrap.

TO COOK BY TIME: Cover with plastic wrap. Cook at **MEDIUM** 5 to 6 minutes, stir once.

TO COMPLETE: Let stand, covered, 3 minutes. Sprinkle lemon juice over shrimp before serving.

Substitution: *1 pound of fresh, shelled and cleaned shrimp may be used in place of the frozen shrimp. Adjust cooking times as follows:*
Cook butter ¾ to 1 minute and shrimp 2½ to 3 minutes.

127

SHRIMP FRA DIAVOLO

1 small onion, chopped
¼ cup finely chopped green pepper
2 cloves garlic, finely chopped
2 tablespoons olive oil
1 can (16 oz.) tomatoes
1 can (6 oz.) tomato paste
¾ teaspoon salt
½ teaspoon basil
½ teaspoon oregano
½ teaspoon thyme
¼ teaspoon crushed red pepper
1¼ pounds medium shrimp, shelled and
    cleaned
1 pound hot cooked spaghetti

Yield: 4 Servings

In 3-quart casserole, combine onion, green pepper, garlic and oil. Cook at **HIGH** 2 minutes. Stir in tomatoes, tomato paste, salt, basil, oregano, thyme and red pepper. Cover with lid. Cook at **HIGH** 8 to 9 minutes; stir once. Add shrimp; cover. Cook at **MEDIUM** 3 to 4 minutes, or until shrimp are opaque; stir twice. Let stand, covered, 1 minute. Serve over spaghetti.

SHRIMP ORIENTAL

½ cup water
3 tablespoons soy sauce
2 tablespoons sherry
⅛ teaspoon hot pepper sauce
1 clove garlic, finely chopped
1½ tablespoons cornstarch
1 package (6 oz.) bamboo shoots, drained
1¼ pounds large shrimp, shelled and
    cleaned
4 green onions, sliced
1 medium tomato, cut into eighths
Hot cooked rice, optional

Yield: 4 Servings

In 3-quart casserole, combine water, soy sauce, sherry, hot pepper sauce and garlic. Blend in cornstarch until smooth. Stir in pea pods and bamboo shoots. Cover with lid. Cook at **HIGH** 4 to 4½ minutes. Add shrimp and green onions; stir to coat. Cover with lid. Cook at **MEDIUM** 4½ to 5½ minutes, or until shrimp are opaque. Stir in tomato. Let stand, covered, 5 minutes before serving. If desired, serve over rice.

SCALLOPS IN WHITE WINE

¼ cup butter or margarine
1 medium onion, chopped
2 cloves garlic, finely chopped
1 pound sea scallops
¼ cup dry white wine
½ teaspoon salt
¼ teaspoon thyme
⅛ teaspoon pepper
½ cup chopped parsley
1 tablespoon lemon juice

Yield: 4 Servings

Combine butter, onion and garlic in 2-quart casserole. Cover with lid. Cook at **HIGH** 2 to 3 minutes, or until onion is tender. Stir in scallops, wine, salt, thyme and pepper; cover. Cook at **MEDIUM** 6 to 7 minutes; stir once. Stir in parsley and lemon juice. If desired, serve with rice.

CLAMS-STEAMER STYLE

12 small clams, scrubbed (littleneck)
¼ cup hot water
Melted butter, or cocktail sauce, optional

Yield: 12 Clams

Combine clams and water in shallow casserole. Cook, covered with glass lid, at **HIGH** 1 minute and at **MEDIUM** 5 to 6 mintues, or until clams are open. Serve, if desired, with melted butter and cocktail sauce.

BAKED STUFFED CLAMS

18 small (littleneck) clams, scrubbed and opened
½ to ⅔ cup seasoned dry bread crumbs
2½ to 3 tablespoons salad oil
¼ teaspoon garlic powder
¼ teaspoon paprika
⅛ teaspoon pepper
3 slices bacon, crisp-cooked and crumbled (see page 83)

Yield: 18 Clams

Arrange clams on the half shell in 12×8-inch dish. With toothpick, pierce each clam several times. Combine bread crumbs, oil, garlic paprika and pepper.

TO COOK BY AUTO SENSOR: Sprinkle crumbs on clams. Top with bacon. Cover completely with plastic wrap. Cook on **COOK A8**. After cooking, release plastic wrap.

TO COOK BY TIME: Cover dish with wax paper. Cook at **MEDIUM** 3½ to 4 minutes, or until clams are tender. Sprinkle crumbs over clams. Top with bacon. Cook at **MEDIUM** 1½ to 2 minutes.

LANDLUBBER'S STUFFED CLAMS

2 cups seasoned croutons, crushed*, divided
1 can (7½ oz.) minced clams
2 tablespoons grated Parmesan cheese
½ teaspoon dried onion flakes
½ teaspoon garlic powder
Dash pepper
1 tablespoon butter or margarine, melted
1½ teaspoons parsley flakes

Yield: 4 Servings

Reserve ¼ cup crouton crumbs. In medium bowl, combine remaining crouton crumbs, clams, cheese, onion, garlic and pepper. Spoon mixture into 4 ramekins or 6-ounce custard cups. Blend reserved crumbs with butter and parsley. Sprinkle on top of clams.

TO COOK BY AUTO SENSOR: Cover each ramekin completely with plastic wrap. Cook on **COOK A7**. After cooking, release plastic wrap.

TO COOK BY TIME: Cook at **MEDIUM-HIGH** 3 to 4 minutes, or until heated through.

***Substitution:** Use 1½ cups dry seasoned bread crumbs for crushed croutons.*

SIMPLE SEAFOOD NEWBURG

1 can (10¾ oz.) condensed cream of
  mushroom soup
1 package (10 oz.) frozen peas, defrosted
  (see page 32)
¼ cup milk or half'n half
1 pound seafood, cooked (see page 121)
  and cut into bite-size pieces
1 jar (2½ oz.) sliced mushrooms, drained
2 to 3 tablespoons sherry

Yield: 4 Servings

In 1½-quart casserole, combine soup, peas
and milk. Cook, covered with lid, at
MEDIUM 4 to 5 minutes; stir once. Add
remaining ingredients. Cook, covered, at
MEDIUM 4 to 5 minutes, or until heated
through; stir once. Let stand, covered, 3
minutes before serving.

OYSTERS ROCKEFELLER EN CASSEROLE

1 can (10½ oz.) condensed oyster stew
3 tablespoons flour
⅔ cup (2⅔ oz.) shredded Cheddar cheese
1 tablespoon dried onion flakes
1 bay leaf, crushed
2 packages (10 oz. ea.) frozen chopped
  spinach, defrosted (see page 32)
1 pint large oysters, drained
½ cup dry bread crumbs
¼ cup grated Parmesan cheese
2 tablespoons butter or margarine, melted
½ teaspoon paprika

Yield: 4 Servings

In medium glass bowl, combine stew, flour,
Cheddar cheese, onion and bay leaf. Cook
at **HIGH** 3 minutes, or until sauce is
thickened; stir twice.
Spread spinach in 2½-quart casserole.
Pour stew mixture over spinach. With
toothpick, pierce each oyster several times
and arrange on stew. Top with bread
crumbs mixed with Parmesan cheese,
butter and paprika. Cook, uncovered, at
HIGH 5 minutes and cook, covered, at
HIGH 5 minutes. Let stand, covered, 5
minutes before serving.

SCALLOPS WITH HERB LEMON BUTTER A

¼ cup butter or margarine
½ teaspoon basil
½ teaspoon crushed rosemary
¼ teaspoon salt
1 pound sea scallops
Juice from 1 lemon (about 2 tablespoons)
Paprika

Yield: 4 Servings

In 8-inch square dish, combine butter,
basil, rosemary and salt. Cook at **HIGH** 1½
minutes, or until melted. Stir in scallops
and sprinkle with lemon juice; spoon
butter mixture over scallops.

TO COOK BY AUTO SENSOR: Cover
completely with plastic wrap. Cook on
COOK A8.

TO COOK BY TIME: Cover with plastic
wrap. Cook at **MEDIUM** 7 to 8½ minutes.

TO COMPLETE: Scallops should be tender.
Sprinkle with paprika. Let stand, covered, 5
minutes before serving.

*Note: For TWO servings, follow above
procedure; halve all ingredients.
Cook butter ½ to 1 minute and
scallops 4½ to 5½ minutes.*

CASSEROLES

Only time for a quick put-something-together supper? You do not have to forfeit a piping hot, hearty meal just because you have only 30 minutes to prepare dinner. With help from your microwave oven you can have a favorite recipe ready and on the table in no time!

BUSY DAY TUNA CASSEROLE A

1 can (6½ oz.) tuna, drained and flaked
4 cups (8 oz.) noodles, cooked and drained
(see pages 180 and 181)
1 can (10¾ oz.) condensed cream of celery
soup
1 can (4 oz.) sliced mushrooms, drained
1 package (10 oz.) frozen peas, defrosted
(see page 32)
¾ cup milk
2 tablespoons chopped pimento
1 cup crushed potato chips

Yield: 4–6 Servings

In 3-quart casserole, combine tuna, noodles, soup, mushrooms, peas, milk and pimento; mix well.

TO COOK BY AUTO SENSOR: Cover with lid. Cook on **COOK A4**. After time appears in display window, stir twice.

TO COOK BY TIME: Cover with wax paper. Cook at **HIGH** 6 minutes and at **MEDIUM-LOW** 10 to 12 minutes. Stir twice.

TO COMPLETE: Top with potato chips. Let stand, uncovered 3 minutes.

Cook noodles according to directions on pages 180 and 181.

In 3-quart casserole, combine tuna, noodles, soup, mushrooms, peas, milk and pimento; mix well.

To Cook by Time: Cover with wax paper. Cook according to recipe; stir twice.
To Cook by Auto Sensor: Cover with lid or completely with plastic wrap. Cook on COOK A4. Stir twice.

Top with potato chips. Let stand, uncovered, 3 minutes before serving.

CHICKEN À LA KING

⅓ cup butter or margarine
2 tablespoons finely chopped green pepper
⅓ cup flour
1 teaspoon salt
⅛ teaspoon pepper
1¼ cups chicken broth
1¼ cups milk or half'n half
3 cups cut-up cooked chicken or turkey
1 jar (4 oz.) sliced pimento, drained
   (about ⅓ cup)
1 can (4 oz.) sliced mushrooms, drained
2 tablespoons dry sherry, optional

Yield: 6 Servings

Combine butter and green pepper in 3-quart casserole dish. Cook at **HIGH** 3 to 4 minutes, or until green pepper is tender. Stir in flour, salt and pepper. Gradually add broth and milk, stir until smooth. Cook at **HIGH** 2 to 3 minutes and at **MEDIUM** 4 to 5 minutes, or until sauce is thickened; stir twice. Add remaining ingredients. Cook at **MEDIUM** 7 to 8 minutes, or until heated through; stir twice. Serve over toast, noodles or rice.

LAST MINUTE DINNER [A]

1 can (10¾ oz.) condensed cream of
   chicken or cream of mushroom soup
1 cup water
¼ cup white wine*
2 teaspoons soy sauce
1½ to 2 cups cut-up cooked chicken or
   turkey
1½ cups instant rice
1 can (16 oz.) green peas, drained
2 tablespoons chopped pimento

Yield: 4 Servings

In 2-quart casserole, blend soup, water, wine and soy sauce. Stir in remaining ingredients. Cover with lid.

TO COOK BY AUTO SENSOR: Cook on **COOK A4**. After time appears in display window, stir twice.

TO COOK BY TIME: Cook at **MEDIUM-HIGH** 9½ to 10½ minutes; stir twice.

TO COMPLETE: Let stand, covered, 5 minutes. Top, if desired, with crushed crackers or buttered bread crumbs.

If desired, omit wine and increase water to 1¼ cups.

SIMPLE CHICKEN POT PIE [A]

2 cups cut-up cooked chicken
1 can (10¾ oz.) condensed cream of
   chicken soup
1 package (10 oz.) frozen mixed
   vegetables, defrosted (see page 32)
½ cup milk
⅛ teaspoon pepper
Dash Worcestershire sauce
2 cups leftover stuffing*

Yield: 4 Servings

In 2-quart casserole, combine chicken, soup, vegetables, milk, pepper and Worcestershire.

TO COOK BY AUTO SENSOR: Cover with a lid. Cook on **COOK A4**. After time appears in display window, stir once.

TO COOK BY TIME: Cook at **MEDIUM-HIGH** 8 to 10 minutes. Stir once.

TO COMPLETE: Crumble stuffing over chicken mixture to form a crust. Cook at **MEDIUM-HIGH** 4 to 5 minutes. Let stand, 5 minutes before serving.

***Substitution:** Use 2 cups seasoned croutons for leftover stuffing.*

133

CHICKEN AND DUMPLINGS

3 pounds chicken parts
3½ cups water, divided
2 bay leaves
2 teaspoons salt
½ teaspoon pepper
1 tablespoon parsley flakes
1 teaspoon thyme
¼ teaspoon dried sage
½ cup flour
1 package (10 oz.) frozen peas and carrots,
   defrosted (see page 32)
Dumplings:
1½ cups buttermilk biscuit mix
½ cup milk
½ teaspoon fine herbes or parsley flakes

Yield: 6 Servings

In 4-quart casserole, combine chicken, 2½
cups water, bay leaves, salt, pepper,
parsley, thyme and sage. Cook, covered
with lid, at **HIGH** 10 minutes and at
MEDIUM 20 minutes, or until chicken is
tender; stir twice. Remove chicken and bay
leaves. Blend flour with remaining 1 cup
water until smooth; stir into dish. Cook at
HIGH 6 to 8 minutes, or until broth is
thickened; stir once.
Meanwhile, remove chicken from bone and
cut into bite-size pieces. Stir into gravy
with peas and carrots.
Cook, covered, at **HIGH** 8 to 12 minutes, or
until hot and bubbly; stir once. Combine
biscuit mix, milk and fine herbes. Spoon
around edge of simmering stew. Cook,
covered, at **MEDIUM** 6 minutes, or until
toothpick inserted in dumpling comes out
clean.

TURKEY TETRAZZINI

¼ cup butter or margarine
¼ cup flour
1 teaspoon salt
¼ teaspoon pepper
1 cup chicken broth
1 cup half'n half
4 cups cut-up cooked turkey or chicken
1 package (8 oz.) spaghetti, cooked and
   drained (see page 180)
1 can (4 oz.) sliced mushrooms, drained
2 tablespoons sherry, optional
¼ cup grated Parmesan cheese
Paprika

Yield: 6 Servings

Heat butter in 3-quart casserole at
MEDIUM-LOW 2 minutes, or until melted;
stir in flour, salt, and pepper. Gradually
add broth and half'n half; stir until
smooth. Cook at **MEDIUM** 7 to 8 minutes,
or until sauce is thickened; stir three
times. Stir in turkey, spaghetti, mushrooms
and sherry.
Cover with plastic wrap. Cook at **MEDIUM**
12 to 14 minutes. Stir twice. Top with
Parmesan cheese and paprika. Let stand,
covered, 5 minutes before serving.

134

HAMBURGER MEDLEY

1 pound ground beef
½ cup chopped green pepper or onion
1 can (15 oz.) tomato sauce
1 cup water
1 can (8 oz.) whole kernel corn, drained
1 cup uncooked elbow macaroni
⅛ teaspoon hot pepper sauce
1 cup corn chips, crushed

Yield: 4 Servings

Crumble ground beef in 3-quart casserole. Stir in green pepper. Cook at **HIGH** 6 minutes, or until beef is browned. Stir once; drain.
Stir in tomato sauce, water, corn, macaroni and hot pepper sauce. Cover with lid.

TO COOK BY AUTO SENSOR: Cook on **COOK A4.** After time appears in display window, stir twice.

TO COOK BY TIME: Cook at **HIGH** 8 minutes and at **MEDIUM-LOW** 10 to 12 minutes, or until macaroni is tender. Stir twice.

TO COMPLETE: Let stand, covered, 10 minutes; top with corn chips and serve.

CHILI 'N RICE CASSEROLE

1 pound ground beef
1 green pepper, chopped
2 medium onions, chopped
1 clove garlic, finely chopped
Water
1 can (16 oz.) whole tomatoes, chopped and drained; reserve liquid
1 can (15 oz.) tomato sauce
1 cup rice
2 to 3 tablespoons chili powder
1 teaspoon salt

Yield: 4 Servings

Crumble ground beef in 4-quart casserole dish. Stir in green pepper, onion and garlic. Cook at **HIGH** 4½ to 5½ minutes, or until beef is browned and onion is tender; stir twice. Drain. Add enough water to reserved liquid to equal 2 cups; add to beef and stir in remaining ingredients. Cook, covered with lid, at **HIGH** 8 to 9 minutes and at **MEDIUM-LOW** 40 minutes, or until rice is almost tender, stir twice. Let stand, covered, 15 minutes before serving.

SATURDAY NIGHT SUPPER

4 slices bacon, diced
1 large onion finely chopped
1 can (10¾ oz.) condensed cream of celery soup
1 can (16 oz.) sliced potatoes, drained (reserve ⅓ cup liquid)
1 package (9 oz.) frozen French-style green beans, defrosted (see page 32)
2 cups cut-up cooked chicken*

Yield: 4 Servings

Cook bacon in 2½-quart casserole at **HIGH** 2½ to 3 minutes; stir once. Remove bacon and add onion to bacon drippings. Cook at **HIGH** 2½ to 3½ minutes, or until onion is tender. Blend in soup and reserved liquid; stir in potatoes, green beans and chicken. Cook at **MEDIUM-HIGH** 12 to 13 minutes, or until hot and bubbly. Stir twice. Let stand, covered, 5 minutes. Top with bacon before serving.

*__Substitution:__ *Use 3 cans (5 oz. ea.) boned chicken or 1 pound frankfurters, cut-up.*

135

CORN DOGGIES

¼ cup butter or margarine
1 medium onion, chopped
1 can (8 oz.) cream-style corn
½ cup milk
1 egg, beaten
⅛ teaspoon hot pepper sauce
¾ cup yellow cornmeal
¾ cup flour
1 tablespoon sugar
2 teaspoons baking powder
½ teaspoon salt
¼ teaspoon dry mustard
4 to 5 frankfurters, cut crosswise in thirds

Yield: 4 Servings

Combine butter and onion in glass bowl. Cook at **HIGH** 2½ minutes; stir once. Stir in corn, milk, egg and hot pepper sauce until smooth. Add cornmeal, flour, sugar, baking powder, salt and mustard. Place frankfurter pieces in spoke fashion in greased 2-quart ring mold. Pour cornmeal mixture over frankfurters. Cook at **MEDIUM-LOW** 13 to 14 minutes, or until toothpick comes out clean. Let stand 5 minutes before serving.

SHEPHERD'S PIE

1 large onion, chopped
3 tablespoons butter or margarine
½ tablespoon parsley flakes
1½ cups beef gravy
2 cups cut-up cooked lamb or beef (about ¾-inch pieces)
1 package (10 oz.) frozen peas and carrots, defrosted (see page 32)
1½ to 2 cups hot mashed potatoes
Paprika

Yield: 4 Servings

Combine onion and butter in 2-quart casserole. Cook at **HIGH** 2 to 2½ minutes, or until onion is tender. Stir in parsley; gradually add gravy. Cook at **HIGH** 3 to 4 minutes, or until gravy is hot; stir twice. Stir in lamb and peas and carrots. Cook at **MEDIUM-HIGH** 10 to 11 minutes, or until heated through; stir twice. Spoon potatoes on top of casserole; sprinkle with paprika. Cook at **MEDIUM-HIGH** 2 to 3 minutes.

QUICK CORNED BEEF AND CABBAGE

2 medium potatoes, thinly sliced (about 2 cups)
1 medium onion, sliced
¼ cup water
¾ teaspoon salt
⅛ teaspoon pepper
1 can (12 oz.) corned beef, crumbled
½ head cabbage, cut into 4 wedges (about 1¼ lb.)
¼ cup butter or margarine, melted

Yield: 4 Servings

In greased 3-quart casserole, layer potatoes and onion. Add water, salt and pepper. Cook, covered with lid, at **HIGH** 8 to 9 minutes. Add corned beef and cabbage; pour butter over cabbage. Cook, covered, at **HIGH** 10 to 12 minutes, or until cabbage is tender. Let stand, covered, 5 minutes before serving.

HOT ENCHILADA DOGS ▪A▪

1 can (16 oz.) chili without beans
3 tablespoons finely chopped green chili
   peppers
⅛ teaspoon hot pepper sauce
8 tortillas, softened*
8 frankfurters, ends slit
1 can (8 oz.) tomato sauce
1 cup (4 oz.) shredded Cheddar cheese

Yield: 4 Servings

Combine chili, chili peppers and hot pepper
sauce. Place 2 tablespoons chili mixture on
each tortilla, place frankfurters in center
and roll up. Arrange tortillas seam-side
down in 12×8-inch dish. Combine tomato
sauce with remaining chili mixture; pour
over tortillas.

TO COOK BY AUTO SENSOR: Cover
completely with plastic wrap. Cook on
COOK A1.

TO COOK BY TIME: Cover with plastic
wrap. Cook at **MEDIUM-HIGH** 6½ to 7½
minutes.

TO COMPLETE: Top with cheese. Let stand,
covered, 5 minutes before serving.

*_Hint:_ To soften tortillas in your
_microwave oven, place tortillas on paper
plate. Cover with wax paper. Heat at
HIGH 40 to 60 seconds, or until softened._

PARTY TUNA CASSEROLE

2 tablespoons butter or margarine, melted
1 tablespoon soy sauce
1 teaspoon garlic powder
1 can (3 oz.) chow mein noodles
1 can (10¾ oz.) condensed cream of
   mushroom soup
1 can (7 oz.) tuna, drained and flaked
2 stalks celery, finely chopped
¼ pound salted cashew nuts
2 teaspoons dried onion flakes
¼ cup water

Yield: 4 Servings

Combine butter, soy sauce, garlic and
noodles; toss well and reserve. In 8-inch
round dish, combine soup, tuna, celery,
nuts, onion and water. Cook at **MEDIUM-
HIGH** 9 to 10 minutes, or until heated
through; stir twice. Top with noodles and
cook at **MEDIUM-HIGH** 1 minute. Let stand,
covered, 5 minutes.

COUNTRY HAM CASSEROLE ▪A▪

1 package (8 oz.) noodles
1 can (10¾ oz.) condensed cream of celery
   soup
¾ cup milk
½ teaspoon dry mustard, optional
2 cups cut-up cooked ham (about ¾ lb.)
1½ cups (6 oz.) shredded Swiss cheese,
   divided
1 can (16 oz.) green peas, drained
French fried onion pieces or crushed
   corn chips

Yield: 4 Servings

TO COOK BY AUTO SENSOR: In 3-quart
casserole, combine uncooked noodles,
ham, 1¼ cups cheese, soup, peas, milk,
mustard and an <u>additional 2¼ cups water.</u>
Cover with lid. Cook on **COOK A4**. When
time appears in display window, stir once.

TO COOK BY TIME: Cook noodles
according to directions on page 180.
In 3-quart casserole, combine soup, milk
and mustard; stir in noodles, ham, 1¼
cups cheese and, peas. Cover with lid.
Cook at **MEDIUM-HIGH** 15 to 17 minutes.
Stir twice.

TO COMPLETE: Top with remaining cheese
and onion pieces. Let stand, covered, 5
minutes before serving.

MERMAID'S IMPERIAL DELIGHT

¼ cup chopped green pepper
2 tablespoons butter or margarine
1 pound medium shrimp, shelled and
   cleaned
2 cups cooked rice (see page 184)
¾ cup mayonnaise
1 can (8 oz.) peas, drained
1 package (6 oz.) crabmeat, drained and
   flaked (canned or frozen, defrosted see
   page 32)
Salt and pepper to taste

Yield: 6 Servings

Combine green pepper and butter in 2-
quart casserole. Cook at **HIGH** 1½ minutes;
stir once. Add shrimp and cook at **MEDIUM**
2 minutes; stir once. Stir in remaining
ingredients. Cook, covered with lid, at
MEDIUM 8 to 9 minutes, or until heated
through, stir twice. Stir gently. Top, if
desired, with buttered bread crumbs.

PAELLA

5½ cups hot tap water
½ teaspoon cinnamon
Pinch saffron
2 packages (6 oz. ea.) chicken flavored rice mix with flavor packet
6 pieces frozen fried chicken, defrosted
1 package (9 oz.) frozen artichoke hearts, defrosted (see page 32)
½ cup sliced pitted ripe olives, optional
3 tablespoons chopped pimento, optional
12 small clams, scrubbed
12 medium shrimp, shelled and cleaned
¾ pound cooked ham, cubed

Yield: 6 Servings

In 5-quart casserole, combine water, cinnamon, saffron and flavor packets from rice mix. Cook, covered with lid, at **HIGH** 10 to 12 minutes, or until liquid is boiling. Add rice and cook, covered, at **HIGH** 10 to 12 minutes. Add chicken, artichokes, olives and pimento. Cook, covered, at **MEDIUM** 10 to 11 minutes, stir once. Add clams, shrimp and ham and cook, covered, at **MEDIUM** 10 minutes; stir twice. Let stand 10 minutes before serving.

SPICY SHRIMP AND SPAGHETTI BAKE

½ cup chopped green pepper
1 medium onion, chopped
3 tablespoons butter or margarine
2 cans (8 oz. ea.) tomato sauce
1 can (16 oz.) whole tomatoes, chopped
1 tablespoon Worcestershire sauce
1 teaspoon salt
⅛ teaspoon crushed red pepper, optional
1 pound medium shrimp, shelled and cleaned
1 package (8 oz.) spaghetti, cooked and drained (see page 180)
¾ cup grated Parmesan cheese, divided

Yield: 4–6 Servings

In 3-quart casserole, combine green pepper, onion and butter. Cook, covered with lid, at **HIGH** 3 to 4 minutes. Stir in tomato sauce, tomatoes, Worcestershire sauce, salt and red pepper. Cook, covered, at **HIGH** 8 to 9 minutes; stir once. Stir in spaghetti and shrimp. Cook, covered, at **MEDIUM** 9 to 11 minutes, or until shrimp are done and mixture is hot, stir twice. Stir in ½ cup cheese. Top with remaining cheese. Let stand 5 minutes.

NONA'S ITALIAN SAUSAGE

1½ pounds Italian sausage links, cut into
    1½-inch pieces
3 medium potatoes, peeled and cut into
    small chunks
1 clove garlic, finely chopped
3 medium green peppers, cut into chunks
3 medium onions, cut into chunks
2 cans (8 oz. ea.) tomato sauce
½ teaspoon salt
½ teaspoon oregano
¼ teaspoon pepper

Yield: 6 Servings

In 3-quart casserole, combine sausage,
potatoes and garlic. Cook, covered with lid,
at **HIGH** 11 to 13 minutes, or until potatoes
are tender; stir twice. Drain; stir in
remaining ingredients and cook, covered,
at **HIGH** 12 to 13* minutes, or until
vegetables are tender; stir twice. Let stand,
covered, 5 minutes before serving.

*If desired, add an additional can (8 oz.)
tomato sauce.*

HONEYED HAM AND APPLE RING

1¼ pounds cooked ham, ground
    (about 3½ cups)
5 small apples peeled, divided
3 eggs
1 cup soft bread crumbs
½ cup milk
⅓ cup finely chopped onion
5 tablespoons honey, divided
¼ teaspoon cloves
⅛ teaspoon ginger
Pepper to taste
2 tablespoons butter or margarine

Yield: 6 Servings

Combine ham, 1 apple, chopped, eggs,
bread crumbs, milk, onion, 4 tablespoons
honey, cloves, ginger and pepper. Spoon
mixture into greased 2-quart ring mold.
Cover with wax paper. Cook at **MEDIUM-
HIGH** 13 to 15 minutes, or until mixture is
set. Let stand, covered, 5 minutes.
Meanwhile, slice remaining apples. In
small glass bowl, combine apples, butter
and remaining honey. Cook, covered with
plastic wrap, at **HIGH** 6 to 7 minutes, or
until apples are tender. Stir once. Invert
ham onto serving platter; arrange apples
on top of ring.

SAUSAGE AND BEAN CASSOULET

1½ pounds Italian sausage links, cut into
    1½-inch pieces
2 small onions, sliced
2 cans (16 oz. ea.) navy or small white
    beans, rinsed*
½ pound cooked ham, cut into 1-inch
    pieces
1 can (8 oz.) tomato sauce
½ cup catsup
¼ cup white wine or water
¼ cup packed brown sugar
1 teaspoon salt
½ teaspoon dry mustard
½ teaspoon pepper

Yield: 6 Servings

Combine sausage and onions in 3-quart
casserole. Cook, covered with lid, at **HIGH**
10 minutes, or until sausage is almost
cooked; stir once. Drain. Stir in remaining
ingredients and cook, covered, at **HIGH** 5
minutes and at **MEDIUM** 10 to 15 minutes,
or until flavors are blended; stir twice.

***Note:** To use dried beans, see page 170.*

139

BAKED ZITI

1 package (8 oz.) ziti macaroni, cooked (see page 180)
1 jar (15½ oz.) spaghetti sauce
½ cup (2 oz.) shredded mozzarella cheese

Yield: 4 Servings

Combine ziti and spaghetti sauce in 2-quart casserole. Cook, covered with lid, at **MEDIUM-HIGH** 9 to 10 minutes; stir twice. Sprinkle with cheese. Let stand, covered, 10 minutes before serving.

EASY LASAGNA

½ pound ground beef
1 jar (32 oz.) spaghetti sauce
½ cup water
1 container (15 oz.) ricotta or cottage cheese
1 egg, slightly beaten
½ teaspoon salt
½ teaspoon pepper
9 lasagna noodles (uncooked)
½ pound mozzarella cheese thinly sliced
½ cup grated Parmesan cheese

Yield: 6 Servings

Crumble ground beef in large glass bowl. Cook at **HIGH** 2 to 3 minutes, or until beef is browned; stir once. Drain. Stir in spaghetti sauce and water. Cook at **HIGH** 4 to 5 minutes or until bubbly. Meanwhile, combine ricotta cheese, egg, salt and pepper. Spoon ½ cup sauce in 12×8-inch dish. Alternately layer noodles, egg mixture, mozzarella cheese and sauce, forming 3 layers. Cook, covered with plastic wrap, at **HIGH** 8 minutes and at **MEDIUM-LOW** 35 to 38 minutes, or until noodles are tender. If necessary, shield ends of dish with foil, during last 10 minutes of cooking time. Sprinkle with Parmesan cheese; let stand, covered, 15 minutes before serving.

EGGPLANT PARMESAN

1 large eggplant (about 1¾ lb.)
1 slice white bread, crumbled
¼ cup grated Parmesan cheese
2 tablespoons butter or margarine, melted
2 cups spaghetti sauce
1½ to 2 cups (6 to 8 oz.) shredded mozzarella cheese

Yield: 4 Servings

Pierce skin of eggplant several times. Place eggplant on paper towel on glass oven tray. Cook at **HIGH** 5 to 6 minutes, or until eggplant is almost tender; roll over twice. Let cool, then peel, if desired, and cut into ½-inch slices.
Meanwhile, combine bread, Parmesan cheese and butter. In 8-inch square dish, alternately layer spaghetti sauce, eggplant, crumb mixture and mozzarella cheese. Cover with wax paper. Cook at **HIGH** 14 to 16 minutes, or until hot and bubbly. Let stand, covered 5 minutes before serving.

EGGS and CHEESES

With the assistance of your microwave oven you can have poached eggs in minutes. Cook directly in the serving bowl. And, you won't be left with the dirty dishes. Creamy scrambled eggs, smooth Welsh rarebit, easy Omelets—all this and more awaits you in this chapter.

DIRECTIONS FOR BAKED EGGS

Generously grease 6-ounce custard cup for each egg. Break egg into cup and with toothpick, pierce egg yolk twice and egg white several times.

Top with one teaspoon milk.

Cover with plastic wrap and cook at MEDIUM according to time indicated in chart.

Let stand before serving. Serve over toast.

BAKED EGGS

NUMBER OF EGGS	APPROX. COOKING TIME (in minutes) at MEDIUM*	STAND TIME
1	¾ to 1	1
2	1¼ to 1½	1
4	1¾ to 2¼	1½
6	2½ to 3	2

*Note: *Eggs will be slightly underdone after cooking time. The cooking will be completed during stand time.*

DIRECTIONS FOR POACHED EGGS

Use 10-ounce custard cup or small glass bowl for each egg. In each cup heat at HIGH ¼ cup hot water and a dash of vinegar and salt.

Break egg into boiling water and with toothpick, pierce egg yolk twice and egg white several times.

Cover with plastic wrap. Cook at MEDIUM according to time indicated in chart.

Let stand, covered, before serving. Serve on buttered toast.

POACHED EGGS

NUMBER OF EGGS	APPROX. COOKING TIME (in minutes)		STAND TIME
	TO BOIL WATER at HIGH	TO POACH EGGS at MEDIUM*	
1	1	½ to ¾	1
2	3	1½ to 1¾	2
4	4	2¼ to 2½	2
6	6 to 6½	3½ to 3¾	2

*Note: *Eggs will be slightly underdone after cooking time. The cooking will be completed during standing time.*

DIRECTIONS FOR SCRAMBLED EGGS

Beat eggs. For each egg add 1 tablespoon milk and dash of salt. Pour into a greased glass container.

Cook at MEDIUM according to time in the chart. Between first and second cooking time, stir eggs. Bring cooked portions along edge of dish to center.

Stir and let stand, covered.

Eggs will continue to cook during stand time and should be slightly underdone after cooking.

SCRAMBLED EGGS

NUMBER OF EGGS	CONTAINER	APPROX. COOKING TIME (in minutes) at MEDIUM*		STAND TIME
		FIRST COOKING	SECOND COOKING	
1	1 cup glass measure	½ to ¾	¼ to ½	1
2	1 cup glass measure	¾ to 1	½ to ¾	1½
4	1 qt. glass bowl	1¾ to 2½	1 to 1½	1½
6	1½ qt. glass bowl	2½ to 3	1 to 1½	2
8	1½ qt. glass bowl	3 to 3¼	2 to 2½	2

***Note**: Eggs will be slightly underdone after cooking time. The cooking will be completed during stand time.*

DIRECTIONS FOR HARD-COOKED EGGS

Eggs should not be hard-cooked in their shell in a microwave oven. Pressure will build up and the egg will explode. However, if the hard-cooked egg will be chopped or sieved, it may be cooked in the microwave oven. Grease 6-ounce custard cups for each egg. Break egg into cup and with toothpick, pierce egg yolk twice and egg white several times.

Cover with plastic wrap and cook at MEDIUM for the time recommended in the chart.

Let stand to cool before slicing, chopping, etc.

HARD-COOKED EGGS

NUMBER OF EGGS	APPROX. COOKING TIME (in minutes) at MEDIUM
1	1 to 1½
2	2 to 2½
4	3½ to 4

NORMANDY OMELET

1 small apple, sliced
2 tablespoons butter or margarine, divided
1 tablespoon honey
Dash cinnamon
4 eggs, separated
Salt and pepper to taste

Yield: 2 Servings

In small glass bowl, combine apple, 1 tablespoon butter, honey and cinnamon. Cook, covered with plastic wrap, at **HIGH** 3 to 4 minutes, or until apples are tender; reserve. Heat remaining butter in 9-inch pie plate at **HIGH** ½ to ¾ minute, or until melted; turn plate to coat bottom with butter.
Meanwhile, beat egg whites until stiff, but not dry; beat egg yolks, salt and pepper until thickened. Fold egg yolks into egg whites; carefully pour mixture into pie plate. Cook at **MEDIUM** 4 to 5 minutes. Let stand 2 minutes. With spatula, loosen edges of omelet from plate; spoon apples onto half. Fold other half omelet over apples. Sprinkle, if desired, with confectioners sugar.

BASIC OMELET

1 tablespoon butter or margarine
2 eggs
2 tablespoons milk
⅛ teaspoon salt
Dash pepper

Yield: 1 Serving

Heat butter in 9-inch pie plate at **HIGH** ½ to ¾ minute, or until melted, turn plate to coat bottom with butter.
Meanwhile, combine remaining ingredients; pour into pie plate. Cook, covered with plastic wrap, at **MEDIUM** 2 to 3 minutes, or until omelet is almost set; stir after 1 minute. Let stand, covered, 2 minutes. With spatula, loosen edges of omelet from plate; fold into thirds to serve.

Note: Try one of these easy variations:
For CHEESE Omelet, before folding, sprinkle ¼ cup shredded cheese down center of omelet.
For HAM Omelet, before folding, sprinkle ¼ cup finely chopped cooked ham down center of omelet.
For HERB Omelet, blend in ⅛ teaspoon basil, thyme or crushed rosemary with eggs and milk.
For JELLY Omelet, before folding, spoon ¼ cup jelly down center of omelet.

BAKED EGGS IN BOLOGNA CUPS

4 slices bologna
4 eggs
Salt and pepper to taste

Yield: 4 Servings

For each serving, line each custard cup (6 oz. ea.) with bologna. Break egg into center. With toothpick, pierce egg yolk twice and egg white several times. Season with salt and pepper. Cover each cup with plastic wrap. Cook at **MEDIUM** 2 to 3 minutes. Let stand, covered, 2 minutes before serving.

NOTE: ***For TWO baked eggs****, follow above procedure; halve all ingredients. Cook 1¼ to 1¾ minutes. Let stand 1 minute.*

EGGS BENEDICT

1 package (1¼ oz.) hollandaise sauce mix
Ingredients as sauce mix package directs
4 eggs
4 thin slices cooked ham
2 English muffins, split and toasted

Yield: 4 Servings

Combine sauce mix and ingredients as package directs in 2-cup glass measure. Cook at **HIGH** 2 to 2½ minutes, or until sauce is thickened; stir once. Prepare Poached Eggs according to chart, page 143. While eggs are standing, cook ham. Arrange ham in single layer on paper towel lined paper plate. Cook at **MEDIUM** 1 to 1½ minutes. To serve, place ham on muffin; top with egg, then sauce. If necessary, reheat at **MEDIUM** ½ to 1 minute.

RANCHERO EGGS

1 can (28 oz.) stewed tomatoes, chopped
3 tablespoons chopped green chilies
1 tablespoon dried onion flakes
⅛ teaspoon garlic powder
Salt and pepper to taste
6 eggs
¾ cup (3 oz.) shredded Monterey jack or
** Cheddar cheese**

Yield: 6 Servings

In 12×8-inch dish, combine tomatoes, chilies, onion, garlic, salt and pepper. Cook, covered with plastic wrap, at **HIGH** 4½ to 5½ minutes; stir once. Break eggs into tomato mixture (around outside edge); with toothpick, pierce egg yolks twice and egg whites several times. Cook, covered, at **MEDIUM** 4½ to 5½ minutes, or until eggs are almost set. Sprinkle with cheese. Let stand, covered, 5 minutes. If desired, serve over corn bread.

SATURDAY'S HAM AND EGG SCRAMBLE

1 cup cut-up cooked ham
2 tablespoons butter or margarine
1 package (3 oz.) cream cheese, softened
  (see page 230)
⅓ cup milk
5 eggs
Salt and pepper to taste

Yield: 4 Servings

Combine ham and butter in 8-inch round dish. Covered with wax paper. Cook at **HIGH** 2 to 3 minutes; stir once. Combine cream cheese and milk; blend in eggs, salt and pepper. Add to ham. Cook, covered, at **MEDIUM** 5 to 6 minutes, or until eggs are almost set; stir twice. Let stand, covered, 3 minutes before serving.

COUNTRY BREAKFAST

2 medium baking potatoes
  (about 6 oz. ea.)*
¼ cup butter or margarine
¼ cup chopped green pepper
¼ cup chopped onion
4 eggs
½ cup milk
½ teaspoon salt
⅛ teaspoon pepper
2 slices American cheese, halved, optional

Yield: 4 Servings

Cook potatoes according to directions for baking potatoes (page 163). Let stand 5 minutes; peel and slice. Meanwhile, in 8-inch round dish, combine butter, green pepper and onion. Cook at **HIGH** 3 to 4 minutes, or until vegetables are tender; add sliced potatoes. Combine eggs, milk, salt and pepper; stir into potatoes. Cook, covered with plastic wrap, at **MEDIUM** 5 to 6 minutes, or until eggs are set; stir twice. Top with cheese. Let stand, covered, 5 minutes before serving.

__Substitution:__ Use 1 or 2 cans (16 oz. ea.) sliced potatoes, drained for baked potatoes.

CORNED BEEF HASH AND EGGS

1 can (24 oz.) corned beef hash
2 tablespoons catsup
1 tablespoon Worcestershire sauce
½ teaspoon onion powder
⅛ teaspoon pepper
4 eggs

Yield: 4 Servings

In 8-inch round dish, combine hash, catsup, Worcestershire, onion powder and pepper. Cook, covered with plastic wrap, at **MEDIUM-HIGH** 3 to 4 minutes; stir. Lightly pat mixture into dish and form 4 wells. Into each well, break 1 egg; with toothpick, pierce egg yolk twice and egg white several times. Cook, covered, at **MEDIUM** 3½ to 4½ minutes, or until eggs are almost set. Let stand, covered, 5 minutes before serving.

148

MACARONI AND CHEESE

**1 package (8 oz.) elbow macaroni, cooked
and drained (see page 180)**
**¾ pound pasteurized process cheese
spread, cut into cubes**
¾ to 1 cup milk
½ to ¾ teaspoon salt
¼ teaspoon onion powder
⅛ teaspoon dry mustard, optional
¼ teaspoon pepper
Buttered bread crumbs

Yield: 4 Servings

In 3-quart casserole, combine macaroni,
cheese, milk, salt, onion, mustard and
pepper. Cook, covered with lid, at **MEDIUM**
9 to 10 minutes; stir twice. Top with bread
crumbs and cook, uncovered, at **MEDIUM** 3
minutes.

Variation: *Use ½ cup tomato sauce for ¼
cup milk and ⅛ teaspoon oregano for dry
mustard.*

SPINACH CHEESE RING 🅰

**2 packages (10 oz. ea.) frozen chopped
spinach, cooked and drained
(see pages 163 and 165)**
1 cup (½ pt.) cottage cheese
2 eggs
1 tablespoon caraway seeds
Dash pepper
¼ cup buttered seasoned bread crumbs
1 tablespoon grated Parmesan cheese
¼ teaspoon paprika

Yield: 4 Servings

In bowl, combine spinach, cottage cheese,
eggs, caraway seeds and pepper. Spoon
into 1-quart glass ring mold.

TO COOK BY AUTO SENSOR: Cover
completely with plastic wrap. Cook on
COOK A8.

TO COOK BY TIME: Cover with plastic
wrap. Cook at **MEDIUM** 4 to 5 minutes, or
until almost set.

TO COMPLETE: Combine bread crumbs,
cheese and paprika. Sprinkle on top. Cook,
uncovered, at **MEDIUM** 1 to 1½ minutes.
Let stand, uncovered, 5 minutes.

149

WELSH RAREBIT

1 pound (4 cups) Cheddar cheese, shredded
3 tablespoons flour
⅔ cup beer
½ teaspoon Worcestershire sauce
½ teaspoon dry mustard

Yield: 4 Servings

In medium bowl, toss cheese with flour. Heat beer in 4-cup glass measure at **HIGH** 1½ to 2 minutes, or until boiling. Gradually add half of cheese, Worcestershire and mustard, stirring until smooth. Cook at **MEDIUM** 1½ to 2½ minutes; stir once. Add remaining cheese. Cook at **MEDIUM** 2 to 3 minutes, or until cheese is completely melted; stir once. Serve, traditionally, over toast points.

CAULIFLOWER AND CARROT QUICHE

1½ cups coarsely chopped cauliflower
1 carrot, shredded
1 tablespoon water
1 9-inch pie shell, baked (see page 219)
1 cup (4 oz.) shredded Swiss cheese
¼ cup grated Parmesan cheese
3 eggs
1 cup (½ pt.) heavy cream
⅛ teaspoon pepper

Yield: 10 Servings

In 1-quart bowl, combine cauliflower, carrot and water. Cover with plastic wrap. Cook at **HIGH** 5½ to 6 minutes. Stir once. Sprinkle vegetables into pie shell. Sprinkle cheeses over vegetables.
Pour cream into 2-cup measure. Cook at **MEDIUM** 2 to 2¼ minutes.
Meanwhile, beat eggs in small bowl. Stir a little hot cream into eggs. Blend eggs back into cream. Pour mixture over ingredients in pie shell. Cook at **MEDIUM-LOW** 15 minutes. Let stand 10 minutes.

SWISS CHEESE FONDUE

1 pound (4 cups) Swiss cheese, shredded
¼ cup flour
⅛ teaspoon garlic powder
⅛ teaspoon pepper
Dash nutmeg
1 cup white wine or apple juice
2 tablespoons Kirsch, optional
French bread, cut into cubes or bread sticks

Yield: 6 Servings

Toss cheese with flour, garlic, pepper and nutmeg. Heat wine in 2-quart casserole* at **HIGH** 2 to 2½ minutes. Gradually add half of cheese; stir until smooth. Cook at **MEDIUM** 2 to 3 minutes; stir once. Add remaining cheese and Kirsch, stir until smooth. Cook at **MEDIUM** 2 to 3 minutes, or until cheese is melted; stir once. Serve hot with French bread.

*If desired, a microwave safe pottery or ceramic fondue dish can be used.

SANDWICHES

Sandwiches have grown to be a lunch and snack time institution. Now, with the help of your microwave oven, those cold luncheon meat sandwiches can turn into something warm and flavorful. When you are in a hurry, you can create a hearty hot meal in minutes...that is better than a cold sandwich from the refrigerator. No extra clean-up...sandwiches with cheeses can be heated on a paper plate covered with a paper napkin. It's that simple.

HEAVENLY FRENCH DIP

1 medium onion, cut into rings
2 tablespoons butter or margarine
½ loaf French bread (about 12 in. long)
¼ to ⅓ pound sliced cooked roast beef
Salt and pepper to taste
1 can (10¼ oz.) beef gravy
2 tablespoons red wine, optional

Yield: 2 Servings

Combine onion and butter in small glass bowl. Cook, covered with plastic wrap, at **HIGH** 2 to 3 minutes, or until onion is tender; stir once.

Meanwhile, slice bread in half lengthwise and then crosswise, forming 2 sandwiches. Arrange beef on 2 pieces bread; top with onions, then season with salt and pepper. Close sandwich; wrap individually in paper napkin.

In same glass bowl, combine gravy and wine. Cook at **HIGH** 1½ to 2 minutes, or until heated through; stir once. Cook sandwiches at **MEDIUM** 1 to 2 minutes, or until warm. Serve with gravy for dipping.

Combine onion and butter in small glass bowl. Cover with plastic wrap. Cook at HIGH 2 to 3 minutes or until onion is tender; stir once.

Slice bread in half lengthwise and then crosswise, forming 2 sandwiches. Arrange beef on 2 pieces of bread; top with onion then season with salt and pepper.

Combine gravy and wine in glass bowl. Cook at HIGH 1½ to 2 minutes, or until heated through; stir once.

Place top of bread on sandwich. Wrap each sandwich in a paper napkin. Cook at MEDIUM 1 to 2 minutes, or until warm.

ARMENIAN LUNCH

1½ pounds ground beef
1 envelope (1 oz.) onion-mushroom soup mix, divided
2 cloves garlic, finely chopped
1 can (8 oz.) stewed tomatoes, chopped and drained
1 tablespoon chopped fresh parsley
1 cup (8 oz.) plain yogurt
½ cup chopped green pepper
Pinch dried mint leaves
4 individual loaves Middle Eastern pocket (pita) bread

Yield: 4 Servings

TO COOK BY AUTO SENSOR: Crumble ground beef in 2-quart casserole. Stir in 3 tablespoons soup mix, garlic, tomatoes and parsley. Cover with lid. Cook on **COOK A8**. After time appears in display window, stir once. After cooking, drain, if necessary.

TO COOK BY TIME: Crumble ground beef in 2-quart casserole dish. Stir in 3 tablespoons soup mix and garlic. Cook, covered with lid, at **HIGH** 4½ to 5½ minutes, or until beef is browned. Stir once; drain. Stir in tomatoes and parsley. Cover. Cook at **HIGH** 1 minute and at **MEDIUM** 3 to 4 minutes. Stir once.

TO COMPLETE: Let stand, covered, 3 minutes. Meanwhile, combine remaining soup mix, yogurt, green pepper and mint. Cut bread in half. Gently open each half and fill "pocket" with beef mixture; top with yogurt dressing.

BARBECUED BEEF SANDWICHES

½ to ¾ pound sliced cooked roast beef
8 slices rye bread or 4 hamburger rolls
¼ to ½ cup barbecue or chili sauce

Yield: 4 Servings

Arrange half of beef on 4 slices bread; spread generously with barbecue sauce. Top with remaining beef, then bread. Wrap each sandwich in paper napkin: arrange on glass oven tray. Cook at **MEDIUM** 3 to 4 minutes, or until heated through.

Note: For TWO sandwiches, follow above procedure. Halve all ingredients; cook 1½ to 2 minutes.
For ONE sandwich, cook 1 to 1¼ minutes.

HAMBURGERS. . . . . . YOUR WAY

1 pound ground beef
4 slices each cheese, onion and tomato
4 hamburger rolls
Catsup or creamy Russian dressing

Yield: 4 Servings

Shape ground beef into 4 patties (about 4-in. in diameter). In 8-inch square dish, arrange patties. Cook **MEDIUM-HIGH** 3½ to 4½ minutes; turn patties over and drain liquid once. Top with cheese. Let stand, covered, 2 minutes. Place each hamburger in roll and top with remaining *ingredients.* as desired.

Note: *For TWO Servings, follow above procedure. Halve all ingredients. Cook patties 1 ½ to 2 minutes.*
For ONE Serving, cook patty ¾ to 1¼ minutes.

CHILI TACOS

1 pound ground beef
1 package (1¼ oz.) taco seasoning mix
½ cup water
12 taco shells
1 cup shredded lettuce
⅔ cup chopped tomatoes
¼ cup chopped green pepper or onion
1 cup (4 oz.) shredded Cheddar or Monterey jack cheese

Yield: 6 Servings

TO COOK BY AUTO SENSOR: In 2-quart casserole, combine ground beef, seasoning mix, and water. Cover with lid. Cook on **COOK A4.** After time appears in the display window, stir once.

TO COOK BY TIME: Crumble ground beef in 2-quart casserole. Heat at **HIGH** 3 to 4 minutes, or until browned. Stir once; drain. Add seasoning mix and water; cover with lid. Cook at **HIGH** 2 minutes and at **MEDIUM** 5 minutes; stir once.

TO COMPLETE: Stir; let stand, covered, 3 minutes. Fill taco shells with 2 tablespoons beef mixture, then top with lettuce, tomato, green pepper and cheese*.

***Hint:** If desired, arrange taco shells in 12×8-inch dish; fill as directed above. Cook at **MEDIUM** 3 to 4 minutes to melt cheese.*

MEAT LOAF MELTWICH

Chili sauce
8 slices rye bread
8 thin slices cooked meat loaf
4 slices (rectangular) Muenster cheese, halved

Yield: 4 Servings

Spread chili sauce on bread. On four slices, place meat loaf and cheese; top with remaining bread. Wrap each sandwich in paper napkin; arrange on glass oven tray. Cook at **MEDIUM** 2½ to 3½ minutes, or until heated through.

Note: *For TWO sandwiches, follow above procedure; halve all ingredients. Cook 1½ to 2 minutes.*
For ONE sandwich, cook 1 to 1½ minutes.

SLOPPY JOES

1 pound ground beef
1 large onion, finely chopped
½ to ¾ cup catsup
¼ cup sweet pickled relish
Salt and pepper to taste
4 hamburger rolls

Yield: 4 Servings

Crumble ground beef in 2-quart casserole.
Stir in onion. Cook at **HIGH** 3 to 4 minutes,
or until beef is browned. Stir once; drain.
Stir in catsup, relish, salt and pepper.
Cover with lid.

TO COOK BY AUTO SENSOR: Cook on
COOK A1.

TO COOK BY TIME: Cook at **HIGH** 1½ to
2½ minutes and at **MEDIUM** 3 to 4
minutes. Stir once.

TO COMPLETE: Serve in split hamburger
rolls.

*Variation: Add ½ pound frankfurters sliced
with ground beef.*

OPEN FACED SANDWICHES WITH GRAVY

1 envelope (⅞ oz.) turkey gravy mix*
1 cup water*
½ pound sliced cooked turkey
4 slices white bread

Yield: 4 Servings

Combine gravy mix and water in 2-cup
glass measure. Cook at **HIGH** 2½ to 3
minutes, or until thickened; stir twice.
Arrange turkey in four piles (to fit bread)
in 8-inch dish. Cook, covered with plastic
wrap, at **MEDIUM-HIGH** 1½ to 2 minutes,
or until heated through. Arrange turkey on
bread; top with gravy.

***Substitution:** Use 1 can (10½ oz.)
mushroom gravy or 1 cup leftover gravy
for mix and water. Cook 1½ to 2 minutes;
stir once.*

> **Note:** *Chicken, pork or beef gravy and
> meat may be used.*

SURPRISE BURGERS

1 pound ground beef
½ teaspoon salt
½ teaspoon pepper
Surprise Fillings*
4 hamburger rolls

Yield: 4 Servings

Combine ground beef, salt and pepper;
shape into 8 thin patties. Arrange Surprise
Filling on 4 patties; top with remaining
patties, sealing edges tightly.
Arrange burgers in 8-inch square dish.
Cook, covered with wax paper, at
MEDIUM-HIGH 5 to 7 minutes. Let stand,
covered, 2 minutes before serving in split
rolls.

***Surprise Fillings:**
Use one of the following; cheese, onion or
tomato slice, sliced mushrooms, pickle
slices or chopped olives.*

MINI-PIZZA SNACKS

2 English muffins, split and toasted
¼ to ½ cup spaghetti sauce
¼ cup (1 oz.) shredded mozzarella cheese
Oregano

Yield: 2 Servings

Arrange muffins on paper plate. Spread with spaghetti sauce. Top with cheese and season with oregano. Cook at **MEDIUM** 1 to 2 minutes, or until cheese is melted.

Note: *For ONE Serving, follow above procedure; halve all ingredients. Cook ½ to 1 minute.*

PIZZA HEROES

1 pound ground beef
1 small onion, finely chopped
½ cup spaghetti sauce
½ teaspoon salt
¼ teaspoon oregano
2 Italian rolls, split lengthwise (about 6 to 8-in, ea.)
Pizza Toppings*
½ to ¾ cup (2 to 3 oz.) shredded mozzarella cheese

Yield: 4 Servings

Crumble ground beef in medium glass bowl. Stir in onion. Cook at **HIGH** 3 to 4 minutes, or until beef is browned; stir once. Drain. Stir in sauce, salt and oregano.
Arrange rolls in 12×8-inch dish. Spoon on beef mixture. Top with Pizza Toppings, then cheese. Cook at **MEDIUM** 3 to 4 minutes, or until cheese is melted and hero is heated through.

***Pizza Toppings**
Use your favorite combination: anchovies, canned sliced mushrooms, green pepper rings, sliced tomatoes or thinly sliced pepperoni.

Note: *For TWO Servings, follow above procedure; halve all ingredients. Cook ground beef 2 to 2½ minutes and cheese 2 to 2½ minutes.*

MEXICAN MEAT PIES

6 corn toaster cakes or English muffins
1 can (16 oz.) chili without beans
½ cup (2 oz.) shredded Monterey jack or Cheddar cheese
Sliced black olives, chopped green pepper and chopped onion

Yield: 3–4 Servings

Arrange corn toaster cakes on 12-inch plate. Spoon on chili. Cook at **MEDIUM-HIGH** 3½ to 4 minutes; top with cheese. Cook at **MEDIUM** 1½ to 2 minutes, or until cheese is melted. Top, as desired, with olives, green pepper and onions.

OPEN FACED TUNA TEMPTER

1 can (7 oz.) tuna, drained and flaked
⅓ cup mayonnaise
Celery seed
Onion powder
Salt and pepper
4 slices whole wheat bread, toasted
4 thin slices tomato
4 slices American cheese

Yield: 4 Servings

Combine tuna and mayonnaise; season with celery, onion, salt and pepper. Spread tuna on toast; top with tomato. On paper plate, cook sandwiches at **MEDIUM** 2 to 2½ minutes. Top with cheese. Cook at **MEDIUM** 1¾ to 2½ minutes, or until cheese is melted.

REUBEN DELI DELIGHT

½ pound thinly sliced cooked corned beef
4 slices rye or pumpernickel bread
¼ cup creamy Russian dressing
1 can (8 oz.) sauerkraut, rinsed and drained
4 slices (rectangular) Swiss cheese, halved

Yield: 4 Servings

Arrange corned beef on bread; top with dressing. Add sauerkraut and arrange sandwiches on paper towel lined glass oven tray. Cook at **MEDIUM-HIGH** 1½ to 2 minutes; top with cheese. Cook at **MEDIUM** 1½ to 2 minutes, or until cheese is melted.

Hint: If a closed sandwich is desired, top with additional bread. Wrap each sandwich in paper napkin and cook ½ to 1 minute.

Note: **For TWO sandwiches,** *follow above procedure; halve all ingredients. Cook sandwiches 1 to 1½ minutes and cheese 1 to 1½ minutes.*
For ONE Serving, *cook sandwich ½ to ¾ minute and cheese ½ to 1 minute.*

RED DELICIOUS SANDWICH

4 slices raisin bread, toasted
Prepared mustard
½ pound sliced cooked ham
½ apple, sliced
4 slices American cheese

Yield: 4 Servings

Spread bread with mustard; arrange on paper plate. Place half of ham on bread; top with apple, then remaining ham. Cook at **MEDIUM-HIGH** 2 to 2½ minutes; top with cheese. Cook at **MEDIUM** 2 to 2½ minutes, or until cheese begins to melt.

Note: **For TWO Servings,** *follow above procedure; halve all ingredients. Cook ham 1 to 1½ minutes and cheese 1½ to 2 minutes.*
For ONE Serving, *cook ham ½ to 1 minute and cheese ¾ to 1¼ minutes.*

157

TEXAS TOMMIES

8 slices bacon
4 frankfurters
1 slice American cheese, cut into thin
   strips
4 frankfurter rolls

Yield: 2 Servings

Cook bacon between layers of paper towel
in 12×8-inch dish at **HIGH** 2½ to 2¾
minutes, or until partially cooked.
Meanwhile, make lengthwise slit in each
frankfurter, leaving ½-inch uncut on each
end; make an "X" cut in each end. Stuff
slit with cheese; wrap 2 slices of bacon
around each frankfurter and secure with
wooden toothpicks. Discard paper towels
from dish and arrange frankfurters in dish.
Cook at **HIGH** 2½ to 3½ minutes, or until
heated through. Remove toothpicks and
serve in split rolls.

*Note: For ONE Serving, follow above
procedure halve all ingredients.
Cook bacon 1 to 1¼ minutes and
frankfurters 1½ to 1¼ minutes.*

SEAFARER'S SANDWICH

1 package (8 oz.) frozen fried fish fillets (4
   fillets)
½ cup cole slaw, optional
4 slices American cheese
4 hamburger rolls
4 tablespoons tartar sauce or cocktail
   sauce

Yield: 4 Servings

Cook fillets in 8-inch square dish at
MEDIUM-HIGH 3½ to 4½ minutes. Top
with cole slaw and cheese. Cook at
MEDIUM 2½ to 3½ minutes, or until
cheese is melted. Place fillet in roll; top
with tartar sauce.

*Note: For TWO Servings, follow above
procedure; halve all ingredients.
Cook fillets 1½ to 2 minutes and
cheese 1¼ to 1¾ minutes.
For ONE Serving, cook fillet ¾ to
1¼ minutes and cheese ½ to 1
minute.*

POTATO DOGS

⅓ cup water
1 tablespoon milk
2 teaspoons butter or margarine
Dash dry mustard, optional
⅔ cup instant mashed potato flakes
2 frankfurters
Pork flavored seasoned coating mix

Yield: 2 Servings

In small glass bowl, combine water, milk,
butter and dry mustard. Cook at **HIGH** 1 to
1½ minutes, or until boiling. Stir in instant
mashed potatoes; cool.
Meanwhile, cut "X" slit in ends of
frankfurters.
Pat potato mixture around frankfurters,
leaving ends exposed; roll in coating mix.
On paper plate, arrange coated
frankfurters. Cook at **HIGH** 2¼ to 2¾
minutes. If potato coating cracks, press
together with fingers.

ROUND-ABOUT DOGS

1 can (8 oz.) pork and beans
1 tablespoon sweet pickle relish or catsup
4 frankfurters
2 slices rye bread
Prepared mustard
2 slices bacon, crisp cooked and crumbled
   (see page 83)
¼ cup (1 oz.) shredded Cheddar cheese

Yield: 2 Servings

Combine beans and relish in small glass
bowl. Cook covered with plastic wrap, at
MEDIUM-HIGH 1½ to 2 minutes, or until
heated through; stir once.
Along one side of each frankfurter, make
deep slits every ¾-inch. Arrange franks
cut-side out on paper towel lined paper
plate. Cook at **MEDIUM-HIGH** 2½ to 3
minutes, or until heated through and
curled.
Spread mustard on bread; place on
serving plate. Arrange two frankfurters on
each bread to form ring. Fill ring with
beans; top with bacon and cheese. Cook at
MEDIUM-HIGH 1 to 1¼ minutes, or until
cheese begins to melt.

*Variation: Arrange cooked frankfurter on
toasted English muffin half; fill center with
heated sauerkraut and top with poppy
seeds.*

158

VEGETABLES and SIDE DISHES

Fresh vegetables retain their vibrant color, delicious flavor and crisp texture. Using only a small amount of water and seasoning the vegetables after cooking will become the easiest way ever to serve garden-fresh tasting vegetables.

Simple ways to heat frozen vegetables in your microwave oven will amaze you...and no added salt to detract from the delicate flavor. Follow the instructions in the chart to prepare frozen vegetables.

DIRECTIONS FOR COOKING FRESH VEGETABLES BY TIME

Weights given in the chart on pages 162 and 163 for fresh vegetables are purchase weights before peeling, trimming, etc.

Place vegetables in a casserole. Add 2 to 3 tablespoons of water per pound of vegetables. Add salt to water or add after cooking. Do not place salt directly on vegetables. Cover dish with lid or plastic wrap.

Vegetables that are to be cooked whole and unpeeled, need to be pierced to allow steam to escape. Arrange vegetables in a circular pattern on a paper towel lined oven tray.

Cook at HIGH according to time recommended in charts. Halfway through cooking, stir, turn vegetables over or rearrange.

Let stand, covered, according to the time indicated in the chart on pages 162 and 163.

DIRECTIONS FOR COOKING FROZEN VEGETABLES BY TIME

Remove vegetable from package and place in an appropriately sized container. Vegetables frozen in a pouch should be placed on a dish and pierce top of pouch.

Cook at HIGH according to directions given in chart on pages 162 and 163. Vegetables should be cooked covered. Cooking vegetables in their package does not alllow for stirring and is not recommended.

Halfway through cooking, stir vegetables and rearrange corn on the cob.

FRESH AND FROZEN VEGETABLE CHART FOR TIME COOKING

VEGETABLES	AMOUNT	APPROX. COOKING TIME, covered, at HIGH (in minutes)	STAND TIME (in minutes)
ARTICHOKES Fresh, about 6 to 8 oz. ea. (3-in. diameter) See recipe, page 172	1 2 4	6 to 7½ 8½ to 10 12½ to 14	5 5 5
Frozen, hearts	1 package (9 oz.)	5 to 6	3
ASPARAGUS Fresh, cut into 1½-in. pieces	1 pound plus ¼ cup water	5 to 6½	3
Frozen, spears	1 package (10 oz.)	5½ to 7	3
BEANS, Green or Wax Fresh, cut into 1½-in. pieces	1 pound plus ¼ cup water	6½ to 8	3
Frozen	1 package (9 oz.)	6 to 8	3
BEETS Fresh, sliced	1½ to 2 pounds plus ¼ cup water	10½ to 12	5
BROCCOLI Fresh, cut into spears	1 pound plus ¼ cup water	6 to 7½	3
Frozen, chopped or spears	1 package (10 oz.)	6½ to 8	3
BRUSSEL SPROUTS Fresh	1 tub (10 oz.) plus 2 tablespoons water 1 pound plus ¼ cup water	5½ to 7 8 to 10	5 5
Frozen	1 package (10 oz.)	7½ to 9	5
CABBAGE, Fresh Chopped or Shredded	4 cups (about 1 lb.) plus ¼ cup water	6½ to 8	5
Wedges	4 (about 1 lb.) plus ¼ cup water	6 to 7½	5
CARROTS, sliced ½-in thick Fresh	1 pound plus ¼ cup water	7 to 8½	5
Frozen	1 package (10 oz.)	5½ to 7	3
CAULIFLOWER Fresh, cut into flowerets	1 pound plus ¼ cup water	6½ to 8	5
whole	1 to 1¼ lb. plus ¼ cup water	11½ to 13	5
Frozen, flowerets	1 package (10 oz.)	5½ to 7	3
CORN, Whole Kernel Frozen	1 package (10 oz.)	4 to 5½	3
CORN, On the cob Fresh (remove husk and silk)	1 ear ⎤ plus 2 to 4 2 ears ⎥ tablespoons 4 ears ⎥ water 6 ears ⎦	2 to 3 3 to 4 8½ to 10 13 to 14½	3 3 5 5
Frozen (rinse off any frost)	1 ear 2 ears 4 ears 6 ears	3½ to 4½ 5 to 6½ 9½ to 11 14 to 15½	3 3 5 5
EGGPLANT, Fresh Cubed	1 pound plus ¼ cup water	7 to 8½	3
Whole (pierce skin)	1 to 1¼ pounds	4½ to 6	3

FRESH AND FROZEN VEGETABLE CHART FOR TIME COOKING

VEGETABLES	AMOUNT	APPROX. COOKING TIME, covered, at HIGH (in minutes)	STAND TIME (in minutes)
LIMA BEANS Frozen	1 package (10 oz.) plus ½ cup water	5½ to 7	3

OKRA, Frozen
    Sliced
    Whole
	1 package (10 oz.)
	1 package (10 oz.)
		5 to 6½
		5½ to 7
			3
			3

ONIONS Fresh, (small, whole)	8 to 10 plus ¼ cup water (about 1 lb.)	6½ to 8	3

PEAS, GREEN
    Fresh
    Frozen
	1½ pounds plus ¼ cup water
	1 package (10 oz.)
		5 to 6½
		5½ to 7
			3
			3

PEAS, Snow (Pea pods) Frozen	1 package (6 oz.)	4½ to 5½	3
PEAS and CARROTS Frozen	1 package (10 oz.)	5½ to 7	3
PEAS, Black-eyed Frozen	1 package (10 oz.) plus ½ cup water	15 to 18	5
POTATOES* Fresh (about 6 oz. ea.)	1 2 4 6	4½ to 5½ 7 to 9 10 to 12 14 to 16	3 to 5 3 to 5 3 to 5 3 to 5

SPINACH
    Fresh, leaf
    Frozen, leaf or chopped
	1 pound plus ¼ cup water
	1 package (10 oz.)
		5½ to 7
		6½ to 8
			3
			3

SQUASH (Summer), sliced
    ½-in. thick
    Fresh
    Frozen
	1 pound plus ¼ cup water
	1 package (10 oz.)
		6½ to 8
		5 to 6½
			3
			3

SQUASH (Winter)
    Fresh, whole
        (pierce skin)
    Frozen, whipped
	1 (1 lb.)
	2 (¾ lb. ea.)
	1 package (12 oz.)
		6 to 7½
		7½ to 9
		6½ to 8
			5
			5
			3

SUCCOTASH Frozen	1 package (10 oz.)	5½ to 7	3
VEGETABLES, mixed Frozen	1 package (10 oz.)	6½ to 8	3

ZUCCHINI, sliced ½-in. thick
    Fresh
    Frozen
	1 pound plus ¼ cup water
	1 package (10 oz.)
		6½ to 8
		5 to 6½
			3
			3

*Potatoes can be wrapped in aluminum foil after cooking to keep warm for serving.

DIRECTIONS FOR COOKING FRESH VEGETABLES BY AUTO SENSOR

Weights given in the chart on page 165 for fresh vegetables are purchase weights before peeling, trimming, etc.

Cut, slice or trim as directed in chart. Cook vegetables in covered casserole, except for whole, unpeeled vegetables. Whole, unpeeled vegetables should be arranged in the oven according to the directions given in the chart.

Cook according to the Auto Sensor Cycle which is indicated in the chart. If softer vegetables are preferred, vegetables cooked on COOK A8 may be cooked on COOK A7. When time appears in display window, stir vegetables.

After cooking, stir vegetables and let stand, covered, 3 minutes before serving.

FRESH VEGETABLE COOKING CHART FOR
AUTO SENSOR COOKING A

VEGETABLES	AMOUNT OF WATER	APPROX. (in minutes) COOKING TIME	AUTO SENSOR CYCLE	SPECIAL INSTRUCTIONS
ARTICHOKES 2 (6 to 8 oz. ea.) 4	rinsed & drained	15 26	COOK A8	Cut stem off; snip leaf tips with scissor.
ASPARAGUS, 1 lb. Cut into 1½-in. pieces or spears	¼ Cup	14	COOK A8	———
BEANS, Green or Wax, 1 lb. Cut into 1½-in, pieces	2 Tablespoons	18	COOK A7	Stir once when cook time appears in display window and begins to count down.
BROCCOLI, 1 lb. Cut into spears	¼ Cup	14	COOK A8	———
BRUSSEL SPROUTS 1 tub (10 oz.) 1 lb.	2 Tablespoons ¼ Cup	12 14	COOK A8	———
CABBAGE, 1 lb. Shredded Cut into wedges	¼ Cup ¼ Cup	12 19	COOK A8	———
CARROTS, 1 lb. Sliced into ¼-in. pieces	¼ Cup	16	COOK A6	———
CAULIFLOWER, 1 lb. Flowerets Whole	¼ Cup ¼ Cup	13 16	COOK A7	———
EGGPLANT, 1 lb. Cubed	¼ Cup	14	COOK A8	———
PEAS, 2 lb. Shelled	¼ Cup	20	COOK A7	———
POTATOES Medium, Baking Potatoes (about 6 oz. ea.)	1 2 4 6	7 9 15 23	COOK A6	Prick skin several times with fork. Arrange in circular pattern on paper towel.
SPINACH, 1 lb. Leaf	¼ Cup	12	COOK A8	———
SUMMER SQUASH, 1 lb. Cut into ½-in. Slices	¼ Cup	13	COOK A8	———
WINTER SQUASH, (ACORN) 1 (1 lb.) 2 (1 lb. ea.)	——— ———	13 26	COOK A6	Choose equal size squash. Arrange stem-down in custard cup. Pierce skin several times. DO NOT cover.
ZUCCHINI, 1 lb. Cut into ½-in. slices	¼ Cup	13	COOK A8	———

DIRECTIONS FOR COOKING FROZEN VEGETABLES ON AUTO SENSOR

Empty 10-ounce package of frozen vegetables into glass container. Add 2 tablespoons water.

Cover dish with lid or completely with plastic wrap. Cook on Froz-Cook A7, or cook on A8.

For frozen vegetables in the pouch, place the pouch on a dish. Pierce a hole in the pouch and cook on FROZ-COOK A1.

After cooking, stir and let stand, covered, 3 minutes before serving.

DIRECTIONS FOR COOKING CANNED VEGETABLES

Empty 8-ounce or 16-ounce can of vegetables into a 1-quart casserole. Include any liquid.

To Cook by Time: Cover casserole with lid. Cook at MEDIUM-HIGH. Cook an 8-ounce size can for 1½ to 2 minutes. Cook a 16-ounce size can for 2½ to 3 minutes.
To Cook by Auto Sensor: Cover casserole with lid or completely plastic wrap. Cook on COOK A1.

After cooking, stir and let stand, covered, 3 minutes.

BLANCHING FRESH VEGETABLES (How to Blanch Fresh Vegetables)

Follow directions in chart for recommended amount of vegetables, water and cooking time. Wash vegetables; slice or chop as directed.

Place amount of vegetable recommended in chart into 2-quart casserole dish; add water.

Cook at HIGH according to time given in chart; stir once. Vegetables will be an even bright color. Plunge vegetables immediately into ice water.

Blot dry on paper towels to remove excess moisture.

Place in freezer containers or bag. Label and date; freeze.

DIRECTIONS FOR COOKING FROZEN BLANCHED VEGETABLES

Empty vegetables into casserole; break up if possible.

Cover with lid. Cook at HIGH according to time recommended in chart.

Let stand, covered, 3 minutes; season to taste.

BLANCHING AND COOKING FRESH VEGETABLES

VEGETABLES	AMOUNT	WATER	APPROX. COOKING TIME TO BLANCH VEGETABLES (in minutes) at HIGH	APPROX. COOKING TIME (in minutes) at HIGH
Asparagus Cut into 2-inch pieces	1 lb.	¼ cup	2 to 2½	5 to 6
Beans, Green Cut into 2-inch pieces	1 lb	¼ cup	5½ to 6	5 to 6
Broccoli Chopped or cut into spears	1 to 1¼ lb.	¼ cup	4 to 4½	5 to 6
Brussel Sprouts	10 oz. tub	¼ cup	3½ to 4	5 to 6
Cauliflower Cut into flowerets	1½ to 1¾ lb.	¼ cup	3½ to 4	4 to 5
Spinach, leaves	1 to 1¾ lb.	———	2½ to 3	6½ to 7½
Zucchini Cut into ½ to ¾-in. pieces	1 lb.	¼ cup	3 to 3½	6½ to 7½

DIRECTIONS FOR PREPARING DRIED BEANS OR PEAS

Combine hot tap water, beans and 2 tablespoons oil in casserole dish.

Cover dish with lid. Bring beans and hot water to a boil at HIGH. Let beans soak, covered, 1 hour. Omit this step for peas and lentils.

To Cook by Time: Cover with lid. Cook according to directions in chart. Stir.

To Cook by Auto Sensor: Cover with lid. Cook on COOK A2. When time appears in display window, stir beans.

One pound of dried beans equals about 6 cups cooked. Use in place of canned beans.

ITEM	CONTAINER	TIME COOKING			AUTO SENSOR COOKING	
		AMOUNT OF HOT WATER	TO BOIL WATER (in minutes) at HIGH	TO COOK BEANS at (in minutes) MEDIUM-LOW	AMOUNT OF WATER	APPROX. COOKING TIME (in hours) on COOK A2
Black-eyed peas (1 lb.)	5-quart casserole	2½ quarts	10 to 12	70	2½ quarts	2
Kidney beans, Lima beans (small) or Northern beans (1 lb.)	5-quart casserole	2 quarts	9 to 11	60	3 quarts	2½
Lima beans (large) (1 lb.)	5-quart casserole	2½ quarts	10 to 12	75	3 quarts	2½
Split peas or Lentils (1 lb.)	4-quart casserole	1½ quarts	8 to 10	45	1½ quarts	1¼

APPLE BAKED SQUASH A

1 medium butternut squash, halved
  lengthwise, peeled and seeded
1 medium apple, cored, peeled, and
  quartered
¼ cup packed brown sugar
¼ cup butter or margarine, softened
1½ teaspoons flour
½ teaspoon salt
¼ teaspoon cinnamon

Yield: 4 Servings

Cut squash into ½-inch slices. Arrange
slices in 12×8-inch dish. Cut apple into thin
slices; place on top of squash. Combine
remaining ingredients until well blended.
Drop by spoonfuls over apple squash
mixture.

TO COOK BY AUTO SENSOR: Cover
completely with plastic wrap. Cook on
COOK A7. After cooking, release plastic
wrap.

TO COOK BY TIME: Cover with plastic
wrap. Cook at **MEDIUM** 17 minutes.

TO COMPLETE: Let stand, covered, 3
minutes before serving.

HONEY ACORN SQUASH

2 acorn squash (about ¾ lb. ea.)
4 tablespoons honey
4 teaspoons butter or margarine
⅛ teaspoon grated lemon peel

Yield: 4 Servings

Pierce skin of squash several times,
arrange on paper towel lined glass oven
tray. Cook at **HIGH** 4 to 5 minutes, turning
squash over once; let stand 3 minutes. Cut
squash in half; scoop out seeds. Arrange
squash, cut-side up in 12×8-inch dish. Top
with honey, butter and lemon. Cook,
covered with plastic wrap, at **HIGH** 4 to 5
minutes, or until squash is tender.
Let stand, covered, 2 minutes before
serving.

*Variations: Use one of the following
toppings for honey, butter and lemon—
For FRUIT'N HONEY SQUASH, use 4
tablespoons finely chopped apple, 2
tablespoons flaked coconut, 4 tablespoons
honey and 2 tablespoons butter.
For HOLIDAY SPECIAL SQUASH, use ½
cup chopped orange, ¼ cup whole berry
cranberry sauce, 2 tablespoons packed
brown sugar and ¼ teaspoon cinnamon.*

ARTICHOKES FOR TWO [A]

8 tablespoons butter or margarine, melted, divided
½ teaspoon garlic salt
2 fresh artichokes (8 oz. ea.)
1 lemon, thinly sliced and halved
¼ cup dry seasoned bread crumbs
2 tablespoons grated Parmesan cheese
¼ teaspoon paprika
¼ teaspoon parsley flakes

Yield: 2 Servings

Combine 6 tablespoons butter with garlic; set aside. Cut stem off artichoke; trim tips of leaves; then rinse. Place lemon in between leaves; arrange artichokes in 1½-quart casserole. Pour butter mixture over artichokes.

TO COOK BY AUTO SENSOR: Cover completely with plastic wrap. Cook on **COOK A7**.

TO COOK BY TIME: Cover with plastic wrap. Cook at **HIGH** 9 to 11 minutes.

TO COMPLETE: Combine 2 tablespoons butter with remaining ingredients. Sprinkle over cooked artichokes. Let stand, covered, 5 minutes before serving.

Note: For FOUR Servings, follow above procedure; double all ingredients. Cook artichokes 13 to 15 minutes. For ONE Serving, halve all ingredients. Cook artichokes 7 to 9 minutes.

CLASSIC COMPANY GREEN BEANS

2 packages (9 oz. ea.) frozen french-style green beans
1 can (10¾ oz.) condensed cream of mushroom soup
1 can (3 oz.) french fried onions

Yield: 6 Servings

Place beans in 2-quart casserole. Cook, covered with lid, at **HIGH** 9 to 11 minutes, or until beans are tender; stir twice. Stir in soup and half of onion pieces; top with remaining onion pieces.
Cook at **HIGH** 5 to 6 minutes. Let stand, 3 minutes before serving.

BROCCOLI EGG DIVINE

1 package (1¼ oz.) hollandaise sauce mix
Ingredients as sauce mix package
  directs
1 pound fresh broccoli spears, cooked
  (see pages 162 and 165)*
4 hard-cooked eggs, chopped
  (see page 145)
2 slices Swiss cheese, cubed
¼ cup dry bread crumbs
2 tablespoons butter or margarine, melted
Paprika

Yield: 6 Servings

Combine hollandaise sauce mix and ingredients according to package directions in 2-cup glass measure. Cook at **HIGH** 2 to 3 minutes, or until sauce is thickened; stir once. In 9-inch pie plate, arrange broccoli in spoke fashion, flowerets toward center (trim stems if necessary); top with eggs and cheese. Pour sauce over cheese and top with bread crumbs blended with butter and paprika. Cook, covered with plastic wrap, at **HIGH** 4½ to 6 minutes or until heated through. Let stand, covered, 5 minutes before serving.

Substitution: Use 2 packages (10 oz. ea.) frozen broccoli spears cooked (see pages 162 and 165) for fresh broccoli.

GREEN BEANS AMANDINE

¼ cup slivered almonds
3 tablespoons butter or margarine
1¼ to 1½ pounds fresh green beans, cut
  into 1½-inch pieces
¼ cup water
½ teaspoon salt
Dash ground nutmeg, optional

Yield: 4 Servings

Combine almonds and butter in 2-cup glass measure. Cook at **HIGH** 3 to 4 minutes, or until almonds are lightly browned; reserve. Combine beans and water in 2-quart casserole. Cook, covered with lid, at **HIGH** 8½ to 10 minutes, or until beans are tender; stir once. Add remaining ingredients, almonds and butter; let stand, covered, 3 minutes before serving.

BETTER BAKED BEANS

3 slices bacon, diced
½ cup chopped green pepper or onion
2 cans (16 oz. ea.) pork and beans
¼ cup molasses
¼ cup catsup
1 tablespoon prepared mustard
½ teaspoon Worcestershire sauce
Dash hot pepper sauce

Yield: 6 Servings

Combine bacon and green pepper in 1½-quart casserole. Cook at **HIGH** 3 to 4 minutes, or until bacon is crisp. Stir in remaining ingredients; cook, covered with wax paper, at **HIGH** 3 to 4 minutes and at **MEDIUM-LOW** 10 to 12 minutes.

CHEESY VEGETABLE CASSEROLE

4 medium onions, sliced (about 1 lb.)
1 teaspoon salt
½ teaspoon basil
¼ teaspoon pepper
3 tablespoons butter or margarine
½ cup seasoned dry bread crumbs
Paprika
4 medium tomatoes (about 1½ lb.), sliced
6 slices American cheese (1 oz. ea.)

Yield: 6 Servings

Cook onions in medium glass bowl, covered with plastic wrap, at **HIGH** 4½ to 5½ minutes; stir once. Stir in salt, basil and pepper.
Heat butter in small glass bowl at **HIGH** 1 to 1½ minutes, or until melted; stir in bread crumbs and paprika. In 2-quart casserole, alternately layer half the tomatoes, onions and cheese; top with remaining tomatoes and onions.
Cover with plastic wrap. Cook at **HIGH** 10 to 12 minutes. Top with remaining cheese, then bread crumb mixture; let stand, covered, 5 minutes before serving.

173

SWISS SCALLOPED CORN A

3 slices bacon, crisp-cooked and crumbled (see page 83)
2 cans (17 oz. ea.) whole kernel corn, drained
1 cup (4 oz.) shredded Swiss cheese
1 egg
1 can (5⅓ oz.) evaporated milk
½ teaspoon onion powder
⅛ teaspoon pepper
1½ tablespoons flour
¼ cup dry bread crumbs
1 tablespoon butter or margarine, melted
Paprika

Yield: 6 Servings

In 12×8-inch dish, combine bacon, corn and cheese. Blend in egg, milk, onion powder, pepper and flour. Top with bread crumbs blended with butter. Sprinkle with paprika.

TO COOK BY AUTO SENSOR: Cover completely with plastic wrap. Cook on **COOK A8**.

TO COOK BY TIME: Cover with plastic wrap. Cook at **MEDIUM** 10 to 12 minutes.

TO COMPLETE: Let stand, uncovered, 5 minutes before serving.

Variation: Use 1 cup (4 oz.) shredded Cheddar cheese for Swiss cheese.

ORANGE GLAZED CARROTS A

¼ cup orange juice
3 tablespoons honey
3 tablespoons butter or margarine, melted
½ teaspoon grated lemon peel, optional
¼ teaspoon salt
Dash nutmeg
2 teaspoons cornstarch
1 pound carrots, sliced ½-inch thick

Yield: 4 Servings

In 2-quart casserole, combine juice, honey, butter, lemon peel, salt and nutmeg. Stir in cornstarch; mix until well blended. Stir in carrots. Cover with lid.

TO COOK BY AUTO SENSOR: Cook on **COOK A7**. After time appears in display window, stir once.

TO COOK BY TIME: Cook at **HIGH** 7 to 8½ minutes; stir once.

TO COMPLETE: Stir; let stand, covered, 3 minutes before serving.

CARAWAY CABBAGE A

¼ cup butter or margarine, melted
1 small head cabbage, cut into 6 wedges (about 1½ pounds)
¼ teaspoon caraway seeds
¼ cup water

Yield: 6 Servings

Brush cabbage with butter. Arrange cabbage in 12×8-inch dish so wide edges are towards rim. Sprinkle with caraway seeds and water.

TO COOK BY AUTO SENSOR: Cover completely with plastic wrap. Cook on **COOK A8**. After heating, release plastic wrap.

TO COOK BY TIME: Cover with plastic wrap. Cook at **HIGH** 8 to 9½ minutes.

TO COMPLETE: Cabbage should be just tender. Let stand, covered, 5 minutes, before serving.

RATATOUILLE

2 medium onions, sliced
1 medium green pepper, cut into ½-inch
   slices
⅓ cup oil
2 cloves garlic, finely chopped
1 medium eggplant (about 1½ lb.), peeled
   and cut into ¾-inch pieces
3 medium tomatoes (about 1 lb.), cut into
   sixteenths
2 medium zucchini (about 1 lb.), cut into
   ½-inch slices
¼ cup vegetable juice cocktail or tomato
   juice
2 teaspoons each basil and parsley flakes
1 teaspoon salt
¼ teaspoon pepper

Yield: 8 Servings

In 5-quart casserole, combine onions, green
pepper, oil and garlic. Cover with lid. Cook
at **HIGH** 4 to 5 minutes; stir once. Stir in
remaining ingredients; cover.

TO COOK BY AUTO SENSOR: Cook on
COOK A8. When time appears in display
window, stir twice.

TO COOK BY TIME: Cook at **HIGH** 16 to 18
minutes; stir twice.

TO COMPLETE: Let stand, covered, 5
minutes before serving.

*Variation: Add ¼ pound fresh mushrooms,
sliced or 1 can (4 oz.) sliced mushrooms,
drained with eggplant.*

HERB BAKED TOMATOES

3 tablespoons seasoned dry bread crumbs
2 tablespoons butter or margarine, melted
2 tablespoons grated Parmesan cheese
½ teaspoon oregano or basil
2 medium tomatoes, cut in half

Yield: 4 Servings

Combine bread crumbs, butter, cheese and
oregano. Arrange tomato halves in 8-inch
square dish; top with bread crumb mixture.
Cook, covered with plastic wrap, at **HIGH**
1½ to 2 minutes or until tomatoes are
tender. Let stand 2 minutes before serving.

GARDEN SUCCOTASH

1 package (10 oz.) frozen lima beans
1 package (10 oz.) frozen whole kernel
   corn
2 tablespoons chopped pimento, optional
¼ cup milk or half'n half
3 tablespoons butter or margarine
1 teaspoon salt
Dash pepper

Yield: 6 Servings

In 2-quart casserole, combine lima beans,
corn and pimento. Cook, covered with lid,
at **HIGH** 9 to 11 minutes, or until
vegetables are tender; stir once. Stir in
remaining ingredients. Cook, covered, at
HIGH 1 to 1½ minutes, or until heated
through.

175

STUFFED ONIONS FLORENTINE

6 large Spanish onions (about 3½ lb.)
¼ cup water
½ pound pork sausage, crumbled
1 package (10 oz.) frozen chopped spinach, defrosted and drained (see page 32)
¾ cup (3 oz.) shredded Cheddar or Swiss cheese
1 egg
6 tablespoons buttered bread crumbs

Yield: 6 Servings

Peel onions; cut ½-inch slice off sprout end and just enough off the root end to sit flat. Arrange onions in 12×8-inch dish; add water. Cook at **HIGH** 11 to 13 minutes, or until onions are partially cooked. (Remove centers as they pop up). Carefully remove centers of onion, leaving a ¼ to ½-inch shell; chop ¼ cup centers.

In glass bowl, combine ¼ cup chopped onion, crumbled sausage and spinach. Cook at **HIGH** 4 to 5 minutes, or until sausage is cooked; stir twice. Drain. Stir in cheese and egg. Fill onion shells with spinach mixture and arrange in baking dish; top with bread crumbs. Cook, covered with plastic wrap, at **HIGH** 6 to 7 minutes, or until heated through. Let stand, covered, 5 minutes before serving. Serve, if desired, with Cheese Sauce (page 56).

ZUCCHINI MEDLEY A

1 can (15 oz.) tomato sauce
4 medium zucchini (about 6 oz. ea.), sliced ¼-inch thick
4 stalks celery finely chopped
2 medium onions, sliced, separated into rings
1 green pepper, chopped
½ teaspoon salt
¼ teaspoon garlic powder
¼ teaspoon oregano
⅛ teaspoon pepper
¼ cup grated Parmesan cheese

Yield: 4 Servings

In 2-quart casserole, combine tomato sauce, zucchini, celery, onions, green pepper, salt, garlic powder, oregano and pepper; mix well. Cover with lid.

TO COOK BY AUTO SENSOR: Cook on **COOK A7**. After time appears in display window, stir twice.

TO COOK BY TIME: Cook at **MEDIUM** 20 minutes; stir twice.

TO COMPLETE: Stir; let stand, covered, 5 minutes. Top with cheese before serving.

ZUCCHINI PARMESAN

4 medium zucchini, sliced into 1-inch pieces (about 1½ lb.)
¼ cup grated Parmesan cheese
1 can (8 oz.) tomato sauce
½ cup (2 oz.) shredded mozzarella cheese

Yield: 4 Servings

In 8-inch round dish, combine zucchini, Parmesan cheese and tomato sauce. Cook, covered with plastic wrap, at **HIGH** 8 to 9 minutes, or until zucchini is tender; stir once. Sprinkle with mozzarella cheese and let stand, covered, 5 minutes before serving.

BAKED STUFFED POTATOES A

4 medium potatoes, baked (see page 163)
½ cup (2 oz.) shredded Cheddar cheese
⅓ to ½ cup milk
2 tablespoons butter or margarine,
  softened
1 egg
Salt and pepper to taste
Paprika

Yield: 4 Servings

Cut a thin slice (lengthwise) from each
potato. Scoop out potato, leaving a thin
shell. In small bowl, combine potato,
cheese, milk, butter, egg, salt and pepper;
mash until smooth. Spoon potato mixture
into shell; sprinkle with paprika. In 8-inch
square dish, arrange potatoes in a circle.

TO COOK BY AUTO SENSOR: Cover
completely with plastic wrap. Cook on
COOK A7.

TO COOK BY TIME: Cover with wax paper.
Cook at **MEDIUM** 4 minutes.

TO COMPLETE: Let stand, uncovered, 3
minutes before serving.

*Note: **For TWO Servings,** follow above
procedure; halve all ingredients (use
whole egg). Cook 2 to 3 minutes.*

QUICK SCALLOPED POTATOES

6 medium potatoes (about 6 oz. ea.)
¼ cup butter or margarine
1 tablespoon dried onion flakes
1 teaspoon salt
½ teaspoon pepper
¼ cup flour
2 cups milk

Yield: 6 Servings

Following procedure for baking potatoes
(page 163.) Cook potatoes at **HIGH** 10 to 11
minutes, or until potatoes are almost
tender. Let stand 5 minutes; peel and slice.
Meanwhile, in 4-cup glass measure,
combine butter, onion, salt and pepper.
Cook at **HIGH** 1 to 1½ minutes, or until
butter is melted. Stir in flour; gradually
add milk, stir until smooth.
Cook at **MEDIUM** 6 to 7 minutes, or until
sauce is smooth; stir twice. In 2-quart
casserole alternately layer potatoes and
sauce forming three layers.
Cover with plastic wrap. Cook at **MEDIUM**
14 to 15 minutes. Let stand, covered,
5 minutes before serving.

177

MASHED POTATOES Ⓐ

6 medium potatoes (about 2 pounds),
  peeled and quartered
½ to ¾ cup milk
¼ cup butter or margarine
Salt and pepper to taste

Yield: 6 Servings

Rinse potatoes; drain. Arrange potatoes in medium glass bowl.

TO COOK BY AUTO SENSOR: Cover completely with plastic wrap. Cook on **COOK A8.** After time appears in display window, stir once. After cooking, release plastic wrap.

TO COOK BY TIME: Cover with plastic wrap. Cook at **HIGH** 9 to 10½ minutes; stir once.

TO COMPLETE: Potatoes should be tender. Let stand, covered, 5 minutes. Drain. Meanwhile, in large glass bowl, combine remaining ingredients. Cook at **MEDIUM** 2 to 3 minutes, or until hot. Add potatoes and mash until smooth.

Note: For INSTANT mashed potatoes, follow package directions. Cook water, milk and salt in bowl at **HIGH** *(see Heating Liquids chart page 52). Stir in butter and instant potato flakes.*

HOT GERMAN POTATO SALAD

4 slices bacon, diced
1 small onion, finely chopped
2 teaspoons flour
⅓ cup cider vinegar
2 tablespoons packed brown sugar
¼ teaspoon celery seed
Salt and pepper to taste
4 medium potatoes, baked, (see page 163)
  peeled and sliced*

Yield: 4 Servings

Combine bacon and onion in 12×8-inch dish. Cook at **HIGH** 3½ to 5 minutes; stir occasionally. Stir in flour, vinegar, sugar, celery seed, salt and pepper. Cook at **HIGH** 1 to 1½ minutes, or until slightly thickened; stir once. Add potatoes. Cook at **HIGH** 3 to 4 minutes, or until heated through; stir once. Serve warm.

***Substitution:** Use 2 cans (16 oz. ea.) sliced potatoes, drained, for baked potatoes.*

SWEET POTATO PONE

¼ cup butter or margarine
2 cans (16 oz. ea.) sweet potatoes or yams,
  drained
1 egg
½ cup milk
2 tablespoons packed brown sugar
2 tablespoons molasses
½ teaspoon cinnamon
¼ teaspoon nutmeg
Dash cloves
½ cup miniature marshmallows, optional

Yield: 6 Servings

Heat butter in 1½-quart casserole dish at **HIGH** 1 to 1½ minutes, or until melted. Combine butter, sweet potatoes, egg, milk, sugar, molasses, cinnamon, nutmeg and cloves; mash until smooth. Spread into same casserole dish.
Cover with plastic wrap. Cook at **HIGH** 8 to 9 minutes, or until heated through. Top with marshmallows. Cook, uncovered, at **HIGH** ½ minute.

POTATO DUMPLINGS

2 quarts hot water or broth
2 cups hot mashed potatoes
½ cup flour
1 egg
½ teaspoon salt
¼ teaspoon parsley flakes
⅛ teaspoon pepper
Dash nutmeg

Yield: 4–6 Servings

Heat water in 3-quart casserole, covered with glass lid, at **HIGH** 10 minutes, or until water is boiling.
Meanwhile, combine remaining ingredients; drop by heaping tablespoons into water. Cook at **HIGH** 3 to 4 minutes, or until dumplings float; drain.

PASTAS, GRAINS and CEREALS

To tempt you into trying rice, pasta and cereals in the microwave oven, here are delicious recipes you will not be able to resist. Microwave cooked pasta and rice will eliminate sticky pans. Microwaved hot cereals are cooked directly in the cereal bowl and makes clean-up easy.

DIRECTIONS FOR COOKING PASTA BY TIME

Follow directions in chart for recommended dish size, amount of water and cooking time. Add pasta to boiling water, with 1 teaspoon salt and 1 tablespoon oil.

Cook, covered, at HIGH. Stir twice. Test pasta for doneness before adding more time. Slightly undercook pasta that will be heated again in casseroles. Stir and let stand, covered, 3 minutes.

Drain and rinse before serving.

ITEM	CONTAINER	AMOUNT OF HOT WATER	APPROX. TIME TO BOIL WATER at HIGH (in minutes)	APPROX. TIME TO COOK PASTA at HIGH (in minutes)	STAND TIME (in minutes)
Egg Noodles medium width (8 oz.)	3-qt. casserole	1½ quart	7 to 8	5 to 6	3
Elbow Macaroni (8 oz.)	3-qt. casserole	1½ quart	7 to 8	7 to 8	3
Lasagna Noodles (8 oz.)	oblong baking*	1½ quart	7 to 8	13 to 15	3
Spaghetti (8 oz.-broken)	3-qt. casserole	2 quarts	8 to 9	7 to 8	3
Specialty Noodles bows, shells, etc. (8 oz.)	3-qt. casserole	1½ quart	7 to 8	10½ to 11	3

*Heat water for lasagna in 2-qt. glass bowl. Pour over noodles in 12×8-inch dish.

DIRECTIONS FOR COOKING PASTA BY AUTO SENSOR A

To cook 8 oz. medium egg noodles or 8 oz. elbow macaroni, place 1½-quarts cold water, 1 teaspoon salt, and 1 tablespoon oil and noodles in 4 or 5-quart casserole.

Cover with lid. Cook on COOK A1. Stir and let stand, covered, 10 minutes.

Drain and rinse before serving.

ITEM	CONTAINER	AMOUNT OF WATER	APPROX. COOKING TIME COOK A1	STAND TIME (in minutes)
Egg Noodles medium width (8 oz.)	4 to 5 qt. casserole	1½ quart	17	5 to 10
Elbow Macaroni (8 oz.)	4 to 5 qt. casserole	1½ quart	13	5 to 10

NOODLE PUDDING

1 package (8 oz.) medium egg noodles
½ cup butter or margarine
4 eggs, beaten
1 cup cottage cheese
1 cup sour cream
¾ cup raisins
½ cup sugar
1 teaspoon cinnamon
¼ teaspoon nutmeg

Yield: 8 Servings

Cook noodles according to chart, page 180. Heat butter in large glass bowl at **MEDIUM** 1 minute, or until melted. Combine remaining ingredients and drained noodles; pour into 2-quart ring mold. Sprinkle, if desired, with additional cinnamon. Cook at **MEDIUM** 18 to 20 minutes until pudding is set. Let stand, covered with wax paper. Serve warm or chilled.

FLORIDA-STYLE NOODLES

1 package (8 oz.) medium egg noodles
½ cup almonds
¼ cup butter or margarine
1 tablespoon poppy seeds
½ tablespoon grated lemon peel
½ tablespoon grated orange peel
½ teaspoon salt
⅛ teaspoon pepper
1 cup sour cream

Yield: 4 Servings

Cook noodles according to chart, page 180. While noodles are standing, in microwave safe serving bowl, combine almonds and butter. Heat at **HIGH** 1 to 1½ minutes, or until butter is melted. Stir in drained noodles, poppy seeds, lemon and orange peel, salt and pepper, toss well. Serve with sour cream.

FETTUCCINE ALFREDO

1 package (8 oz.) fettuccine
1 cup grated Parmesan cheese
½ cup butter or margarine, cut into quarters
½ cup heavy cream
Pepper to taste

Yield: 4 Side-Dish Servings

Cook fettuccine according to directions for egg noodles in chart, page 180. While noodles are standing, combine cheese, butter and cream in microwave-safe serving bowl. Cook at **MEDIUM** 3 to 4 minutes, or until butter is melted; stir twice. Stir in drained noodles; toss well. Season with pepper.

DIRECTIONS FOR COOKING RICE AND OTHER GRAINS BY TIME

Follow directions in chart for recommended dish size, amounts of water and cooking time. Add grain to boiling water. Add salt and butter according to package directions.

Cover with lid. Cook at MEDIUM-LOW for time recommended in chart. Let stand covered before serving.

For instant (no cook) products, follow package directions. Bring hot water to boil on HIGH. Stir in product and let stand covered for time given on package.

For special rice, substitute beef or chicken broth for water. Add cooked onions, mushrooms or crumbled bacon before serving.

DIRECTIONS FOR COOKING RICE ON AUTO SENSOR

Place 2 cups water, 1 cup long grain rice and 1 teaspoon of salt in a 4-quart casserole.

Cover with lid. Cook on COOK A3. Cooking time is about 20 minutes. Stir, let stand, covered, 10 minutes before serving.

183

RICE AND OTHER GRAINS CHART

ITEM	CONTAINER	AMOUNT OF HOT WATER	APPROX. TIME TO BOIL WATER at HIGH (in minutes)	APPROX. TIME TO COOK GRAIN at MEDIUM-LOW (in minutes)	STAND TIME (in minutes)
RICE Brown (1 cup)	2-qt. casserole	3 cups	5 to 6	45 to 50	15
Flavored Rice Mix (6 oz.)	2-qt. casserole	as package directs	4 to 5	20	10
Long Grain (1 cup)	2-qt. casserole	2 cups	4 to 5	13½ to 16½	10
Long Grain & Wild Rice Mix (6 oz.)	2-qt. casserole	2½ cups	4½ to 5	23 to 25	5
Quick Rice (1 cup)	1-qt. casserole	1 cup	2 to 3	5	5
Short Grain (1 cup)	2-qt. casserole	2 cups	4 to 5	10 to 12	10
BARLEY Quick Cook (1 cup)	2-qt. casserole	3 cups	5 to 6	5½ to 6½	3 (then drain)
GRITS (⅔ cup)	3-qt. casserole	3⅓ cups	5 to 6	10	10

SPANISH RICE

1 large onion, chopped
¼ cup finely chopped green pepper
2 tablespoons butter or margarine
Water
1 can (16 oz.) stewed tomatoes, chopped
    and drained; reserve liquid
1 cup long grain rice
1½ teaspoons salt
⅛ teaspoon pepper

Yield: 6 Servings

In 2-quart casserole, combine onion, green pepper and butter. Cook at **HIGH** 2½ to 3½ minutes; stir once. Add enough water to reserved liquid to equal 2 cups. Add to dish with tomatoes, rice, salt and pepper. Cook, covered with lid, at **HIGH** 4 to 5 minutes and at **MEDIUM-LOW** 16 to 17 minutes, or until rice is tender; stir once. Let stand, covered, 5 minutes before serving.

RICE PILAF

¼ cup butter or margarine
1 cup long grain rice
2¼ cups chicken broth
¼ cup raisins, optional
1 to 1½ teaspoons curry powder

Yield: 6 Servings

Heat butter in 2-quart casserole at **HIGH** 1 minute, or until melted; stir in rice. Cook at **HIGH** 2 to 3 minutes, or until rice is browned; stir once. Add remaining ingredients and cook, covered with lid, at **HIGH** 4 to 5 minutes and at **MEDIUM-LOW** 12 to 14 minutes, or until rice is tender. Let stand, covered, 5 minutes.

Variation: Cook ¼ cup slivered almonds with butter.

185

HOPPIN' JOHN

4 slices bacon, diced
1 medium onion, chopped
2½ cups hot water
1½ cups cooked black-eyed peas
1 cup long grain rice
1 teaspoon salt
¼ teaspoon pepper
Dash hot pepper sauce, optional

Yield: 6 Servings

Combine bacon and onion in 2½-quart casserole. Cook at **HIGH** 4 to 5 minutes, or until bacon is crisp; stir once. Stir in remaining ingredients. Cook, covered, with lid, at **HIGH** 5 to 7 minutes and at **MEDIUM-LOW** 11 to 13 minutes, or until rice is tender; stir once. Let stand, covered, 5 minutes before serving.

BARLEY MUSHROOM CASSEROLE

6 tablespoons butter or margarine
2 medium onions, finely chopped
3 cloves garlic, finely chopped
1 pound fresh mushroom, sliced
1 cup quick cooking barley
½ cup chicken broth
¼ cup chopped parsley
2 teaspoons basil
1 teaspoon salt
¼ teaspoon pepper

Yield: 6 Servings

In 2½-quart casserole, combine butter, onion and garlic. Cook, covered with lid, at **HIGH** 3 to 4 minutes, or until onion is tender. Stir in remaining ingredients. Cook, covered, at **HIGH** 5 minutes and at **MEDIUM-LOW** 5½ to 6½ minutes, or until barley is tender. Let stand, covered, 5 minutes before serving.

DIRECTIONS FOR COOKING HOT CEREAL

Follow directions in chart for recommended dish size, amount of water, cooking time and power level. Combine cereal and hot water in dish. For Cream of Wheat and Farina, add cereal to boiling water.

Cook; stir once halfway through cooking time.

Let stand 1 to 2 minutes before serving. Top as desired with sugar or spices.

CEREAL	CONTAINER	AMOUNT OF HOT WATER	AMOUNT OF CEREAL	APPROX. COOKING TIME (in minutes)		STAND TIME (in minutes)
				at HIGH	at MEDIUM	
Cream of Wheat						
1 serving	2-cup glass bowl	1¼ cups	2½ tablespoons	1	4 to 6	1
2 servings	1-qt. glass bowl	2 cups	⅓ cup	1½	6 to 7	1
4 servings	2-qt. glass bowl	3¾ cups	⅔ cup	2	7 to 8	2
Farina						
1 serving	individual serving dish	⅔ cup	2 tablespoons	1½ to 2	——	1
2 servings	2 individual serving dishes	1⅓ cups	¼ cup	3¼ to 3¾	——	1
4 servings	2-qt. glass bowl	2⅔ cups	½ cup	4½ to 5½	——	2
Oatmeal (Quick)						
1 serving	individual serving dish	¾ cup	⅓ cup	1 to 1½	——	1
2 servings	2 individual serving dishes	1½ cups	⅔ cup	2 to 2½	——	1
4 servings	2-qt. glass bowl	3 cups	1⅓ cups	3½ to 4	——	2
Wheat-Bran Cereal						
1 serving	individual serving dish	¾ cup	¼ cup	3	——	1
2 servings	2 individual serving dishes	1½ cups	½ cup	5 to 6	——	1
4 servings	2-qt. glass bowl	3 cups	1 cup	7 to 8	——	2

GRANOLA CEREAL

2 cups quick or old fashion oats
⅔ cup soy nuts or coarsely chopped nuts
⅓ cup wheat germ, optional
¼ cup packed brown sugar
¼ cup honey
1 teaspoon vanilla
⅓ cup raisins or coconut

Yield: 3 Cups

Cook oats in 12×8-inch dish at **HIGH** 3 to 5 minutes; stir occasionally. Add nuts, wheat germ, and brown sugar; stir in honey and vanilla. Cook at **HIGH** 3 to 5 minutes; stir twice. Add raisins. Cool completely, stirring occasionally to crumble mixture. Store in airtight container.

Note: *To make GRANOLA SNACK, follow above procedure. Add ¼ cup oil with honey.*

NICE AND SPICY OATMEAL

4 cups hot water
2 cups quick-cooking oats
½ cup chopped dried apricots or raisins
¼ cup packed brown sugar
¼ teaspoon salt
½ cup wheat germ, optional
1 teaspoon cinnamon

Yield: 4 Servings

In 2-quart casserole, combine water, oats, apricots, sugar and salt. Cook at **HIGH** 4 to 5 minutes, or until slightly thickened; stir once. Stir in wheat germ and cinnamon. Let stand 3 minutes before serving.

QUICK BREADS

Now, you do not have to get up hours before everyone else to surprise them with a freshly baked treat or plan in advance for something to serve with coffee.

Your microwave oven brings you flexibility for spur of the moment fun. Most breads and coffee cakes bake in 15 to 20 minutes, muffins or buns in about 6 minutes.

DIRECTIONS FOR QUICK BREADS

Prepare batter according to package or recipe directions.

Use recommended dish size. Glass dishes allow bottom of baked goods to be checked visually for doneness. After cooking visually check bottom for doneness.

Grease bottom of dish when cakes are served from the dish. Grease bottom and sides and line bottom of dish with wax paper when the product is inverted and removed from dish. Never flour the dish.

When necessary, shield ends of loaf dishes with 3-inch strip of foil. Shield square dishes with triangle of foil on each corner; mold around dish.

When cooking muffins, line microwave muffin pans with paper baking cups. Fill paper baking cups ⅔ full.

Check during cooking since brands and cooking times vary. After cooking, tops may be sticky, but a toothpick inserted near center should come out clean.

Let stand, uncovered, on a flat surface for 5 to 15 minutes. Stand time is important to allow product to finish cooking

Cakes and breads that are to be inverted should be loosened from the sides of the dish. Carefully turn product out of dish and peel off wax paper. Store, covered, until ready to serve.

QUICK BREAD MIX CHART

Most package mixes benefit from 2-stage cooking. We have given these directions where they are helpful.

Item	Amount of Batter	Dish Size/Preparation	First Stage →	Second Stage	Special Instructions	Stand Time
Coffee Cake Fruit Variety (16 to 19 oz.)	All batter	Grease 8 or 9-inch round dish.	**LOW** 6 minutes	**MEDIUM-HIGH** 4 to 5 minutes	To dry top, cover with wax paper during last minute of cooking.	10 minutes, uncovered
Coffee Cake Streusel Variety (10.5 oz.)	All batter	Grease 8 or 9-inch round or square dish.	**LOW** 6 minutes	**MEDIUM-HIGH** 2½ to 3 minutes	Shield each corner of square dish with a triangle of foil	10 minutes, uncovered
Quick Bread (14½ to 17 oz.)	All batter	Grease 9×5×3-inch loaf dish. Line bottom with wax paper.	**LOW** 10 minutes	**MEDIUM-HIGH** 3½ to 4 minutes	Shield each end with a 3-inch strip of foil. Mold foil around handle.	15 minutes, uncovered
Corn Bread (10 to 12 oz.)	All batter	Grease 8 or 9-inch round or square dish.	**LOW** 6 minutes	**MEDIUM-HIGH** 2½ to 3½ minutes	Increase milk by 2 Tbsp. Add 1 Tbsp. oil to batter. Shield each corner of square dish with a triangle of foil. Mold foil around dish.	10 minutes, uncovered
Gingerbread (14 oz.)	All batter	Grease 8-inch square dish.	**MEDIUM** 8½ to 9½ minutes	————	————	15 minutes, uncovered
Muffins (cook 6 at a time)	Scant ¼ cup per muffin	6-cup muffin pan lined with paper baking cups.	**MEDIUM-LOW** 4½ to 5½ minutes	————	————	5 minutes, uncovered

IRISH SODA BREAD

2¾ cups flour
3 tablespoons sugar
¾ teaspoon salt
¾ teaspoon baking powder
4 tablespoons butter or margarine
1½ cups raisins
1 tablespoon caraway seeds
1 cup buttermilk
1 egg
¾ teaspoon baking soda

Yield: 6 Servings

Sift together flour, sugar salt and baking powder; cut in butter. Stir in raisins and caraway. Combine buttermilk, egg and baking soda; add to dry ingredients. Stir only until flour is moistened. On floured board, lightly knead dough until smooth, about 3 minutes. Shape into ball and place in 1½-quart glass bowl, bottom lined with wax paper; cut an "X" across top of dough. Cover with wax paper. Cook at **MEDIUM** 7 to 9 minutes. Let stand uncovered, 10 minutes; turn out of bowl. Let stand upside-down an additional 10 minutes; store, covered, until ready to serve.

BOSTON BROWN BREAD

1 cup buttermilk
½ cup molasses
½ cup raisins
½ teaspoon baking powder
½ teaspoon baking soda
½ teaspoon salt
½ cup whole wheat flour
½ cup yellow cornmeal
¼ cup flour

Yield: 1 Loaf

Combine buttermilk and molasses; stir in raisins, baking powder, baking soda and salt. Add flours and cornmeal, stir only until moistened. Pour batter into generously greased 4 cup-glass measure. Cover loosely with plastic wrap; hold wrap in place with rubber band secured under handle of glass.
Place on inverted pie plate microwave oven. Cook at **MEDIUM** 8 to 9 minutes. Let stand, uncovered, 10 minutes. Remove from dish; let stand 5 minutes. Store, covered, until ready to serve.

SOUTHERN CHEESE SPOON BREAD

½ cup yellow cornmeal
2 cups milk
½ teaspoon salt
2 eggs, beaten
1 cup (4 oz.) diced American cheese
2 tablespoons butter or margarine

Yield: 6 Servings

In medium glass bowl, combine cornmeal, milk and salt. Cook at **HIGH** 3 minutes and at **MEDIUM** 3 to 4 minutes, or until cornmeal is thickened; stir twice. Stir until smooth; add eggs, cheese and butter. Stir until cheese and butter are almost melted. Pour into greased 1-quart casserole dish. Cook covered with lid, at **MEDIUM** 2 minutes. Stir well; recover. Cook at **MEDIUM** 5 to 7 minutes, or until center is almost set. Let stand 10 minutes before serving.

BASIC NUT BREAD

½ cup packed brown sugar
3 tablespoons butter or margarine
2 eggs
¾ cup buttermilk
½ teaspoon vanilla
1¼ cups flour
¾ cup chopped nuts
1½ teaspoons baking powder
½ teaspoon cinnamon
½ teaspoon salt
Cinnamon sugar

Yield: 1 Loaf

Cream together sugar and butter; stir in eggs, buttermilk and vanilla. Add flour, nuts, baking powder, cinnamon, and salt, stirring only until flour is moistened. Spoon batter into 9″×5″×3″ greased glass loaf dish, bottom lined with wax paper. Sprinkle with cinnamon sugar. Shield ends of dish with 3-inch strip of foil, mold foil around dish. Cook at **LOW** 10 minutes and at **MEDIUM-HIGH** 4 to 5 minutes, or until toothpick inserted near center comes out clean. Let stand, 15 minutes. Invert and remove wax paper; let stand 5 minutes. Store, covered, until ready to serve.

SIESTA CORNBREAD

1 package (12 oz.) corn muffin mix
½ cup chopped onion
2 tablespoons chopped pimento
1 to 2 tablespoons chopped jalapeno peppers
1 can (8¼ oz.) cream-style corn
1 egg
¼ cup milk
2 tablespoons oil

Yield: 6 Servings

Combine corn muffin mix, onion, pimento and peppers; stir in corn, egg, milk and oil. Spoon batter into greased 2-quart ring mold. Cook at **LOW** 6 minutes, or until **MEDIUM-HIGH** 5 to 6 minutes, or until bread pulls away from center and sides of dish. Let stand 10 minutes. Invert from dish and serve warm.

193

CHERRY BRUNCH ROLLS

½ cup packed brown sugar
¼ cup chopped maraschino cherries
¼ cup flaked coconut
1 tablespoon water
¼ teaspoon cinnamon
1 can (8 oz.) refrigerated biscuits
3 tablespoons butter or margarine, melted

Yield: 10 Rolls

In small glass bowl, combine brown sugar, cherries, coconut, water and cinnamon. Stir until smooth. Cook at **HIGH** 2 to 2¼ minutes. Pour into a greased 5-cup ring mold. Dip each biscuit into melted butter. Arrange biscuits on top of cherry mixture. Cook at **MEDIUM** 4 to 4½ minutes. Let stand, covered, 5 minutes before inverting on serving platter. Store, covered, until ready to serve.

PECAN STICKY BUNS

½ cup brown sugar
⅓ cup finely chopped pecans
1 teaspoon cinnamon
¼ cup butter or margarine, melted
1 can (8 oz.) refrigerated crescent dinner rolls

Yield: 8 Buns

In small bowl, combine sugar, pecans and cinnamon. Unroll the 2 sections of dough, but do not separate. On each long rectangle, brush on 1 teaspoon butter. Spoon 2 tablespoons pecan mixture; re-roll. Cut each into quarters, forming 8 buns. Dip each bun into butter and then into pecan mixture. In 8-inch round dish, arrange biscuits in ring (do not place any in center); sprinkle remaining pecan mixture over ring. Cook at **MEDIUM** 4½ to 5½ minutes. Let stand, covered, 5 mintues before inverting onto platter. Cover until ready to serve.

PUMPKIN PECAN MUFFINS

1 cup flour
⅔ cup sugar
1¼ teaspoons pumpkin pie spice
1 teaspoon baking powder
⅛ teaspoon salt
½ cup chopped nuts
½ cup raisins
½ cup cooked pumpkin
¼ cup milk
3 tablespoons oil
1 egg, beaten

Yield: 12 Muffins

Combine flour, sugar, pumpkin pie spice, baking powder and salt. Stir in nuts and raisins. Add pumpkin, milk, oil and egg; stir until flour is moistened. Line 6-cup muffin pan with paper baking cups; fill ¾ full. Cook at **MEDIUM-LOW** 5½ to 6½ minutes, or until toothpick inserted near center comes out clean. Let stand 5 minutes. Repeat procedure with remaining batter. Store covered.

EASY MORNING MUFFINS

2 cups flour
½ cup sugar
1 tablespoon baking powder
½ teaspoon salt
½ cup milk
½ cup oil
2 eggs, beaten
3 tablespoons butter or margarine, melted
Cinnamon sugar

Yield: 12 Muffins

Combine flour, sugar, baking powder and salt. Add milk, oil and eggs; stir until flour is moistened. Line 6-cup muffin pan with paper baking cups; fill ¾ full. Cook at **MEDIUM-LOW** 4½ to 5½ minutes, or until toothpick inserted near center comes out clean. Let stand 5 minutes. Repeat procedure with remaining batter. If desired, dip tops of muffins in melted butter and then in cinnamon sugar. Store covered.

Variations: Add any ½ cup of the following, tossed with 1 tablespoon flour.
●*Blueberries*
●*Chopped nuts*
●*Raisins*

RAISIN BRAN MUFFINS

2¼ cups raisin bran cereal
⅔ cup milk
6 tablespoons oil
2 eggs, beaten
⅔ cup flour
6 tablespoons packed brown sugar
1 tablespoon baking powder
½ teaspoon cinnamon

Yield: 12 Muffins

Combine cereal, milk, oil and eggs. Stir until cereal is moistened. Let stand 5 minutes. Combine flour, sugar, baking powder and cinnamon. Add to cereal mixture; stir until well blended. Line 6-cup muffin pan with paper baking cups; fill ¾ full. Cook at **MEDIUM-LOW** 5½ to 6½ minutes, or until toothpick inserted near center comes out clean. Let stand 5 minutes. Repeat procedure with remaining batter. Serve warm.

PEACHY MUFFINS

1 can (8¾ oz.) sliced peaches, drained; reserve ¼ cup
   liquid
⅓ cup packed brown sugar
3 tablespoons butter or margarine
1 egg, beaten
¼ cup milk
1 cup flour
½ cup chopped pecans
1½ teaspoons baking powder
½ teaspoon salt
½ teaspoon nutmeg

Yield: 12 Muffins

Finely chop peaches; set aside. Cream together sugar and butter. Stir in egg, milk and reserved syrup. Add flour, pecans, baking powder, salt and nutmeg. Stir only until flour is moistened. Stir in peaches. Line 6-cup muffin pan with paper baking cups; fill ¾ full. Cook at **MEDIUM-LOW** 5½ to 6½ minutes, or until toothpick inserted near center comes out clean. Let stand 5 minutes. Repeat procedure with remaining batter. Store covered.

HOLIDAY CRANBERRY COFFEE CAKE

1 can (8 oz.) whole berry cranberry sauce
6 tablespoons sugar, divided
¼ cup chopped nuts, optional
1 tablespoon butter or margarine, melted
2 cups buttermilk biscuit mix
1 cup orange juice or apple juice
1 egg

Glaze:
1 cup confectionters sugar
1 to 2 tablespoons water
½ teaspoon vanilla

Yield: 8 Servings

In small bowl, combine cranberry sauce, 4 tablespoons sugar, nuts and butter. Cook at **HIGH** 2 minutes. Spread into 8 or 9-inch round baking dish, bottom lined with wax paper. Combine biscuit mix, juice, egg and remaining sugar; blend until smooth, about ½ minute. Spoon batter over cranberry mixture. Cover with wax paper. Elevate dish in oven on inverted pie plate. Cook at **LOW** 8 minutes and at **MEDIUM-HIGH** 3½ to 4½ minutes, or until toothpick inserted near center comes out clean. Let stand, uncovered, 10 minutes before inverting onto platter; carefully peel off wax paper. Store, covered, until ready to serve.
Meanwhile, prepare glaze. In bowl, combine sugar, water and vanilla; stir until smooth. Drizzle with glaze just before serving.

SOUR CREAM COFFEE CAKE

½ cup sugar
¼ cup butter or margarine
1½ cups flour
1 cup sour cream
2 eggs
1½ teaspoons vanilla
1 teaspoon baking powder
1 teaspoon baking soda
½ teaspoon salt

Topping:
⅓ cup chopped walnuts
¼ cup sugar
½ teaspoon cinnamon

Yield: 8 Servings

Cream sugar and butter in large bowl, with electric mixer. Add remaining ingredients. Beat at low speed 30 seconds and at medium speed 2 minutes. Pour into greased 8-inch square dish. In small bowl, combine topping ingredients; sprinkle over batter. Shield each corner of dish with a triangle of foil; mold foil around dish. Cook at **LOW** 8 minutes and at **MEDIUM-HIGH** 4½ to 6 minutes. Let stand 10 minutes. Serve immediately.

GRAHAM STREUSEL COFFEE A CAKE

½ cup butter or margarine, melted
1 cup graham cracker crumbs
½ cup packed brown sugar
⅓ cup chopped nuts
¾ teaspoon cinnamon
1 package (18¼ oz.) yellow cake mix
4 eggs
1 cup water
⅓ cup oil

Vanilla Glaze:
2 cups confectioners sugar
2 to 3 tablespoons water
1 teaspoon vanilla

Yield: 10 Servings

In medium bowl, combine butter, crumbs, sugar, nuts and cinnamon. Divide crumb mixture into two 8 or 9-inch round baking dishes, bottoms lined with wax paper. Spread to cover bottom of dishes. In large bowl, with electric mixer, blend cake mix, eggs, water and oil at low speed ½ minute; beat at medium speed 3 minutes. Pour 2 cups batter into each dish.

TO COOK BY AUTO SENSOR: Cover completely with plastic wrap. Cook on **COOK A8**.

TO COOK BY TIME: Cook at **LOW** 6 minutes and at **MEDIUM-HIGH** 2 to 3 minutes, or until toothpick inserted near center comes out clean. To dry top of cake cover with wax paper last minute of cooking.

TO COMPLETE: Let stand, uncovered, 10 minutes. Repeat procedure with remaining cake.
Meanwhile, prepare glaze. In bowl, combine sugar, water and vanilla; stir until smooth. With knife, loosen cake from sides of dish. Invert one cake onto serving platter; carefully peel off wax paper. Invert second layer onto paper plate; carefully peel off wax paper. Cover until cool; just before serving spread half of glaze on cake on serving platter; top with second layer. Drizzle with remaining glaze.

BANANA NUT COFFEE A CAKE

¼ cup oil
¼ cup milk
1 egg
½ cup mashed ripe banana (about 1)
½ cup packed brown sugar
¾ cup flour
½ cup chopped nuts
¾ teaspoon baking powder
¼ teaspoon salt
¼ teaspoon baking soda

Nut Topping:
¼ cup packed brown sugar
¼ cup chopped nuts
2 tablespoons flour
⅛ teaspoon cinnamon
1 tablespoon butter or margarine, softened

Yield: 8 Servings

In medium bowl, combine oil, milk, egg, banana and sugar; add flour nuts, baking powder, salt and baking soda. Stir only until flour is moistened. Pour into greased 8 or 9-inch round baking dish. Combine brown sugar, nuts, flour and cinnamon. Blend in butter. Sprinkle on top of coffee cake.

TO COOK BY AUTO SENSOR: Cover dish completely with plastic wrap. Cook on **COOK A4**.

TO COOK BY TIME: Cook at **MEDIUM** 7½ to 9 minutes, or until toothpick inserted near center comes out clean.

TO COMPLETE: Let stand, uncovered, 10 minutes. Store, covered, until ready to serve.

PROOFING (RISING) BREAD DOUGH

Make your favorite yeast bread recipe and follow these basic directions for proofing dough.

Prepare dough according to recipe directions. Do not select a recipe that yields more than two (2) loaves.

Place dough in a well greased large glass bowl. Brush top of dough with oil. Cover loosely with plastic wrap.

Place 3 cups of warm water in a 10-inch glass or glass ceramic pie plate or 10-inch glass or glass ceramic square dish. Place bowl with dough in water.

Set oven at **WARM**; heat for 25 to 30 minutes or until dough doubles in size. Dough has risen when two fingertips lightly pressed about ½-inch into dough leave an impression.

Punch dough down; shape into loaves. Place dough into well greased 8½"×4½"×2½" glass or glass ceramic loaf dishes. Repeat proofing procedure if your recipe directs. Note: Two (2) 8½"×4½"×2½" loaf dishes will fit into a 10-inch square dish.

Bake conventionally according to recipe directions.

DESSERTS and CANDIES

This chapter offers a wide variety of popular dessert recipes; cakes, pies, bar cookies and fruit-type desserts. We have included both recipes from scratch and convenience mixes. Many of these can be cooked during dinner and served warm.

DIRECTIONS FOR CAKES AND CUPCAKES

Prepare batter according to package or recipe directions. Layer cakes must be baked one layer at a time. Or, the entire cake mix may be baked in a 16 cup fluted tube dish.

Use dishes recommended in chart or recipes. Glass baking dishes allow the bottom of the cakes to be checked for doneness. When the product is removed from the oven, visually check bottom.

Grease the bottom of the baking dish when cakes are to be served directly from the dish. Grease the bottom and sides of dish when cake is to be inverted and removed from dish, such as layer cakes, upside-down cakes. If desired, bottom of dish may be lined with wax paper. Never flour cake dishes and fluted tube dishes.

Use only 2¼ cups of batter for an 8 or 9-inch round or square dish. Cook second layer immediately after the first. The remaining batter can be used for cupcakes.

When using fluted tube dish, be sure to grease sides and "tube". All the batter from a 2 layer cake mix may be poured into a 16 cup fluted tube dish.

When necessary, square dishes can be shielded on each corner with a triangle of foil. Mold foil around dish.

When cooking cupcakes, line microwave muffin pans with paper baking cups. Fill paper baking cups half full.

Cover with wax paper when indicated in chart or recipe. Most package mixes and some recipes benefit from 2-stage cooking. We have given 2-stage cooking directions where they are helpful.

Check cakes during cooking since brands and cooking times vary. After cooking, tops may be sticky, but a toothpick inserted near the center should come out clean.

Let stand, uncovered on a flat surface for 5 to 15 minutes. Stand time is important to allow cakes and cupcakes to finish cooking.

To invert loosen cakes from sides of dish, carefully turn out. Store, covered, until ready to serve. Cool completely to frost. Apply frosting with light pressure.

CAKE MIX CHART

ITEM	Amout of Batter	Dish Size/ Preparation	First Stage	→	Second Stage	Special Instructions	Stand Time
Cake Mix (18¾ to 20¼ oz.)	2¼ cups	Grease 8 or 9-inch round or square dish.	**LOW** 6 minutes	→	**MEDIUM-HIGH** 3 to 4 minutes	Shield each corner of square dish with triangle of foil.	10 minutes, uncovered
Cake Mix (18¾ to 20¼ oz.)	All batter	Grease 16-cup fluted tube dish.	**LOW** 10 minutes	→	**MEDIUM-HIGH** 6½ to 7 minutes	Cover dish with wax paper during last minute of cooking.	15 minutes, uncovered
Brownies (15 oz.) Cake-Like	All batter	8 or 9-inch round or square dish.	**MEDIUM** 8 to 9 minutes		——————	Shield each corner of square with triangle of foil.	until completely cool
Cupcakes	2 rounded table-spoons per cup cake	Muffin pan lined with paper baking cups 1 2 4 6	**MEDIUM** ½ to 1 1 to 1¼ 2 to 2½ 3 to 4 minutes		——————	Place muffin pan on inverted pie plate	5 minutes, uncovered
Mix-in-Dish Cake (15 oz.) without frosting	All batter	Grease 8 or 9-inch round or square dish.	**LOW** 8 minutes	→	**MEDIUM-HIGH** 3½ to 4½ minutes	Shield each corner of square dish with triangle of foil. Cover dish with wax paper last minute of cooking.	10 minutes, uncovered
Mix-in-Dish Cake (11.4 oz.) with frosting	All batter	Cardboard pan provided with mix.	**LOW** 5 minutes	→	**MEDIUM-HIGH** 1½ to 2 minutes	——————	until cool, uncovered

DIRECTIONS FOR COOKING CAKE MIXES BY AUTO SENSOR

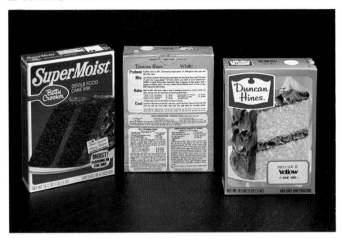

Prepare basic cake mix or cake mix with pudding according to package directions.

Grease 8 or 9-inch round or square cake dish. Pour 2¼ cups of batter into dish. If desired, line bottom of dish with wax paper.

Mix-in-Dish Cakes (15 oz.) should be prepared directly in a 8 or 9-inch round or square cake dish. Bake entire batter.

Cover dish completely with plastic wrap. Cook on COOK A4.

After cooking, release plastic wrap. Let stand, covered, on flat surface 10 minutes.

Turn out of dish and carefully peel off wax paper, or let cake cool completely in dish. Store, covered, until served. Frost, if desired, when completely cooled.

CARROT SPICE CAKE 🅰

1¼ cups flour
1 cup packed brown sugar
1 teaspoon baking powder
1 teaspoon baking soda
2 teaspoons cinnamon
½ teaspoon allspice
½ teaspoon salt
1¼ cups shredded carrot
⅔ cup oil
2 eggs
1 can (8 oz.) crushed pineapple, drained
1 teaspoon vanilla
½ cup chopped nuts
¼ cup raisins

Yield: 8 Servings

In large bowl, with electric mixer, combine flour, sugar, baking powder, baking soda, cinnamon, allspice, salt and carrot. Stir in oil, eggs, pineapple and vanilla; beat 2 minutes, at medium speed. Stir in nuts and raisins. Pour batter into a greased 10 to 12 cup fluted tube dish.

TO COOK BY AUTO SENSOR: Cover completely with 2 pieces of plastic wrap. Cook on **COOK A3.**

TO COOK BY TIME: Cover with wax paper. Elevate pan in oven on inverted pie plate. Cook at **MEDIUM** 10 to 11 minutes, or until toothpick inserted near center comes out clean.

TO COMPLETE: Let stand, uncovered, 10 minutes. Store, covered, until ready to serve.

YELLOW CAKE

¾ cup sugar
⅓ cup butter or margarine
1 egg
⅔ cup milk
1 teaspoon vanilla
1 cup flour
1½ teaspoons baking powder
¼ teaspoon salt

Yield: 1 Layer

Cream sugar and butter in large bowl, with electric mixer. Add egg, milk and vanilla, mixing until blended. Stir in remaining ingredients. Beat 1 minute at medium speed. Grease an 8 or 9-inch round baking dish with wax paper. Pour batter into dish; cover with wax paper. Elevate dish, in oven, on inverted pie plate. Cook at **LOW** 6 minutes and at **MEDIUM-HIGH** 5 to 5½ minutes, or until toothpick inserted near center comes out clean. Let stand, uncovered, 15 minutes. Invert on serving plate; peel off wax paper. Store covered.

APPLESAUCE CAKE

2 cups flour
1 cup chopped walnuts
3 teaspoons cinnamon
2 teaspoons baking soda
1½ teaspoons salt
1 teaspoon baking powder
1 teaspoon nutmeg
¼ teaspoon cloves
2 cups sugar
½ cup oil
3 eggs
1 jar (15 oz.) applesauce

Yield: 12 Servings

Mix flour, walnuts, cinnamon, baking soda, salt, baking powder, nutmeg and cloves; set aside. In large bowl, with electric mixer, beat sugar, oil and eggs at high speed for 5 minutes. Alternately blend in flour mixture and applesauce; beat until smooth. Pour batter into well greased 16-cup fluted tube dish. Cover with wax paper. Elevate dish in oven on inverted pie plate. Cook at **LOW** 10 minutes and at **MEDIUM-HIGH** 9 to 10 minutes, or until toothpick inserted in center comes out clean. Let stand, uncovered, 15 minutes. Invert onto serving plate.

FESTIVE RUM CAKE

1 cup finely chopped pecans or walnuts
1 package (18¼ oz.) yellow cake mix
1 package (3¾ oz.) instant vanilla pudding
 mix
4 eggs
½ cup water
½ cup oil
½ cup dark rum

Rum Glaze:
½ cup butter or margarine, melted
1 cup sugar
¼ cup water
¼ cup dark rum

Yield: 12 Servings

Sprinkle nuts in well-greased 16-cup fluted
tube dish. In large bowl, with electric
mixer, combine cake mix, pudding mix,
eggs, water, oil and rum; beat at medium
speed 4 minutes. Pour batter evenly over
nuts. Cook at **LOW** 10 minutes and at
MEDIUM-HIGH 6 to 8 minutes, or until
toothpick inserted near center comes out
clean. To dry top of cake, cover with wax
paper last 2 minutes of cooking.
Let stand, uncovered, 15 minutes.
Meanwhile, in 2-cup measure combine
butter, sugar and water; mix well. Cook at
HIGH 2 to 2½ minutes; stir in rum. Prick
top of cake; drizzle half of Rum Glaze over
cake (to absorb). Invert cake onto serving
platter and prick top and sides of cake;
drizzle cake with remaining glaze. Store,
covered, until ready to serve.

GERMAN CHOCOLATE A UPSIDE-DOWN CAKE

¾ cup packed brown sugar
3 tablespoons butter or margarine
Pecan halves (about ½ cup)
½ cup flaked coconut
2 tablespoons milk
Single layer chocolate cake mix*
Ingredients as cake package directs

Yield: 8 Servings

Cook sugar and butter in small glass bowl
at **HIGH** ½ minute, or until butter is
melted. Stir until smooth. Spread butter
mixture into 8 or 9-inch round baking dish,
bottom lined with wax paper. Arrange
pecans on top. Sprinkle with coconut and
drizzle with milk.
Prepare cake mix according to package
directions; pour over coconut.

TO COOK BY AUTO SENSOR: Cover
completely with plastic wrap. Cook on
COOK A3.

TO COOK BY TIME: Cook at **LOW** 6
minutes and at **MEDIUM-HIGH** 4 to 5
minutes, or until toothpick inserted near
center comes out clean.

TO COMPLETE: Let stand, uncovered, 10
minutes. Invert onto serving platter;
carefully peel off wax paper. Cool
completely. Store, covered.

***Note:** For HOMEMADE German Chocolate
Cake, use Devil's Food Cake recipe (page
206); cook 9 to 10 minutes.*

205

PINEAPPLE UPSIDE-DOWN CAKE A

6 tablespoons butter or margarine
1 cup packed brown sugar
Water
1 can (20 oz.) sliced pineapple, drained; reserve syrup
10 maraschino cherries
1 package (18 oz.) yellow cake mix
Ingredients as cake package directs

Yield: 2 Layers

In small glass bowl, cook butter, brown sugar and 2 tablespoons water at **HIGH** 3 to 4 minutes, or until mixture boils 1 minute. In 2 (8 or 9-inch) round dishes, spread sugar-butter mixture; arrange pineapple and cherries.
Prepare cake mix according to package directions using reserved syrup as part of water. Pour 2 cups of batter into each dish. Cover with wax paper.

TO COOK BY AUTO SENSOR: Cover completely with plastic wrap. Heat on **COOK A3**. After heating, release plastic wrap.

TO COOK BY TIME: Cook at **LOW** 6 minutes and at **MEDIUM-HIGH** 4½ to 5½ minutes, or until toothpick inserted near center comes out clean.

TO COMPLETE: Let stand 10 minutes. Repeat with remaining layer.
With knife loosen cake from sides of dish, invert onto serving platter. Store covered.

DEVIL'S FOOD CAKE

¾ cup sugar
⅓ cup shortening
1 egg
⅔ hot water
¾ cup flour
¼ cup unsweetened cocoa
½ teaspoon baking soda
½ teaspoon salt
½ teaspoon vanilla
¼ teaspoon baking powder

Yield: 1 Layer

Cream sugar and shortening in large bowl, with electric mixer. Add egg and water. Stir in remaining ingredients and blend until smooth. Pour batter into greased round 8 or 9-inch dish, bottom lined with greased wax paper. Cook at **LOW** 6 minutes and at **MEDIUM-HIGH** 3 to 5 minutes, or until toothpick inserted near center comes out clean. Let stand 15 minutes. Invert cake from dish; peel off wax paper. Cool completely. Store covered.

CHOCOLATE POUND CAKE

1 package (18¼ oz.) chocolate cake mix*
1 package (4½ oz.) instant chocolate pudding mix*
4 eggs
1¼ cups water
⅓ cup oil

Yield: 12 Servings

In large bowl, combine all ingredients; with electric mixer, beat at medium speed 2 minutes. Pour batter into greased 16-cup fluted tube dish. Cook at **LOW** 10 minutes, and at **MEDIUM-HIGH** 6 to 7 minutes, or until toothpick inserted near center comes out clean. To dry top, cover with wax paper during last minute of cooking.
Let stand, uncovered, 15 minutes before inverting onto serving plate; let stand, until cool. Store covered.

***Variation:** Use yellow cake mix and instant lemon pudding mix for chocolate cake and pudding mixes. Reduce water to 1 cup.*

PLANTATION COCONUT CAKE

1 package (18¼ oz.) yellow cake mix
1 package (3¾ oz.) insant coconut cream
 or toasted coconut pudding mix or
 instant vanilla pudding mix
4 eggs
1 cup water
⅓ cup oil
1 jar (12 oz.) strawberry or raspberry
 preserves

Creamy Glaze:
1½ cups confectioners' sugar
2 to 2½ tablespoons milk
2 tablespoons butter or margarine,
 softened
Flaked coconut

Yield: 8 Layers

In a large bowl, with electric mixer,
combine cake mix, pudding mix, eggs,
water and oil; beat at medium speed 2
minutes. Pour batter into greased 16-cup
fluted tube dish. Elevate dish on inverted
pie plate in oven.

Cook at **LOW** 10 minutes and at **MEDIUM-
HIGH** 6 minutes, or until toothpick inserted
near center comes out clean. To dry top of
cake, cover with wax paper during last
minute of cooking.
Let stand, uncovered, 15 minutes before
inverting on plate. Let stand until cool.
Store covered.
Meanwhile, prepare glaze. In bowl,
combine sugar, milk and butter; stir until
smooth. Split cake into 3 layers; spread
preserves between layers. Drizzle with
creamy glaze and top with coconut. Store
covered.

CREAMY CHEESECAKE

1 package (8 oz.) cream cheese, softened
½ cup sugar
1 egg
1 teaspoon vanilla
1 cup sour cream
9-inch graham cracker crumb crust, baked
 (see page 219)

Yield: 8 Servings

In medium bowl, combine cream cheese,
sugar, egg and vanilla until smooth; stir in
sour cream. Cook at **MEDIUM** 3½ to 4
minutes; stir twice. Pour cheese mixture
into pie crust. Cook at **MEDIUM-LOW** 3½ to
5 minutes, or until center is almost set.
Chill at least 3 hours or overnight.

Variations:
*For CHOCOLATE Cheesecake, add 1 packet
(1 oz.) pre-melted unsweetened chocolate
to cream cheese mixture; increase sugar to
⅔ cup.*
*For FRUIT-TOPPED Cheesecake, top chilled
pie with canned fruit pie filling.*
*For PRALINE Cheesecake, brush top of
chilled pie with maple syrup; garnish with
chopped pecans.*
*For PINWHEEL Cheesecake, cook ½ cup
raspberry jam ½ minute at HIGH; swirl
into pie before cooking filling in pie crust.*

207

COCONUT NUT TOPPING FOR CAKE

1 cup evaporated milk
1 cup sugar
½ cup butter or margarine
¼ cup flour
1⅓ cups flaked coconut
1 cup chopped nuts
1 teaspoon vanilla

Yield: 2¼ Cups

In medium glass bowl, combine milk, sugar, butter and flour. Cook at **HIGH** 4½ to 5½ minutes, or until mixture is thickened; stir twice. Add remaining ingredients; cool until spreadable. Stir occasionally.

SUPER CHOCOLATE FROSTING

3 squares (1 oz. ea.) semi-sweet chocolate
1 can (14 oz.) sweetened condensed milk
½ teaspoon salt
½ teaspoon vanilla

Yield: 1½ Cups

In medium glass bowl, heat chocolate at **MEDIUM-LOW** 3½ to 4 minutes, or until melted. Stir in milk and salt. Cook at **MEDIUM-LOW** 5 minutes, stirring twice. Stir in vanilla. Cool completely before frosting cake.

CARAMEL CREAM FROSTING

8 caramels
1½ to 2 tablespoons water
1 package (3 oz.) cream cheese, softened (see page 230)
2 cups confectioners sugar

Yield: Frost Single Layer

Combine caramel and 1 tablespoon water in medium glass bowl. Cook at **HIGH** 1½ to 2 minutes; stir until smooth. With electric mixer, blend in cream cheese, then sugar; add ½ to 1 tablespoon water to reach desired consistency.

JAM BARS

¼ cup butter or margarine, softened
¼ cup sugar
1 egg
½ cup flour
¼ cup ground walnuts
½ teaspoon grated lemon peel
¼ teaspoon cinnamon
⅛ teaspoon salt
½ cup raspberry or strawberry jam

Topping:
½ cup flour
¼ cup packed brown sugar
3 tablespoons butter or margarine, softened

Yield: 16 Bars

Cream butter and sugar with electric mixer. Add egg, flour, walnuts, lemon peel, cinnamon and salt. Mix well. Pat mixture into an 8-inch square dish. Cook at **HIGH** 2½ to 3½ minutes or until center is slightly firm.
Meanwhile, mix together topping ingredients until mixture resembles coarse crumbs. Spread jam on top of baked crust; sprinkle topping over jam. Cook at **HIGH** 3 to 3½ minutes or until jam bubbles around edge. Let stand until cool.

MARBLE BROWNIES

1 package (22½ to 23¾ oz.) fudge brownie mix
Ingredients as brownie package directs for cake-like brownies
2 packages (3 oz. ea.) cream cheese
2 tablespoons butter or margarine
1 egg
¼ cup sugar
1 tablespoon flour
½ teaspoon vanilla

Yield: 32 Brownies

Prepare cake-like brownies according to package directions. Spread 1 cup batter into each of 2 greased (8 or 9-inch) square baking dishes. Combine cream cheese and butter in small glass bowl. Cook at **MEDIUM-LOW** 1½ to 2 minutes, or until softened; blend in remaining ingredients. Evenly divide cheese mixture into baking dishes; spoon remaining brownie batter on top. With knife, swirl gently to marble. Shield each corner with triangle of foil; mold foil around dish. Cook at **LOW** 6 minutes and at **MEDIUM-HIGH** 5 to 6 minutes, or until set. Repeat procedure with remaining dish. Let stand, uncovered, until cool. Store, covered, until ready to serve.

S'MORES

8 graham cracker squares
2 milk chocolate candy bars (1¼ oz. ea.), halved
4 marshmallows

Yield: 4 Cookies

For each cookie, arrange 1 graham cracker in center of paper napkin or paper towel; top with chocolate and marshmallow. Cover with graham cracker and wrap in napkin. Arrange on oven tray. Heat at **HIGH** ¾ to 1 minute. Let stand 2 minutes before unwrapping.

CRISPY MARSHMALLOW TREATS

1 package (10 oz.) marshmallows
¼ cup butter or margarine
5 cups toasted rice cereal

Yield: 2½ Dozen

Combine marshmallows and butter in large glass bowl. Cook at **HIGH** 3 to 4 minutes; stir twice. Stir until smooth. Add cereal and stir to coat well. Press into greased oblong dish. Cool; cut into squares to serve.

Variation: Stir in 1 cup salted peanuts or raisins with cereal.

NUTTY CHIP CHEWS

¾ cup packed brown sugar
½ cup butter or margarine, softened (see page 230)
1 egg
1 teaspoon vanilla
1 cup flour
¼ teaspoon baking powder
¼ cup chopped nuts
1 cup semi-sweet chocolate pieces, divided

Yield: 16 Bars

With electric mixer, cream sugar and butter; add egg and vanilla. Stir in flour and baking powder until well blended; add nuts and ½ cup chocolate pieces. Spread batter in 8-inch square dish. Top with remaining chocolate. Cook at **LOW** 6 minutes and **MEDIUM-HIGH** 3½ to 4½ minutes, or until top springs back when lightly pressed. To dry top, cover with wax paper last minute of cooking. Let stand, uncovered, until cool. Store, covered, until ready to serve.

QUICK BAR COOKIES (FROM MIX)

1 package (14 oz.) chocolate chip cookie mix
Ingredients as package directs
2 tablespoons water

Yield: 16 Bars

Prepare mix according to package directions. Spread dough into ungreased 8-inch square baking dish. Shield each corner with a triangle of foil; mold foil around dish. Cook at **LOW** 8 minutes and at **MEDIUM-HIGH** 2½ to 3 minutes, or until toothpick inserted near center comes out clean. Let stand, uncovered, until cool. Store, covered, until ready to serve.

COOKING PUDDING AND PIE FILLING MIXES

In a container twice the volume of the mix, combine ingredients according to package directions.

Cook at MEDIUM according to the time recommended in the chart. Stir twice during cooking time.

Chill before serving. Stir rice and tapioca pudding occasionally. Egg custard, rice pudding and tapioca pudding will thicken as they chill.

ITEM	APPROX. COOKING TIME at MEDIUM (in minutes)
Regular Pudding and Pie Filling 4 servings (3¼ to 4⅛ oz.) 6 servings (4¾ to 5½ oz.)	7½ to 9 11½ to 13
Egg Custard* (3 oz.)	7 to 8½
Rice Pudding* (3¾ oz.)	7½ to 9
Tapioca Pudding* (3½ oz.)	7 to 8½

*Mixture will thicken as it chills.

CHILLED CHOCOLATE ALMOND SOUFFLE

1 envelope unflavored gelatin
¾ cup sugar
3 eggs, separated
1 cup milk
2 squares (1 oz. ea.) unsweetened chocolate, melted (see page 229)
¼ teaspoon almond extract
1 cup heavy cream, whipped

Yield: 8 Servings

Mix gelatin and ½ cup sugar in large glass bowl. Stir in egg yolks beaten with milk. Cook at **MEDIUM-LOW** 5 to 6 minutes, or until gelatin is dissolved; stir occasionally. With wire whip, stir in chocolate and almond extract; chill until mixture mounds slightly, stir occasionally.
Meanwhile, beat egg whites until soft peaks form; gradually add remaining sugar and beat until stiff. Fold in chocolate-almond mixture; fold in whipped cream. Turn into small souffle dish with 2-inch collar or 6-cup bowl and chill until firm. Garnish, if desired, with slivered almonds and additional whipped cream.

SUPERB STRAWBERRY SOUFFLE

Water
2 packages (10 oz. ea.) frozen sliced strawberries in heavy syrup, defrosted (see page 32) and drained, reserve syrup
4 eggs, separated
2 envelopes unflavored gelatin
6 tablespoons sugar, divided
1 cup heavy cream, whipped

Yield: 6–8 Servings

Add water to reserved syrup to equal 1½ cups; stir in egg yolks. In large glass bowl, mix unflavored gelatin and 4 tablespoons sugar; stir in syrup mixture.
Cook at **MEDIUM** 5 to 6 minutes, or until gelatin is dissolved; stir occasionally. Stir in an additional 1 cup cold water.
Chill until mixture mounds slightly, stir occasionally. Fold in strawberries. Beat egg whites until soft peaks form; gradually add remaining sugar and beat until stiff. Fold in gelatin mixture, then whipped cream. Turn into small souffle dish with 3-inch collar or 6 cup bowl; chill until firm.

BASIC EGG CUSTARD

2 cups milk
4 eggs, beaten
¼ to ⅓ cup sugar
½ teaspoon vanilla
Nutmeg

Yield: 6 Servings

Heat milk in 1-quart glass measure at **MEDIUM** 4 to 5 minutes, or until scalded. Quickly stir in eggs, sugar and vanilla. Pour into 6 greased custard cups (6 oz. ea.); sprinkle with nutmeg. On oven tray, arrange dishes in circular pattern. Cook at **MEDIUM-LOW** 9 to 11 minutes. Remove custards as they are cooked. Custards are cooked when they are firmly set about 1-inch from edge and center is thickened but not set. Center will set as custard cools. Let stand until cool.

STEAMED DATE-NUT PUDDING

1¼ cups flour
½ cup <u>each</u> chopped walnuts and dates
½ cup raisins
1 teaspoon cinnamon
½ teaspoon baking soda
½ teaspoon salt
¾ cup hot water
½ cup molasses
1 egg
2 tablespoons butter or margarine, melted

Yield: 8 Servings

In medium bowl, combine flour, walnuts, dates, raisins, cinnamon, baking soda and salt. Stir in water, molasses, egg and butter. Pour batter into a greased 10 cup fluted tube dish or 6 cup fluted glass mold. Cover completely with plastic wrap.

TO COOK BY AUTO SENSOR: Cook on **COOK A8**.

TO COOK BY TIME: Cook at **MEDIUM** 7 to 9 minutes, or until pudding is set.

TO COMPLETE: Release plastic wrap. Let stand, covered, 10 minutes. Invert onto serving platter; serve warm or cover until cool.
Serve, if desired, with Vanilla Sauce (see page 60) flavored with whisky or brandy.

QUICK RICE PUDDING

3 cups milk
½ cup instant rice
1 package (3 oz.) vanilla pudding and pie filling mix
3 tablespoons raisins*
¼ teaspoon cinnamon or nutmeg*

Yield: 6 Servings

Combine all ingredients in 2-quart glass bowl. Cook, covered with wax paper, at **MEDIUM** 11 to 13 minutes, or until pudding is thickened; stir three times. Chill before serving.

*Variation: Use 1 tablespoon orange liqueur and ½ cup chopped candied fruit for raisins and cinnamon.

RAISIN BREAD PUDDING

2 cups milk
¼ cup butter or margarine
5 eggs, beaten
1 cup sugar, divided
1 teaspoon vanilla
4 cups cubed raisin bread
  (about 16 slices)
⅛ teaspoon cinnamon

Yield: 6 Servings

Combine milk and butter in 1-quart glass measure. Cook at **MEDIUM** 4½ to 5½ minutes, or until milk is scalded; quickly stir in eggs, ½ cup sugar and vanilla. Meanwhile, arrange bread cubes in 2-quart ring mold; sprinkle with remaining sugar and cinnamon. Pour milk-egg mixture over bread. Cook, covered with plastic wrap, at **MEDIUM** 17 to 19 minutes, or until pudding is set. Serve warm or chilled.

APPLE BETTY A

4 cups peeled, cored, apple slices (about 4 to 5 medium)
2 tablespoons sugar
2 tablespoons lemon juice
½ cup old-fashioned or quick oats
⅔ cup packed brown sugar
1 teaspoon cinnamon
1 teaspoon nutmeg
⅓ cup butter or margarine
½ cup chopped walnuts

Yield: 6 Servings

Arrange apple slices in a greased 8-inch round dish. Sprinkle with sugar and lemon juice. Combine oats, sugar, cinnamon and nutmeg; cut in butter until mixture resembles coarse crumbs. Add nuts; mix. Crumble mixture over apple slices.

TO COOK BY AUTO SENSOR: Cover completley with plastic wrap. Cook on **COOK A7**.

TO COOK BY TIME: Cook at **MEDIUM** 20 minutes.

TO COMPLETE: Let stand, uncovered, 5 minutes.

BAKED APPLES

4 large baking apples (about 6 oz. ea.)
¼ cup packed brown sugar
2 tablespoons finely chopped nuts or raisins
¼ teaspoon cinnamon
2 tablespoons butter or margarine
¼ cup water

Yield: 4 Servings

Core apples, leaving small plug in blossom end; peel skin 1-inch from top. Combine sugar, nuts and cinnamon; fill apples with mixture.
Arrange apples in 8-inch square dish. Dot with butter and sprinkle with water. Cook, covered with plastic wrap, at **HIGH** 7 to 9 minutes. Let stand 5 minutes; serve warm or chilled, spooning sauce over apples.

Note: For TWO Servings, follow above procedure. Halve all ingredients. Cook apples 3 to 4 minutes.
For ONE Serving, cook apples 1½ to 2½ minutes.

CHUNKY APPLESAUCE A

3 pounds baking apples, peeled, cored and sliced (about 5½ cups)
¾ cup sugar or to taste
½ cup water
½ to 1 teaspoon cinnamon

Yield: 5½ Cups

Combine all ingredients in large glass bowl.

TO COOK BY AUTO SENSOR: Cover completely with plastic wrap. Cook on **COOK A1**. After cooking, release plastic wrap.

TO COOK BY TIME: Cover with wax paper. Cook at **HIGH** 7 to 10 minutes, or until apples are tender; stir once.

TO COMPLETE: Let stand, covered, 7 minutes. Mash apples until chunky; serve warm or chilled.

CARAMEL APPLES

1 package (14 oz.) caramels
1 tablespoon hot water
4 to 5 medium apples
Wooden ice cream sticks
Finely chopped nuts

Yield: 4–5 Servings

Combine caramels and water in 1-quart glass measure.
Cook at **HIGH** 2 to 3 minutes, or until melted; stir twice
until smooth. Insert sticks into stem of apples. Dip each
apple into caramel mixture turning and tipping dish to coat
apples; sprinkle with chopped nuts. Place on greased
waxed paper lines cookie sheet. Store in a cool place.

*Tip: If caramel mixture becomes too stiff while dipping
apples, return to oven and cook at* **HIGH** *½ to ¾ minute.*

FRUIT COBBLER

Filling:
2 cans (30 oz. ea.) peach slices or other canned fruit*,
  drained; reserve ¼ cup syrup
3 tablespoons flour
½ tablespoon lemon juice
½ teaspoon vanilla
½ teaspoon cinnamon

Topping:
1 cup buttermilk biscuit mix
¼ cup packed brown sugar
¼ cup butter or margarine, softened (see page 230)
2 tablespoons hot water

Yield: 6 Servings

Combine Filling ingredients in 8-inch dish. Combine
Topping ingredients, stir until dough pulls away from sides
of bowl and forms a ball. Gently spread topping onto filling
(topping will spread slightly when cooked). Sprinkle, if
desired, with additional cinnamon. Cook at **MEDIUM-HIGH** 9
to 11 minutes, or until topping is set.
Let stand to cool.

Variations:
  *For **FRESH PEACH** Cobbler, combine 1½ pounds peeled
  and sliced peaches and ¼ to ⅓ cup packed brown sugar;
  cook, covered, at* **HIGH** *3½ to 4 minutes or until tender.
  Follow above procedure, omitting ¼ cup reserved syrup.
  For **QUICK** Fruit Cobbler, substitute 2 cans (21 oz. ea.)
  fruit pie filling and ¼ cup water for Filling ingredients.*

CURRIED FRUIT COMPOTE

1 can (17 oz.) apricot halves, drained,
  reserve syrup
1 can (16 oz.) peach slices, drained,
  reserve syrup
¼ teaspoon curry powder
¼ teaspoon cinnamon
1 tablespoon cornstarch
¼ cup water
½ cup raisins

Yield: 6 Servings

In 2-cup glass measure, combine 1 cup reserved syrups, curry and cinnamon. Heat at **HIGH** 2 to 3 minutes. Blend cornstarch with water until smooth. Stir into syrup. Cook at **HIGH** 1½ to 2 minutes, or until slightly thickened; stir occasionally. In 8-inch square dish, combine apricots, peaches and raisins. Cook at **HIGH** 3½ to 4½ minutes, or until heated through, stir once. Pour sauce over fruit. Cook at **HIGH** 1 to 1½ minutes. Serve warm or chilled.

BAKED GRAPEFRUIT

2 medium grapefruit
8 teaspoons packed brown sugar,
  granulated sugar or maple syrup
Cinnamon

Yield: 4 Servings

With sharp knife, cut each grapefruit in half; remove seeds and cut around each section. Arrange grapefruit on oven tray. Sprinkle with brown sugar. Cook at **HIGH** 3½ to 4½ minutes. Sprinkle with cinnamon before serving.

Note: For TWO Servings, *follow above procedure. Halve all ingredients; cook 2 to 3 minutes.*
For ONE Serving, *cook 1 to 2 minutes.*

PEARS IN WINE SAUCE **A**

2 cinnamon sticks
¼ cup sugar
½ teaspoon whole cloves
¼ teaspoon grated lemon peel
½ cup port wine
2 tablespoons water
2 tablespoons apricot preserves
2 tablespoons apricot brandy
6 small pears, halved lengthwise, peeled,
  cored

Yield: 6 Servings

Combine cinnamon, sugar, cloves, lemon, wine, water, preserves and brandy. Arrange pears, cut-side down in 8-inch round dish. Pour sauce over pears.

TO COOK BY AUTO SENSOR: Cover completely with plastic wrap. Cook on **COOK A8**. After cooking, release plastic wrap.

TO COOK BY TIME: Cover with plastic wrap. Cook at **MEDIUM** 11 minutes.

TO COMPLETE: Let stand, covered, 5 mintues. To serve; baste pears with sauce. Remove cinnamon stick and cloves before serving.

216

BRANDIED PEACHES A

1 can (29 oz.) cling-peach halves, drained,
  reserve ½ cup syrup
⅔ cup peach or pineapple preserves
¼ to ⅓ cup brandy
1 teaspoon lemon juice
Toasted coconut (see page 229)

Yield: 4 Servings

Arrange peaches in 8-inch round dish.
Combine reserved syrup, preserves, brandy
and lemon juice. Pour over peaches; top
with coconut.

TO COOK BY AUTO SENSOR: Cover
completely with plastic wrap. Cook on
COOK A1. After cooking, release plastic
wrap.

TO COOK BY TIME: Cover with plastic
wrap. Cook at **HIGH** 3 to 4 minutes, or
until heated through.

TO COMPLETE: Serve warm or chilled.

PEARS WITH CARAMEL SAUCE

6 large pears (6 oz. ea.)
1 tablespoon sugar
Dash cinnamon
½ cup water
30 caramels (about 10 oz.)
2 tablespoons butter or margarine
2 tablespoons rum, optional
1 tablespoon water
½ teaspoon cinnamon
Sweetened whipped cream

Yield: 6 Servings

Core pears and peel skin 1 inch from top.
Combine sugar and dash cinnamon;
sprinkle inside pears.
Arrange pears in 12×8-inch dish. Sprinkle
with water. Cook, covered plastic wrap, at
HIGH 8 to 9 minutes, or until pears are
tender, cool or chill.
Just before serving, in glass bowl,
combine caramels, butter, rum, water and
cinnamon. Cook at **HIGH** 2 to 3 minutes,
stir twice until smooth. Spoon sauce over
pears; top with whipped cream.

PREPARING PIE CRUSTS

Prepare pastry according to recipe or package directions.

If desired, for a single crust scratch pastry recipe, substitute ½ cup whole wheat flour for ½ cup all-purpose flour.

Microwave pie crusts are light in color. A few drops of yellow food coloring may be mixed with the liquid before adding liquid to the flour mixture. This will give the crust a pale yellow color.

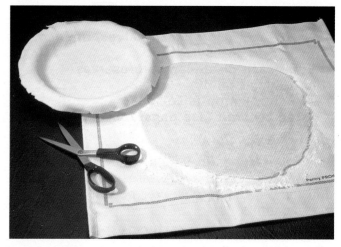

Roll dough out and gently place in pie plate. Trim edge so a ¾-inch overhang remains. Roll overhand down to rim of pie plate. Flute edge.

Prick bottom and sides of pastry with fork. Let pie crust rest 10 minutes. The rest time helps reduce shrinkage.

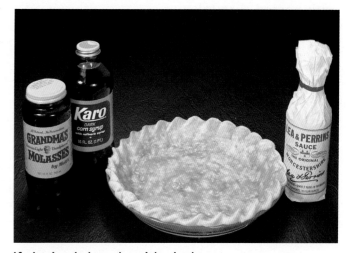

If desired, brush with dark corn syrup or molasses for sweet fillings, or brush with Worcestershire or soy sauce for savory fillings.

218

CRUMB CRUSTS

For crumb crusts combine ⅓ cup butter and ¼ cup sugar in glass bowl.

Heat until butter is melted. Combine 1¼ cups crumbs (graham crackers, chocolate or vanilla wafers).

Firmly pat into 9-inch pie plate.

For frozen crust, thaw and remove from foil pie plate and place in an 8 or 9-inch glass pie plate.

Heat ½ minute, then prick crust and, if desired, brush with dark corn syrup, molasses. Worcestershire or soy sauce.

BAKING PIE CRUST

ITEM	POWER	APPROX. COOKING TIME (in minutes)
From Scratch or Mix	HIGH	3½ to 5
Frozen	HIGH	4 to 5½
Graham Cracker or Cookie Crumb	MEDIUM	2 to 2½

Cook according to directions given in chart. Visually check for doneness. Pastry crusts should be opaque. If crust is undercooked, add cooking time in 15 second increments. Let stand until cool. Chill crumb crusts.

FRESH PEACH PIE

2 pounds fresh peaches, peeled and
sliced*
½ cup packed brown sugar
2 teaspoons lemon juice
1½ teaspoons cornstarch
½ teaspoon cinnamon, optional
9-inch pastry shell, baked (see page
219)

Crumb Topping:
½ cup flour
⅓ cup packed brown sugar
¼ cup butter or margarine, softened
(see page 230)
⅓ cup finely chopped nuts, optional
¼ teaspoon cinnamon

Yield: 8 Servings

Toss peaches with sugar, lemon juice,
cornstarch and cinnamon; arrange in
prepared shell. Cook, covered with wax
paper, at **HIGH** 4 to 6 minutes, or until
peaches are almost tender.
Meanwhile, prepare crumb topping. In
bowl, combine flour, brown sugar, butter,
nuts and cinnamon.
Sprinkle pie with crumb topping. Cook at
HIGH 4 to 5 minutes, or until topping is
set. Let stand until cool.

*Variation: For FRESH APPLE PIE, use 2
pounds apples for peaches.*

ORCHARD FRUIT PIE

1 can (21 oz.) favorite pie filling
¼ cup raisins, optional
1 teaspoon lemon or orange juice
⅛ teaspoon cinnamon
8 or 9-inch pastry shell, baked
(see page 220)
½ cup flour
¼ cup packed brown sugar
¼ cup butter or margarine, softened

Yield: 8 Servings

Combine pie filling, raisins, lemon juice
and cinnamon; pour into prepared crust.
Blend together remaining ingredients;
crumble over filling. Cook at **MEDIUM-HIGH**
6 to 8 minutes, or until heated through.
Cool before serving.

CRANBERRY-NUT PIE

1 pound cranberries, coarsely chopped
1½ cups sugar
⅛ teaspoon salt
½ cup coarsely chopped walnuts
½ cup raisins
1 teaspoon orange peel
3 tablespoons butter or margarine, melted
½ cup water
¼ cup strained orange juice
1½ tablespoons cornstarch
9-inch graham cracker crust, baked
  (see page 220)
Sweetened whipped cream or
  whipped topping

Yield: 8 Servings

In 2½ quart bowl, mix cranberries, sugar and salt. Stir nuts, raisins, peel and butter. Mix cornstarch with water and juice and stir into cranberry mixture. Cook at **HIGH** 12 to 14 minutes, or until mixture thickens. Stir occasionally. Pour into cool crust and refrigerate until cool. To serve, top with sweetened whipped cream around the edge of the pie.

GREAT GRAPE PIE

1 envelope unflavored gelatin
¾ cup water
1 can (6 oz.) frozen grape juice concentrate
1 cup heavy cream, whipped
9-inch graham cracker crumb crust, baked*
  (see page 220)
Sugared grape clusters, optional

Yield: 8 Servings

In large glass bowl, sprinkle unflavored gelatin over water. Cook at **HIGH** 1¼ to 1¾ minutes, or until gelatin is dissolved; stir twice. Stir in grape juice concentrate until melted; chill until mixture mounds slightly. Stir occasionally. Fold in whipped cream; turn into prepared crust and chill until firm. Garnish, if desired, with sugared grape clusters.

***Hint:** When preparing ingredients for crust, add ¼ cup finely chopped nuts and ¼ teaspoon each allspice, cinnamon and nutmeg.*

CHOCOLATE ROCKY ROAD PIE

1 package (3⅝ oz.) chocolate pudding and
  pie filling mix
1¾ cups milk
1 to 1½ cups miniature marshmallows
½ to 1 cup coarsely chopped walnuts
9-inch chocolate cookie crumb crust, baked
  (see page 220)

Yield: 8 Servings

Combine pudding mix and milk in 4-cup glass measure. Cook at **MEDIUM** 7 to 8½ minutes, or until pudding is thickened; stir twice. Cool 5 minutes; fold in marshmallows and nuts. Turn into prepared crust; chill until firm.

GRASSHOPPER PIE

3 cups miniature marshmallows
½ cup milk or half'n half
3 tablespoons creme de cocoa
3 tablespoons creme de menthe
1 cup heavy cream, whipped
9-inch chocolate cookie crumb crust, baked
 (see page 220)

Yield: 8 Servings

Combine marshmallows and milk in large glass bowl. Cook at **MEDIUM** 3½ to 4½ minutes; stir until smooth. Stir in creme de cocoa and creme de menthe; chill until mixture mounds slightly. Fold in whipped cream and turn into prepared crust. Chill until firm.

COCONUT LEMON MERINGUE PIE

1½ cups sugar
⅓ cup cornstarch
¼ teaspoon salt
1½ cups boiling water
3 eggs separated
½ cup lemon juice
3 tablespoons butter or margarine
Grated rind of 1 lemon
9-inch pie shell, baked (see page 220)
⅓ cup sugar
¼ cup toasted coconut (see page 229)

Yield: 8 Servings

In 3-quart casserole, combine 1½ cups sugar, cornstarch and salt; stir in boiling water. Cover with lid. Cook at **HIGH** 9 to 10 minutes, or until thickened.
Stir in small amount of hot mixture into egg yolks; return to hot mixture, beating until well blended. Add lemon juice, butter and lemon rind. Pour into pie shell; set aside.
Meanwhile, beat egg whites until soft peaks form, gradually add remaining sugar and beat until stiff. Spread meringue over filling, making sure it touches crust all around. Sprinkle with coconut. Cook at **HIGH** 3 to 4 minutes, or until meringue is set. Cool completely.

ORANGE MANDARIN CHIFFON PIE

1 envelope unflavored gelatin
⅓ cup sugar
4 eggs, separated
1 can (11 oz.) mandarin orange sections, drained; reserve ⅔ cup syrup
2 tablespoons lemon juice
½ teaspoon grated lemon peel
½ cup sugar
9-inch graham cracker crumb crust, baked
 (see page 220)

Yield: 6 Servings

In medium glass bowl, mix gelatin and ⅓ cup sugar; stir in egg yolks blended with reserved syrup, lemon juice and lemon peel. Cook at **MEDIUM-HIGH** 5 to 6 minutes, or until gelatin is dissolved; stir twice.
Chill until mixture mounds slightly, stir occasionally. Meanwhile, beat egg whites until soft peaks form; gradually add ½ cup sugar and beat until stiff. Fold in gelatin mixture and ½ oranges; turn into prepared crust. Chill until firm; garnish with remaining oranges.

223

PUMPKIN PIE

1 can (16 oz.) cooked pumpkin
1 cup evaporated milk
2 eggs
½ cup sugar
¼ cup packed brown sugar
½ teaspoon salt
1 teaspoon cinnamon
½ teaspoon ginger
¼ teaspoon cloves
9-inch pastry shell, baked (see page 220)

Yield: 8 Servings

Combine pumpkin, milk, eggs, sugars, salt and spices. Pour into prepared shell. Cook at **MEDIUM** 20 to 22 minutes, or until center is almost set. Let stand until cool.

PECAN PIE

1 cup dark corn syrup
¼ cup packed brown sugar
3 eggs
2 tablespoons butter or margarine, melted
1 teaspoon vanilla
¾ cup chopped pecans
9-inch pastry shell, baked (see page 220)
Sweetened whipped cream, optional

Yield: 8 Servings

Combine syrup, sugar, eggs, butter and vanilla; stir in pecans. Pour into prepared crust. Cook at **MEDIUM** 7 to 9 minutes, or until pie is set. Let stand until cool. Garnish, if desired, with sweetened whipped cream.

MAMA'S CHESS PIE

1 cup packed brown sugar
½ cup sugar
3 eggs
½ cup evaporated milk
½ cup chopped walnuts, optional
1 teaspoon vanilla
⅛ teaspoon lemon extract
9-inch pastry shell, baked (see page 220)
Sweetened whipped cream or whipped topping

Yield: 8 Servings

Combine sugar, eggs, milk, walnuts, and extracts; pour into prepared shell. Cook at **MEDIUM** 8½ to 10 minutes, or until center is almost set. Let stand until cool. Just before serving, top with whipped cream.

PEANUT BRITTLE

½ cup water
2 tablespoons butter or margarine
1 jar (8¼ oz.) dry roasted peanuts
  (about 1½ cups)
1½ cups sugar
2 tablespoons molasses
1 teaspoon baking soda

Yield: 1½ Pounds

Combine water and butter in 4-quart glass ceramic casserole. Cook at **HIGH** 1½ to 2 minutes, or until boiling; stir in peanuts, sugar and molasses. Cook at **HIGH** 13 to 14 minutes, or until mixture reads 300°F when tested with candy thermometer*. Quickly stir in baking soda, stir until soda foams. Pour onto well greased cookie sheet; spread thin. Let stand until candy is hardened; break into small pieces.

***Important:** Do not use conventional candy thermometer in dish while operating the microwave oven.*

Place water, and butter in a 4-quart glass ceramic casserole. Cook at HIGH 1½ to 2 minutes.

Stir in one 8¼ oz. jar peanuts, 1½ cups sugar and 2 tablespoons molasses.

Cook at HIGH 13 to 14 minutes, or until candy thermometer reads 300°F.

Quickly stir in 1 teaspoon baking soda.

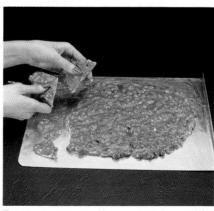

Pour onto well greased cookie sheet. Stand until hardened. Break into small pieces.

225

BUTTERSCOTCH FUDGE

3 cups sugar
¾ cup butter or margarine
1 can (5⅓ oz.) evaporated milk
1 package (12 oz.) butterscotch flavored pieces*
1 jar (7½ oz.) marshmallow creme
1 cup chopped walnuts
1 teaspoon vanilla

Yield: 3 Pounds

In 2½-quart casserole, combine sugar, butter and milk. Cook at **HIGH** 9 to 10½ minutes, or until sugar is dissolved; stir twice. Add remaining ingredients and stir until butterscotch is melted. Turn into well greased 12×8-inch dish. Cool; cut into squares to serve.

Variation: For CHOCOLATE Fudge, use 1 package (12 oz.) semisweet chocolate pieces.

FAST FIXIN' CHOCOLATE FUDGE

2 packages (16 oz. ea.) confectioners sugar
1 cup unsweetened cocoa
½ cup milk
1 cup butter or margarine
1½ cups chopped nuts, optional
2 tablespoons vanilla

Yield: 3 Pounds

Mix sugar and cocoa in large glass bowl. Add milk and butter (do not stir). Cook at **HIGH** 4½ to 6 minutes, or until butter is melted; add nuts and vanilla; stir until smooth. Spread into well greased 12×8-inch dish. Chill until firm. Cut into squares to serve.

Note: For 1½ pounds Fudge, follow above procedure. Halve all ingredients, cook 2 to 3 minutes; pour into greased loaf dish.

Variation: For ROCKY ROAD Fudge, coarsely chop nuts and add 1 cup miniature marshmallows.

PECAN PRALINES

1 cup packed brown sugar
1 cup sugar
⅓ cup light corn syrup
¼ cup water
1½ cups coarsely chopped pecans
1 tablespoon butter or margarine
1 teaspoon vanilla

Yield: 1½ Dozen

In medium glass bowl, combine sugars, corn syrup and water. Cook at **HIGH** 7 to 9 minutes, or until mixture reads 238°F (soft ball stage) when tested with candy thermometer*. Stir in pecans, butter and vanilla. Let stand 2 minutes. Drop by tablespoonfuls onto well greased wax paper lines cookie sheet; chill until set.

*__Important:__ *Do not use conventional candy thermometer in dish while operating the microwave oven.*

TOFFEE FONDUE

1 package (14 oz.) caramels
¼ cup strong coffee
2 to 4 tablespoons milk
½ cup milk chocolate pieces, optional
Dippers*

Yield: 6 Servings

In medium glass bowl, combine caramels, coffee, milk and chocolate. Cook at **MEDIUM** 5 to 6 minutes; stir twice until smooth. Serve with assorted Dippers. If Fondue gets cool, reheat 1 to 2 minutes.

*__Dippers:__ *Apple and pear slices, banana chunks, large marshmallows, angel food or yellow cake, cut into 1½-inch cubes.*

ALMOND BUTTER CRUNCH

½ cup butter or margarine
1½ cups sugar
3 tablespoons water
1 tablespoon light corn syrup
4 (1⅕ oz. ea.) milk chocolate candy bars
½ cup finely chopped almonds

Yield: 1¼ Pounds

Heat butter in 3-quart glass ceramic casserole at **HIGH** 1½ to 2 minutes, or until melted; stir in sugar, water and corn syrup. Cook at **HIGH** 8 to 9 minutes, or until mixture reads 290°F (soft crack stage) when tested with candy thermometer*. Pour onto <u>well</u> greased wax paper; let stand ½ minute. Arrange chocolate on candy; as chocolate melts, spread evenly over candy. Top with nuts, pressing nuts into chocolate. Chill until chocolate is set; break into small pieces.

*__Important:__ *Do not use conventional candy thermometer in dish while operating the microwave oven.*

RAISIN CLUSTERS

8 squares (1 oz. ea.) semi-sweet chocolate
⅔ cup sweetened condensed milk
1 cup raisins*

Yield: 2 Dozen

In medium glass bowl, heat chocolate at **MEDIUM-LOW** 3 to 4 minutes, or until chocolate is melted; stir in milk until smooth, then raisins. Drop by teaspoonfuls onto greased wax paper lined cookie sheet; chill.

***Variations: For ELEPHANT Clusters,** use 1 cup unsalted peanuts for raisins.
For CHINESE Clusters, use 1 cup crisp chow mein noodles for raisins.

SWEET SPICED NUTS

½ cup packed brown sugar
1½ tablespoons water
½ teaspoon salt
½ teaspoon cinnamon
¼ teaspoon allspice
⅛ teaspoon cloves
⅛ teaspoon nutmeg
1½ cups almond, cashew, pecan or walnut halves or combination

Yield: 1½ Cups

In 2-quart casserole, combine sugar, water, salt, cinnamon, allspice, cloves and nutmeg. Cook at **HIGH** 1 to 1½ minutes, or until sugar is melted; stir in nuts. Cook at **HIGH** 4 to 5 minutes, or until syrup begins to harden. Immediately pour nut mixture onto a well greased cookie sheet. Spread thin. Cool; break into small pieces.

MICROWAVE SHORTCUT

To further illustrate the versatility of your microwave oven, here are some of our favorite tips to help you save more time.

Because all times given are approximate and may vary do not leave the oven unattended.

To Soften Dried Fruits, place fruit in a small bowl and sprinkle with water. Cover with plastic wrap and heat at **HIGH** 30 to 40 seconds.

To Melt Butter or Chocolate, place ¼ pound butter or 1 square (1 oz.) of chocolate in dish. Heat butter 1 to 2 minutes and chocolate 2 to 3 minutes at **MEDIUM-LOW**. Check before adding more time.

To Toast Coconut, spread ⅓ cup coconut in a 9-inch pie plate. Cook at **HIGH** 1 to 1½ minutes, or until golden brown; stir twice.

To Remove Oven Odors, combine water with the juice and peel of one lemon in a small bowl. Heat at **HIGH** 5 minutes; wipe oven interior with damp cloth.

To Dry Herbs, place a few sprigs or ½ cup leaves between paper towels. Heat at **HIGH** 1 to 1½ minutes or until dry and crumbly. Check frequently. Timings may vary with different herbs.

To Dry Lemon or Orange Peel, place grated peel in glass bowl. Heat at **HIGH** 30 to 60 seconds, or until dry; stir once.

To Soften 3 oz. Package of Cream Cheese or ¼ pound of Butter, remove from wrapper and place on a dish. Heat at LOW 30 to 60 seconds.

To Reheat a Slice of Cold Fruit Pie, place on a dish. Reheat at **MEDIUM-HIGH** 15 to 45 seconds.

To Reheat an 8 oz. Baby Bottle of cold milk or formula to luke-warm, remove cap and nipple from bottle. Cook at **MEDIUM** 30 to 60 seconds. Screw nipple on bottle, gently shake bottle and stand 1 to 2 minutes before using. Do not heat bottles with disposable linings in the microwave oven.

To Shorten Barbecue Cooking Time, partially cook chicken, ribs, etc. in the microwave oven. Then season and finish cooking on a barbecue grill.

Cook Chicken pieces at **HIGH** when you need chicken for salad, sandwiches or casseroles. One pound of chicken should cook 7 to 8 minutes.

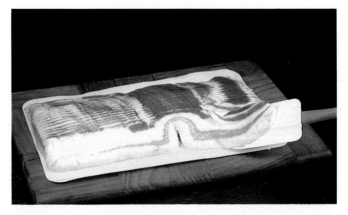

To Separate Cold Bacon, heat package at **HIGH** 15 to 30 seconds.

To Soften Hard Ice Cream, warm a half gallon at **WARM** 3½ to 5 minutes.

To Heat Liqueurs for Flaming Desserts, place ¼ cup liqueur in glass measure. Heat at **HIGH** 15 to 25 seconds. Pour over dessert and ignite.

To Roast Nuts, place 1½ cups nuts in 9-inch glass pie plate. Heat at **HIGH** for 3 to 4 minutes; stir twice.

To Toast Sesame Seeds, place ¼ cup of sesame seeds in a small bowl. Cook at **HIGH** for 2½ to 3½ minutes; stir twice.

To Make Croutons, cut enough dry bread to make 2 cups of bread cubes. Spread cubes in a shallow dish. Cook at **HIGH** 3 to 4 minutes; stir occasionally.

To Soften Brown Sugar, place 1 cup hard brown sugar in dish with a slice of bread or a wedge of apple. Cover with plastic wrap. Heat at **HIGH** 30 to 60 seconds.

231

INDEX

233

234

237

Printed in Japan
(X40AP) 85. 9. ⑨